Pluriversal sovereignty and the state

Manchester University Press

THEORY FOR A GLOBAL AGE

Series Editor: Gurminder K. Bhambra, Professor of Postcolonial and Decolonial Studies in the School of Global Studies, University of Sussex

Globalization is widely viewed as a current condition of the world, but there is little engagement with how this changes the way we understand it. The Theory for a Global Age series addresses the impact of globalization on the social sciences and humanities. Each title will focus on a particular theoretical issue or topic of empirical controversy and debate, addressing theory in a more global and interconnected manner. With contributions from scholars across the globe, the series will explore different perspectives to examine globalization from a global viewpoint. True to its global character, the Theory for a Global Age series will be available for online access worldwide via Creative Commons licensing, aiming to stimulate wide debate within academia and beyond.

Previously published by Bloomsbury:

Connected sociologies
Gurminder K. Bhambra

Eurafrica: The untold history of European integration and colonialism
Peo Hansen and Stefan Jonsson

On sovereignty and other political delusions
Joan Cocks

Postcolonial piracy: Media distribution and cultural production in the global south
Edited by Lars Eckstein and Anja Schwarz

The Black Pacific: Anti-colonial struggles and oceanic connections
Robbie Shilliam

Democracy and revolutionary politics
Neera Chandhoke

Published by Manchester University Press:

Race and the Yugoslav region: Postsocialist, post-conflict, postcolonial?
Catherine Baker

Diaspora as translation and decolonisation
Ipek Demir

Debt as power
Tim Di Muzio and Richard H. Robbins

Subjects of modernity: Time-space, disciplines, margins
Saurabh Dube

Frontiers of the Caribbean
Phillip Nanton

John Dewey: The global public and its problems
John Narayan

De-centering queer theory: Communist sexuality in the flow during and after the Cold War
Bogdan Popa

Bordering intimacy: Postcolonial governance and the policing of family
Joe Turner

Pluriversal sovereignty and the state

Imperial encounters in Sri Lanka

Ajay Parasram

MANCHESTER UNIVERSITY PRESS

Copyright © Ajay Parasram 2023

The right of Ajay Parasram to be identified as the author of this work has been asserted in accordance with the Copyright, Designs and Patents Act 1988.

Published by Manchester University Press
Oxford Road, Manchester M13 9PL

www.manchesteruniversitypress.co.uk

British Library Cataloguing-in-Publication Data
A catalogue record for this book is available from the British Library

ISBN 978 1 5261 4840 7 hardback
ISBN 978 1 5261 4839 1 open access

An electronic version of this book is also available under a Creative Commons (CC-BY-NC-ND) licence.

First published 2023

The publisher has no responsibility for the persistence or accuracy of URLs for any external or third-party internet websites referred to in this book, and does not guarantee that any content on such websites is, or will remain, accurate or appropriate.

Typeset
by Cheshire Typesetting Ltd, Cuddington, Cheshire

Contents

List of figures	vi
Preface and dedication	vii
Introduction: total territorial rule and the universal state	1
1 Colonial contamination and the postcolonial moment	32
2 Universal sovereignty: externalizing violence, relational state formation, and empire	48
3 Universal gaze and pluriversal realities	75
4 Ontological collision and the Kandyan Convention of 1815	103
5 The coloniality of the archives	136
Conclusion: pluriversal sovereignty and research	168
References	177
Index	194

Figures

4.1 Milky Way and Andromeda galaxies colliding (Time 1). NASA artistic prediction, May 31, 2012. 127

4.2 Milky Way and Andromeda galaxies in Time 2, having "passed through" each other. NASA artistic prediction, May 31, 2012. 128

C.1 Convergence of Milky Way and Andromeda galaxies. NASA, artistic prediction, May 31, 2012. 175

Preface and dedication

Working in colonial archives is a lot like working in a coal mine – without constant attention to the canary that judges the quality of air one is breathing and when one might need to resurface for fresh air, one could easily fall victim to the noxious fumes. I have learned an enormous amount about early nineteenth-century empire from the scholarship of late-colonial and postcolonial historians. Studying colonial state formation has had the unexpected side effect of reflecting on the context of first- and second-generation scholars who were "postcolonial" before it was a term, venturing into the archival coalmines without canaries. In their time, they had to first make the case to their professors (many of whom were former colonial administrators) that they even belonged in the university before they could conduct their research. Each time I emerged from the "coalmine" for a drink of water outside the Asia and Africa reading room of the British Library I was greeted by a bust of W. M. G. Colebrooke, a British military officer who oversaw the legislative and geographic restructuring of Ceylon in the late 1820s and early 1830s, but who also had extensive experience in India, Java, the Caribbean, and British North America. I regularly ate lunch in Torrington Square – a constant reminder of George Byng, seventh Viscount Torrington and the Governor of Ceylon during the Matale Rebellion in 1848. While there are large parts of this book in which I engage postcolonial histories critically, I do this from a place of appreciation and respect, in solidarity with intergenerational anti-colonial scholarly labour.

Through the process of researching this book, I came to understand myself as a transnational, multigenerational byproduct of

viii *Preface and dedication*

empire. My ancestors left South Asia in the nineteenth century as indentured labourers to Kairi, a southern Caribbean island arrogantly renamed "Trinidad" by a famously lost Spaniard in 1498. In my lifetime, my family migrated to Canada and I have lived, learned, and struggled with allies against ongoing post-British Canadian colonialism in the Coast Salish, Algonquin, and Mi'kmaq regions that I have lived in. Being engaged in anti-colonial work in one part of the world while studying colonial state formation and the making of the system of states in another has helped me to understand that a transnational diasporic position is not only a "lack" but potentially an important point of connectivity. Empire was always a global phenomenon, and working to understand its deep knots in the colonial present needs to be global as well.

I am grateful to have been able to access so many records at the (Wesleyan) Methodist Missionary Society Archive at the School of Oriental and African Studies, University of London, the British Library, and The National Archives of the United Kingdom. Not even half of what I was able to read make it into these pages; I appreciate the interest and helpfulness of the staff I interacted with in these locations. While I was conducting much of the early research, I had the benefit of learning how to engage with archival collections with a view to centring the humanity of the colonized through a series of generous conversations with Robbie Shilliam. I am also grateful to Gurminder K. Bhambra, who had taken an interest in the concept of pluriversal sovereignty since I shared the first conference paper on the subject in 2015. Being able to publish this work as part of the series Theory for a Global Age is a special honour. Towards that end, I am grateful for the comments, guidance, and help offered to me in earlier versions and drafts of this work from the many brilliant minds I have had the privilege to engage: Chinnaiah Jangam, Cristina Rojas, Hans-Martin Jaeger, Anupama Ranawama-Collie, Jaipersad Parasram, Seromanie Parasram, Jivesh Parasram, Nissim Mannathukkaren, Priyamvada Gopal, John Munro, Giorgio Shani, Navnita Behara, Somdeep Sen, Anu Pandey, Fazeela Jiwa, Colin Mitchell, Christopher Austin, Jai Sen, Amaan Kazmi, Masuma Khan, and Mithey Augustine, who also worked on this book as my research assistant. I am also grateful to the editorial team at MUP, and to the anonymous reviewers whose thoughtful, helpful, and insightful engagements with the text have greatly improved it. One reviewer in particular really went above and beyond in their engagement with the text, and the book is much better as a result. While all these wonderful people have contributed to the book, all its faults rest with me alone.

I dedicate this book to the late Mat Nelson. He carried the burden of his genius with considerable grace, generosity, curiosity, and fierce commitment to building a better world with one foot in the present, one foot in the past, and both eyes staring down the future. Mat's passing is a loss not only to those who knew him, but also to future generations of scholars and students, now denied the critical insights his work promised.

Introduction: total territorial rule and the universal state

On May 18, 2009, the then Sri Lankan President Mahinda Rajapaksa declared victory over terror and invited the world, embroiled in a "global" war on terror, to be his pupil in counter-terrorism. Rajapaksa won the 2005 presidential elections with a promise to end to the island's longstanding civil war between the Liberation Tigers of Tamil Eelam (LTTE), which controlled a large crown of territory in the north and east of the island, and the Sri Lankan government based in the rest of the island. The central government based in Colombo appealed to two powerful but related discourses anchored to the international community's defining norm of state sovereignty: the right to defend the state from terror on the one hand, and the right of postcolonial states to exercise total territorial rule without foreign interference on the other.

Rajapaksa spent his first term as President diplomatically strengthening his stability in parliament by winning over small parties to his coalition. Paired with military successes and the establishment of new Cabinet positions, he was especially successful in relocating the basis of populist nationalism away from parliament and centring it into the presidency. As Venugopal (2018: 197) explains, "the presidency was an attempt to recalibrate the elite-mass equation in favour of elites" when it was established, and the domestic as well as global military context of counter-terrorism enabled Rajapaksa to strengthen his position as a strong-man Asian leader who would not be bullied into missing the military opportunity to end the war by Western pressure (de Alwis, 2010). Armed with these political tools in the international arena, Colombo skilfully manoeuvred Chinese diplomatic, military, and financial assistance to prevent the

2 *Pluriversal sovereignty and the state*

international community from violating the government's sovereign right to re-assert total territorial rule over the island (Parasram, 2012; de Alwis, 2010; Venugopal, 2018). At the height of Tamil Eelam's power, it operated a judiciary, bank, army, navy, air force, and government with centres in the north and east of the island. Competition to establish and normalize space and territory at the liminal boundaries of Tamil Eelam and Sri Lanka took the form of performing the function of the state, with the two sides at different points using civilians as "marginal placeholders" during the war and in the militarized development and resettlement initiatives that followed the formal end of the war (Klem and Kelegama, 2020). After more than a decade of varying degrees of semi-autonomy in Tamil Eelam, Colombo's ability to isolate the LTTE by blocking naval transportation routes and extra-territorial financing networks forced the LTTE leader, Velupillai Prabhakaran, into a dangerous gamble. He wagered that the international community would not stand by while Colombo's aggressive and anachronistic military campaign into Tamil Eelam continued to escalate.

He was wrong. Despite international concern and mass mobilization of the global Tamil diaspora, the discursive power of sovereign state legitimacy was deemed more important than the lives of internally displaced, kidnapped, or generally terrorized civilians by both the state and the LTTE. The military drove the LTTE from its *de facto* capital of Kilinochchi by January 2, 2009 and contained it, along with thousands of civilians, into approximately 250 square kilometres of coastal forest terrain (Shekhawat, 2010: 208). The war ended, according to a May 28, 2009 article in the *Economist*, when two LTTE leaders and their cadres agreed to lay down arms and return to the negotiating table ("After the Slaughter," 2009). As the cadres raised white flags and crossed the battlefield with their families, the military cleared the field with machine guns. Most of the LTTE leadership was crushed amid the last physically defendable assertion of the geopolitical entity of Tamil Eelam. Prabhakaran's corpse, his forehead bearing a bullet hole, was displayed soon thereafter across state media.

As the Sri Lankan military advanced into Eelam, small areas of land were designated "cleared" when political control shifted from Eelam to Lanka; and the people caught between the warring factions

Introduction: total territorial rule 3

were declared "liberated." Those Tamil civilians in "cleared" zones would be ushered into guarded open-air holding camps so that "terrorists" could be separated from civilians and the government in Colombo could plan its resettlement agenda. A key component of this resettlement was aimed at establishing military and Sinhala settlements alongside areas resettled by Tamils displaced by the war ("Plan to Resettle Tamil IDPs," 2009; DeVotta, 2009). Huge amounts of civilian land in the north and east of the island were seized by the Sri Lankan military during the civil war, and more than a decade afterwards, civilians were still unable to return to their homes and fields ("Why Can't We Go Home?," 2018). As Klem and Kelegama (2020) explain, both Tamil and Sinhala communities operated as "marginal placeholders" in the post-war development and resettlement context. Comparing the Tamil community of Sampur with the Sinhala settlement of Weli Oya, they argue that ethnic nationalism operates differently in the two communities, because Sinhala nationalism has long centred the importance of peasants and land, while Tamil nationalism under the LTTE centred liberation, which at times was at odds with aspects of Hindu, agrarian, Tamil identity in the eastern region. Sinhala settlements operate as a "spearhead" of the nation under President Mahinda Rajapaksa, and settlers were given land in exchange for *de facto* becoming "guardian prisoners" tied to the frontier. For Tamils, long displaced from Sampur, which had operated as a bureaucratic and operational hub during the LTTE period, the right to return was as much about access to land as it was about re-establishing Tamil space.

On May 19, 2009, President Rajapaksa announced for the world to hear, "We are a government who defeated terrorism at a time when others told us that it was not possible. The writ of the state now runs across every inch of our territory" ("No Mention of Prabhakaran in Rajapaksa's Victory Speech," 2009). Rajapaksa's second sentence has stayed with me for fourteen years and has haunted my research ever since. How did such a chilling and absolute spatial ontology of sovereignty become the universal model upon which human political society ought to be ordered in the modern, allegedly "post-colonial" world? Today, the civil war is long concluded, and yet aggressive ethno-nationalism persists, with

4 *Pluriversal sovereignty and the state*

the country's Muslim, Tamil, and Christian minorities together with dissidents of all communities bearing much of the brunt of Sinhala-Buddhist nationalism. While there was some reprieve under the one-term Sirisena presidency, Sirisena was ultimately replaced by Gotabaya Rajapaksa, the brother of Mahinda who served as Defence Secretary under the two Mahinda Rajapaksa terms. More than a decade since the formal end of the civil war, ethno-nationalism and the will to write minorities out of public monuments and national histories continue to occur, as does the scapegoating of minority populations by Sinhala-Buddhist populists. Under the "new patriotism" of the post-war period, Mahinda Rajapaksa pushed hard to present a vision of the national polity as being one that has moved beyond ethnicity and into a period of "those who love the country" and those "that have no love for the land of their birth" (quoted in Wickramasinghe, 2009: 1045). As Nira Wickramasinghe (2009) argues, the left and right political parties are constructed as having no meaningful role to play because love of the homeland ought to overcome ideology and ethnic differences. She situates the contemporary political predicament in the Donoughmore Commission, which introduced universal suffrage and the removal of colonial-era ethnic representation (Wickramasinghe, 2009: 1049). Following the 2019 Easter terrorist attacks claimed by the extra-territorially based ISIS, local Muslim-owned businesses faced boycotts and endured mob violence and murder (Ethirajan, 2019). While the first Rajapaksa administration grew over-confident in its undemocratic conduct in the post-war period and was ultimately ousted from power in 2015, it has since regained what was lost and more. The Sirisena administration, which ran and won a surprising victory in 2015 on the basis of reform and anti-corruption, was ultimately seen as "weak" in the face of a mounting debt crisis, rising political instability, and being unable to prevent the 2019 Easter attacks. In the elections later that year, Gotabhaya Rajapaksa, the military officer who steered the draconian war strategy under his brother, the then President Mahinda Rajapaksa, in the later stages of the civil war, was elected President. Despite a constitutional crisis in 2018 that saw the Supreme Court battle the Executive over the appointment of Mahinda Rajapaksa to the Prime Ministerial role, upon election

Introduction: total territorial rule 5

Gotabaya Rajapaksa appointed Mahinda as Prime Minister, and the brothers Rajapaksa, elevated by populist response to their appeals to national strength buttressed by Sinhala ethno-nationalism, ran the country until the economic crisis and popular uprisings forced them from office in 2022.

Amid such a compelling political present, it might seem strange to turn to the relatively late colonial period of the early to mid nineteenth century, but this period has much to teach us in the present about structural violence and its imbrication in the modern state. The universalization and normalization of the territorial nation state is one of the most important issues of global social theory, as it literally conditions the territory beneath us while limiting the social and political imagination of what might else may be possible. State sovereignty is the taproot of the modern and colonial state system, imperially rooted in the nineteenth century and blossoming into a post-colonial and ostensibly democratic world system with the formation of the United Nations after the Second World War. Modern, world-making empire of the last two hundred years enforces a system of global order that centres the territorial state as its ontological basis, but before and ever alongside this hegemonic system, pluriversal sovereignty was the norm across most of the world. Stated simply, practices of sovereignty relied on ontological starting points grounded more closely in local practices, and scholars of Buddhist and Hindu state theory in southern Asia more generally, but in Sri Lanka in particular, have argued that these ontological distinctions need greater consideration (Tambiah, 2013; Seneviratne, 1987; Wijeyeratne, 2014; Obeyesekera, 2006; 2017). I do not wish to offer a broad description of the many examples of pluriversal sovereignty in this book: there are many rich examples available that detail the pluriversality of sovereign practices and ways of being that are life-affirming alternatives to the territorial nation state (A. Simpson, 2014; Coulthard, 2014; L. Simpson, 2020; Wijeyeratne, 2014; N. Perera, 1998; Bernard, 2017; de la Cadena, 2010, 2015; Escobar, 2015). My interest in this book is in describing the process through which universal sovereignty displaced and replaced pluriversal sovereignty through ontological conflict as represented in one empirical case: the collision(s) of Kandyan and British notions of sovereignty in the early to mid nineteenth century.

6 *Pluriversal sovereignty and the state*

Through emphasizing one important manifestation of modernity and coloniality – the territorial state – I seek to contribute to three areas of scholarly discussion: (1) the political ontologies of sovereignty, (2) postcolonial and decolonial international relations, and (3) globalisation through the colonial encounter.

This is an important thing to do, because despite the excellent developments in postcolonial and decolonial international relations, the territorial state remains an organizing background and an ontological assumption that is necessary in order to build other important ideas and contributions. Accepting the state without appreciating the histories through which the territorial state was universalized has limited both our political and intellectual efforts to escape statist, universal thinking and all that comes with that. For example, many, though not all, scholarly accounts of the origins of the Sri Lanka–Tamil Eelam civil war start with the struggle for political independence from the British – including mine (DeVotta, 2004; Chandra R. de Silva, 1987; Parasram, 2012). I joined others in situating the conflict's origins in the rise of Sinhala-Buddhist nationalism, which dethroned the more elite-driven United National Party for the populist-driven Sri Lanka Freedom Party of S.W.R.D. Bandaranaike in 1955. Although Bandaranaike was himself part of the young national elite, his discursive appeal and willingness to decry hundreds of years of Christian rule in the Buddhist homeland empowered the very same Buddhist ethno-nationalism that would take his life before the end of the decade. As H. L. Seneviratne (2001: 17) explains, following Bandaranaike's nationalist victory in 1956, he sought to cool ethnic tensions in collaboration with the Tamil leader S. J. V. Chelvanayagam through brokering a power-sharing agreement that would have granted relative autonomy through self-government to the Tamil-dominated north and east. Bandaranaike quickly reversed course on the so-called B-C Pact after monks staged a sit-in in front of his official residence. The shift in institutional biases and contestations over public state resources stratified Ceylon along ethnic lines, gradually giving rise to militant resistance when civil disobedience proved ineffective (A. J. Wilson, 2000; Krishna, 1999; Wijimanne, 1996; DeVotta 2009; K. M. de Silva, 1984). Although it is generally accepted that had the B-C Pact gone ahead, the civil war might not have developed, I believe that

Introduction: total territorial rule   7

long before the post-colonial period, the naturalization of "total territorial rule" encoded into the very function of the modern/ colonial nation state created a geopolitical and ethno-nationalist context in which another conflict would probably have emerged. This is true of Sri Lanka, as I will argue in this book, but I believe it is also true more generally, though my work on the subject has been so far limited to Sri Lanka, Canada, Trinidad and Tobago, India, and to a lesser extent Pakistan and Afghanistan. As Manu Goswami (2004: 5) argues with reference to India, there is a need to study the socio-cultural, political, economic, and global contexts within which national space is produced:

> The very idea of India as a bounded national space and economy, as first elaborated in the last third of the nineteenth century, has made possible both a universal language of national unity and development and engendered terrifying violence and social conflict.

The same is true of Ceylon, but whereas Goswami and many other excellent scholars focus on the nation, broadly defined, my focus is on the making and normalization of the territorial state that came prior to the rise of anti-colonial nationalism in the late nineteenth century (Goswami, 2004, Chatterjee, 1986; 1993).

State before nation

Lanka was a vibrant hub of international relations long before Europeans were discovered off its shores in the early sixteenth century. Multiple sovereigns existed simultaneously across the territory until the nineteenth century, and while many of these sovereigns laid claim symbolically to control of the entire island, total territorial rule was neither truly accomplished nor required for legitimacy in the way it is today (Wickramasinghe, 2014; Obeyesekere 2020). The transformations of the nineteenth century mark a particularly important critical juncture requiring study, and this work has to some important extent been done in a number of studies that focus on the sweeping and important legal reforms of the Colbrooke–Cameron Commission of 1829–1833 (K. M. de Silva, 1965; 1984; Mendis, 2005; D. Scott, 1999; Duncan, 2007;

8   *Pluriversal sovereignty and the state*

N. Perera, 1998; Banderage, 1983); and in some cases, its antecedents (Casinader et al., 2018; Sivasundaram, 2007). This book is not a history of Sri Lanka, Tamil Eelam, Ceylon, Sinhala nationalism, or Tamil nationalism – all of which are worthy studies that would be in excellent company amid the many wonderful studies written by Sri Lankan and Sri Lanka-focused scholars in the last seventy years. While I draw on these texts as well as colonial archival materials, this book is a story of becoming a modern/colonial state through a particular colonial encounter which is woven into the global imperial system of the nineteenth century. It is a story of transformations bound up in colonizing and anti-colonizing vectors and out of which a new spatial ontology of state sovereignty not only has emerged, but has presented itself as the universal option for organizing human political life. Within this struggle exist fragments of different kinds of sovereignty, and I focus on the contestation over sovereignty in the coming chapters.

Because it is the state, rather than the nation, that is my primary focus, I emphasize the early to mid nineteenth century rather than the late nineteenth century. By the late nineteenth century, we see the rise of sovereignty seeking postcolonial nationalism in much of "British" South Asia. The process of becoming the modern territorial state, and with it the contemporary requirement to extend the "writ of the state" to "every inch of territory," emerged out of a series of colonial and anti-colonial struggles that was already global by the mid nineteenth century. The chapters pick up on threads connecting the ontological and cosmological differences separating British and Kandyan (in particular) understandings of sovereignty and the associated spatial politics that worked to naturalize the modern state-nation on top of older South Asian spatial practices like a palimpsest. Of course, sovereignty in Sri Lanka is of a much older vintage than even the earliest forms of spatial organization in Britain, and no part of this book is intended to suggest otherwise. As historians of Sri Lanka have demonstrated, the rise and decline of empires and political associations which incorporated parts of the island were not always limited geographically to the island, some stretching into continental South Asia. What Agnew (1994) has called the territorial assumptions of international relations theory have always attempted to see a world already formed by "container-like" states that are

Introduction: total territorial rule   9

geographically pre-configured (Taylor, 1994), but this has rarely ever reflected reality. Indeed, the spatial logic of what S. J. Tambiah (1977: 69) has described as the "galactic polity" system of states was already centuries old at the time when the British arrived in the Kandyan highlands, and this Ashokan-inspired practice of sovereignty was itself the outcome of previous ontological collisions with older practices of sovereignty on the island.

The bulk of the book focuses on the years between 1815 and 1848. This was a transformative time not only in Ceylon, but also across much of the globe. "Pax Britannia" ushered in what is generally historicized as one of the most "peaceful" periods of international history, but there was no peace for those resisting colonial rule. The violent events unfolding in Ceylon and the colonial world more generally offer a counterpoint to the false narrative of peace within the historical international relations literature (Barkawi, 2016). I emphasize this period because while the latter half of the nineteenth century and first half of the twentieth century have much to offer those interested in the development of ethno-religious nationalism and institutional development, in my reading, these issues were already operating by the late nineteenth century within a sovereign ontological framework in which "total territorial rule" under a central government went unquestioned. Emphasizing the contamination of South Asian sovereignty, the story of the state unfolds in three periods in this book. In the first instance and prior to the arrival of the British (yet overlapping with the Portuguese and the Dutch) is the *rajamandala* system that has developed over approximately the last 2,200 years in South Asia. The period of British presence in Ceylon in the early to mid nineteenth century is the main period of sovereign contamination or ontological collision that I focus on. The third period of state formation followed the mid to late nineteenth century, after total territorial rule was normalized and the project of anti-colonial activism sought to displace the British and take over the reins of the territorial state. It was in this most recent period, from the late nineteenth century onwards, that the calcification of modern identities, including formal institutional religious identities, began to be leveraged to defeat the colonial occupiers at their own game, that is, through using the liberal/colonial institutions of the state against the British.

10 *Pluriversal sovereignty and the state*

In focusing on the middle period of ontological collision between a British-Christian understanding of sovereignty and a Kandyan-Buddhist sovereignty, I revisit the important 1815 Kandyan Convention as a key text in international relations. The Kandyan Convention was an agreement signed by the main chiefs of the independent kingdom of Kandy and by the British government represented by Governor Robert Brownrigg. In most historical accounts, this convention marks the period of British rule over the entirety of the island of Ceylon, and with good reason, as this was the main subject of the Convention. I detail the events and diplomatic intrigue leading to the Kandyan Convention in Chapter 4, but my point of departure from the secondary histories of the Convention is that rather than seeing it as the birth of British rule, I instead see it as the beginning of a deep ontological contestation of the meaning of sovereignty, represented in a Kandyan-Buddhist genealogy of sovereignty conflicting with a British-Christian genealogy of sovereignty.[1] Signed on March 2, 1815, the Convention was the formal end of a longer process of removing the reigning monarch, Sri Vikrama Rajasinha. In essence, this was an internal, elite, Kandyan feud between the monarch and the aristocracy that extended at least to the diplomatic intrigues that led to his installation as king as a teenager under the guidance of his *Maha Adikar* (Prime Minister), Pilimatalava, in 1798 (Mendis, 2005: 19–22).

Vikrama Rajasinha's *Maha Adikar* in the lead-up to the Convention was a man named Ahelepola Wijayasundara Wickramasinghe Chandraskara Amarkoon Wasala Ranamuka Mudiyanse. Ahelepola was the nephew of Pilimatalava, who had occupied the position of *Maha Adikar* until being charged with treason for conspiring against the king in 1811 (Vimalananda, 1984). Ahelepola succeeded his uncle as *Maha Adikar*, and continued his uncle's practice of being in communication with the British government through its chief translator, John D'Oyly. The king's policies were increasingly alienating him from the aristocracy, and the delicate balance of power at the elite level that had helped Rajasinha fend off attempts to dethrone him in the past were severely compromised when he issued an arrest warrant for Ahelepola, seizing his wife and children and ultimately having them put to death in accordance with legal conventions.

Introduction: total territorial rule 11

While Kandyan legal precedent allowed the king to hold captive and execute the family of a person charged with treason who failed to turn up when summoned, the act of cruelty would ultimately become a discursive justification to facilitate British intervention in Kandyan affairs in opposition to the orders of the Colonial Office in London. Ahelepola fled south to British territories and then brokered passage for the British forces under Governor Brownrigg through the Kandyan provinces, unchallenged by Kandyan soldiers, and ultimately into the capital city ("The Case of Eyhelapola Maha Nilime," 1828). It is unlikely that without Ahelepola's assistance, the British would have been either interested in pursuing their rule over the entire territory of the island or able to do so, as past attempts had failed miserably, and guidance from the Colonial Office in London was to avoid interference in the affairs of Kandy (Chandra R. de Silva, 1987; Vimalananda, 1984; K. M. de Silva, 1981). While this paraphrases the hegemonic representation of the last king of Kandy in the historical literature on the period, recent scholarship has sought to question the representation of Vikrama Rajasinha as a villain, highlighting the ways in which the historical material relied heavily on colonial representations of the king and how such representations went on to normalize a largely ahistorical narrative of the Nayaka kings as being "foreigners" (Obeyesekere, 2017; 2006). Indeed, the early Kandyan period has been interpreted as a form of cosmopolitanism by Gananath Obeyesekere (2020), whose recent study of the pre-Nayaka Kandyan kings shows that under the reign of Vimaladharmasuriya I there was no problem in welcoming Hindu, Buddhist, and Catholic influences into Kandy, with the understanding that sovereignty took the form of fulfilling Buddhist obligations. In this period Vimaladharmasuriya I would serve guests wine produced from his own vineyard and the king and his family and court would dress in stylish Portuguese tradition; and this cultural cosmopolitanism continued into the nineteenth century, impacting what is now seen as "traditional" Kandyan clothing that weds European, Kandyan, and southern Indian styles and traditions (Wickramasinghe, 2015). As the Dutch were driving out the Portuguese in the coastal areas of the country, Kandy would offer refuge to Catholics fleeing Protestant aggression, even making space in Buddhist temples for Christian worship and conversion if desired.

12   *Pluriversal sovereignty and the state*

Although the Nayaka kings, whose lineage hails in part from Madurai in southern India, tend to be historicized as the emergence of foreign influence on Kandyan society, this is an exaggeration, since it had long been the tradition for Kandyan kings to forge alliances in southern India and to marry women from Madurai. South Indian Hindu influence and Portuguese Catholic influence were not uncommon, but it was under the reign of the last three kings of Kandy that the visible performance and urban geographical development of Kandy took on an overtly and more purist Buddhist requirement. It is important to keep in mind that these last three kings who emphasized Buddhist ceremony and tradition as part of their sovereign practice were men ostensibly hailing from South India, and this practice was related to demonstrating their "Buddhification," as will be explored later.

I emphasize the middle period of sovereign ontological collision of British and Kandyan sovereignties (a) in order to describe how the Kandyan Convention was one document that speaks to at least two distinct ontological sovereign traditions, and (b) because despite the fact that Kandy interacted, warred with, and at times brokered diplomatic relations with other European powers, neither the Portuguese nor the Dutch ever succeeded in controlling the interior of the island. Thus there is something both conceptually and materially important about the Kandyan Convention that needs to be emphasized in order to understand the ontological politics at play between 1815 and 1850, acknowledging the importance of the reforms of 1833 but broadening the process of state-making beyond any particular date or legal arrangement.

Colonial powers more generally did not operate within South Asia through direct and alien sovereign rule initially; rather, different colonial states and state-supported corporations like the British and Dutch East India Companies sought to understand regional geopolitical dynamics and exploit them for economic and political-administrative purposes. At the same time, since the 1757 Battle of Plassey, through which the British East India Company asserted itself on the subcontinent by defeating the Nawab of Bengal and his French allies, the British East India Company invested scholarly and administrative efforts towards language and cultural learning in order to systematize and adjust administrative tactics to reflect

Introduction: total territorial rule   13

British understandings of South Asian history. The British East India Company's official presence in Ceylon, however, lasted only between 1796 and 1802. A system of dual rule operated from 1797 to 1802 in which Britain, through its governor in Colombo, administered the territories politically, and the British East India Company looked after economic and trade affairs with the promise of monopoly control of cinnamon. "Ceylon," as a colonial geographic imaginary, described territory little more than 20 kilometres from the coast and consisted largely of mercantilist trading forts, eventually administered with some centrality out of the fort town of Colombo in the south west. Only after 1815 was the island even conceptually thought of as being a single political entity in a totalizing material sense, though sovereigns often made claims to the entire island throughout its history (Wickramasinghe, 2014).

Within the period of colonial contamination, monumental transformations occurred, from the forced labour construction of early military roads to the privatization and enclosure of Kandyan land and to mass demographic and economic transformations that integrated Ceylon definitively into the rapidly developing imperial political economy of the nineteenth century. Not all of these events can be discussed in this short book, and I focus on the significance of pluriversal sovereignty and ontological collision rather than mapping out the specific empirical events that are generally well documented in other secondary histories of the period (Banderage, 1983, K. M. de Silva, 1987; Wickramasinghe, 2014; Jayawardena, 2010; Mendis, 2005). Alongside these physical, political, and economic changes, missionary education created a political need for secularism as Christian-educated pupils began to use their education to calcify and discipline the philosophical and monastic practices of Buddhism (and to lesser extent, Hinduism) into "religions" that could confront colonial and spiritual aggression on common battlefields. Similar to Orientalist scholarship of the late eighteenth century in India, Eurocentric Orientalist scholars were interested in *Buddagama*, which they translated and rationalized in early nineteenth-century Orientalist European scholarship as "Buddhism." As Elizabeth Harris (2006) notes, in the attempt to rationalize "Buddhism" and "Hinduism" with a monotheistic sensibility, the historical figure of the Buddha needed to be placed into

14 *Pluriversal sovereignty and the state*

the general narrative of historical events as understood within an Abrahamic worldview. This led early Western scholars to hypothesize that the Buddha might be Noah, Moses, or other Biblical figures. British support for Christian schools and institutions at the expense of other religious education gave rise to the association of the "Buddhist revival" with anti-British nationalism by the late nineteenth century (DeVotta, 2004; Jayawardena, 1995; Gokhale, 1973). As interesting as these issues are, they too became possible in a milieu wherein anti-colonial activists began to use the apparatus of the liberal-colonial state of Ceylon to make claims on it, rather than organize against it. While the late nineteenth century and early twentieth century were periods of enormous importance to an understanding of the development of ethno-religious nationalism, in relation to the processes that led to state naturalization, that period represents a time when the peoples of Ceylon articulated their resistance to colonialism through organizing to challenge the newly established assemblage of colonial religion, schools, and state institutions; the "state" in this period was already formed, even if the "nation" was still very much taking shape (Perera, 2002; Jeganathan and Ismail, 1995). In contrast, the tumultuous period under study here brings to light the contestations over land, sovereignty, economy, and spirituality, at times spanning the British Empire, that eventually normalized the political territorial foundations over which ethno-nationalism would later make its claims. In other words, the material and ontological contestations from 1815 to 1848 were the basis upon which the modern/colonial meaning of state territory took shape in Ceylon, as part of an expansive assemblage of global colonial violence that characterized the period of alleged "great peace" in the international realm.

Archiving in relief

As a contribution to theory for a global age, this book seeks to de-centre Eurocentric ontological assumptions in the study of postcolonial place. De-centring is important, as it does not mean rejecting or moving past ideas of a Eurocentric ilk; Europe is a *part* of the world, but its localized experiences and ways of making sense of the world have been over-privileged in social science research concerning the nature of global politics and society. In order to tell stories about Europe, scholars defocus on what to them is a "periphery" in order to focus on what they see to be the "core." I defocus on Europe, and the result of doing so makes a geographical region that is very familiar to Western-trained readers seem, at times, over-simplified. This is not because I think that I can collapse the many intricate processes and practices that give meaning to British expressions of sovereignty by the nineteenth century, for example, when I conflate them as "British-Christian" ontologies of sovereignty contrasted with an equally over-simplified notion of "Buddhist-Kandyan" ontologies of sovereignty. In historical research, when moving beyond the biases of the colonial archives and the epistemic colonialism inoculated in secondary literature, one must purposefully defocus on Europe in order to focus on something else. Larissa Lai (2014: 14), working from G. C. Spivak's work on "reading against the grain," describes the process of postcolonial research as "reading official documents for the truths that might emerge in their gaps, counter to their intended purpose and thus counter to their overt framing." Histories of colonialism talk about colonial territory as if Ceylon (as a pre-configured and already existing political entity) simply "fell" to the British from the Dutch, despite the knowledge that Kandy was long independent and operating according to its own sovereign system. That the two conditions coexist in historical records speaks not to a lack of knowledge about territorial diversity and the multiple ontological starting points that inform them but, rather, to an intellectual consensus that this diversity and ontological difference do not matter. I disagree; and in my reading, taking pluriversal sovereignty seriously helps us to understand contemporary ethno-nationalist conflicts that speak to fragments of national memory that are too often stripped of its depth and instead mobilized for modern/colonial political purposes (Korf, 2009). As anyone who has spent time in colonial archives can attest, the records speak to the fact that colonial archives were not only disinterested in what ordinary people thought and did; colonial administrators and missionaries were, at times, unaware of the significance of their actions. The archives can only take us so far; there are necessary, albeit speculative, leaps that must be made to

16   *Pluriversal sovereignty and the state*

connect the dots in order to glimpse the agency of colonized people and the pluriversal sovereignty in motion.

When researching this book I practised "archiving in relief," which refers to a sculpting metaphor applied to archiving. When a sculptor carves their piece in relief, it gives the impression that the sculpted material has been raised above the background. Yet to carve in relief, the sculptor starts with a flat surface, and chisels away the background to elevate the carving. To "archive in relief" is to use elevated historical artefacts (government ordinances, legal reforms, correspondences, diaries, missionary publications, newspapers, court martials, etc.) in order to better understand the background that has been discarded in mainstream historical accounts that have been collected to consciously or subconsciously serve a vested political interest. The archivist, like the sculptor, chisels away the parts of the material that are not relevant to the hegemonic historical framing – hegemonic because it need not be and often is not a purposeful exercise in exclusion – and these are the parts they study to see the background more clearly. In this way, I am indebted to scholars working in the subaltern studies tradition, but as I have argued elsewhere and will elaborate in due course, subaltern studies tend to privilege epistemic problems of archives instead of ontological ones. I agree with much of the subaltern position that liberal historiography's emphasis on statecraft artificially elevates stories of kings and already constituted states (Guha, 2002; Chakrabarty, 2000; Chatterjee and Jeganathan, 2001). However, around these elevated objects, a background is still visible. By examining the background in particular, I strive to understand how the colonial encounter helped produce the state, which would then go on to create the norms and conditions for Sri Lanka's postcolonial sovereign conflicts.

The problem of the "pre-political"

The epistemic violence within historical research and the idea of the archive as a container of facts about the past take on important implications in the writing of post-colonial histories (Nandy, 1995; Chatterjee, 1993; 1986; Guha, 2002; Parasram,

Introduction: total territorial rule   17

2020; Munslow, 2010). In this section, I discuss some of these assumptions in terms of thinking through the moment of modern territorial state formation, as well as the normalization of developmentalist reasoning as it relates to state formation. As noted above, most of the secondary literature identifies the 1815 Kandyan Convention or the 1833 Colebrooke–Cameron reforms as the central issues of concern to the consolidation of British administrative rule. The Colebrooke–Cameron reforms were extremely important in terms of the reorganization of the colonial government as well as political, juridical, and geographical transformations on the island (Mendis, 2005: 56–58). They were steeped in both liberal and colonial values: liberal in the establishment of a legislative council to advise the governor and centralizing of the administrative hub of the island in the coastal colonial fort-city of Colombo,[2] and colonial in the powerlessness of the "unofficial" members of that assembly. These unofficial positions were reserved for three "native" members representing Sinhalese, Burgher, and Tamil people respectively.[3] As unofficial members, they were unable to compel changes in the legislative agenda that were not first agreed on by the governor. While the overarching philosophical motivation guiding colonial governance as articulated in the Colebrooke–Cameron reforms can be considered "liberal" in terms of promoting institutions and law and order, the inclusion of an assembly of "natives" to advise the governor should not be confused with ambition for gradual representative government at this time. As K. M. de Silva (1981: 262) writes,

> The Colonial Office, like Colebrooke, did not regard it [legislative council] as a representative assembly in embryo, but looked upon it as a check upon the Governor in the sense that it was an independent and fairly reliable source of information for the Secretary of State who would otherwise be dependent on the Governor alone for information with regard to the colony and its affairs.

Another particularly colonial and liberal attribute of the reforms was the attempt to chip away at Kandyan autonomy by administratively incorporating the interior into the maritime provinces and the overarching administrative capital in Colombo (K. M. de Silva, 1981: 262; Chandra R. de Silva, 1987; 149).

18   *Pluriversal sovereignty and the state*

While dates are often used in the writings of histories as a kind of aid to the reader to imagine great shifts or "critical junctures," such moments speak to the broad array of contradicting forces that manifest themselves, often in hindsight, as the pivotal change in affairs (Hardt, 2002). My problem with stating that 1815 or 1833 marked the birth of the centralized colonial state under British authority is that it does not adequately capture the important political agency and fundamental equality of the people and worldviews involved in the creation of state territory, albeit under extremely unequal terms. Politics, as Jacques Rancière (2001) argues, is not a conflict within the *arche*; it is a rupture in the logic of that *arche*, the re-inscribing of meaning into social relations that comes from rejecting the logic of the existing order. Though Rancière's thinking developed in the socio-political context of 1968 Paris, this approach to understanding the nature of politics offers an important lens through which to rethink the thirty-year period of colonial state formation in Ceylon, because the majority of secondary history conceives of ordinary people in this time period as "looking backwards" to pre-political times. The secondary historical literature on the early to mid-nineteenth century in Ceylon is forthcoming about the obvious crimes committed by the British against the different people living on the island, but the authors tend to accept many of the subtler normative assumptions about the placement of the British as being more advanced in historical development or accomplishment. Partha Chatterjee (1993) explores this in the context of India, distinguishing between "internal" and "external" understandings of nation, but even this nuanced reading of nationalism comes after the normalization and consolidation.

Rancière's conception of politics insightfully focuses analytical attention on a non-hierarchical understanding of politics that breaks with conventional histories (both South Asian and Western) of this time period that historicize ordinary people as "pre-political," or, in Rancière's (2001: 6) terms, the *demos*, which is not meant to speak or is unable to speak sensibly. I agree with Rancière (2001: 10) that "politics is first and foremost an intervention upon the visible and the sayable," which requires close attention to how "natives" appear in the colonial archives.[4] Like Rancière's description of the demonstration that resists the police order to "move along, there's

Introduction: total territorial rule 19

nothing to see here," disturbances, arrests, and failed attempts that have occurred and are visible – at least when we are archiving in relief – ought to be interpreted as democratic politics that shaped the evolution of anti-colonial political organizing and the colonial state, which had to respond to this subversive activity. My point differs from Rancière's in that I am not proposing a binary opposition in which elite interests serve as a kind of police power; I mean instead to argue that elites and ordinary people respond to one another in tandem and through what Mignolo (2011) and others have described as a "colonial matrix of power" within which multiple forms of structural power intersect. Through these dynamic and ever-unfolding conflicts, colonized territory became satellite states within an embryonic imperial world system.

It is possible to re-read colonial archives "in relief" through looking for the enactment of "politics" in the way Rancière describes: because policies and taxes were often discussed between London and Colombo, the fear of rebellion was part of the policy approach taken by the colonial government. Although the Uva (1817–1818) and Matale (1848) rebellions have been historicized as being relevant because of the actions they compelled out of the colonial authorities, smaller-scale protests and interventions occurred as well, as Kumari Jayawardena's important book *Perpetual Ferment* (2010) covers in great detail. They represent "dissensus," in that they interrupt the normal order of society by "making visible that which had no reason to be seen" (Rancière, 2010: 38). In this way, Rancière's radical egalitarianism, though steeped in Western thought, is useful in making visible "subaltern" politics that have influenced the normalization of Eurocentric stateness. Indeed, the secondary literature and the archival material on which much of this is based take as their frame of reference the material accomplishment or official failure of a military action as the marker of importance. Rancière's definition of politics as interruption helps us to take more seriously the impact of *failed* attempts, as they influenced the culture of governance and the expected order and predictability of resistance in this period of colonial state formation. Not only did they inflect the development of police power (broadly speaking), but they arguably laid the ground for a democratic politics that eventually became subsumed by more institutional (and

20 *Pluriversal sovereignty and the state*

thus less radical) forms of resistance through the state by the second half of the nineteenth century (Perera, 2002). Amid these transformations, a generation of youth were coming of age in the context of watching their relatives being forced to labour to construct military roads under brutal conditions, and struggled to find a place in a society that was rapidly globalizing and integrating into broader imperial economic networks.

While I do not emphasize the political economy of "improvement" in this project, the logic of civilizational improvement as an antecedent to more contemporary "development" thinking can be seen in the proliferation of and justifications for plantations as an essential part of the early colonial project following the Uva Rebellion of 1817–1818 in particular. In the aftermath of the Uva Rebellion, the British government adopted the concept of *rajakariya* and forced the local populations to build roads connecting Colombo to Kandy. *Rajakariya* was a form of corvée labour through which public works like irrigation of communal lands were carried out. It was a localized practice, however, within a spatial organization of power in the Kandyan kingdom and its orbits of influence, which were held in balance by the symbolic and ceremonial role of the Kandyan king and the semi-autonomous provinces. Applying *rajakariya* beyond the limits of Kandy and for the purposes of public works beyond agriculture broke the precedent that had developed over centuries in Kandy; it also transformed a practice that had gained legitimacy based on the material benefits accrued by access to communal lands and converted it instead into a kind of colonial prison labour used to punish the most marginal through colonial-liberal policies steeped in the discourse of improvements. Rather than *rajakariya* producing a public good as understood by people, the word "public" was instead understood and practised by the British to mean the state, which itself represented the class of white men charged with the administration and integration of territory. Thus, a local practice of cashless labour intended to better serve communal lands became the means through which privatization and commercialization instead would gain a footing. Military working parties alongside forced labourers were responsible for constructing the colonial road system under Governor Brownrigg's successor, Edward Barnes. As the bureaucrat

Introduction: total territorial rule 21

J. W. Bennet reflected in 1843, it was Barnes's "zeal" and "devotion" to commerce and agricultural development alongside the military necessity of easing the travel between the fertile interior and the capital in Colombo that motivated the rapid construction of roads (Bennet, 1843). Barnes, aside from being known as the "roads" governor following the military governorship of Robert Brownrigg, represented commercial development interests, as he and many of his bureaucrats would go on to earn fortunes from establishing and servicing the coffee and later tea plantations in the island's centre (Bandarage, 1983; Duncan, 2007). The working conditions that locals were forced to endure were so harsh that even a generation later, the long-term effects on those made to labour on the roads evoked sympathy from Bennet. In making a plea for some financial compensation for the widows and families of the men who built the military and plantation roads connecting the Kandyan area to the colonial administrative centre in Colombo, Bennet (1843: 173) highlighted that compulsory labour "has secured possession of the interior and ensured the safety of the maritime provinces from a foe in their rear, prompted the commercial interests of the colony, and augmented its resources and revenue." Road construction brought with it more than transportation: it broke the "frontier" barrier used by anti-colonial Kandyan soldiers for generations to keep Europeans close to the shore and away from a jungle terrain they could not navigate. As Manu Goswami (2004: 46), working from Henry Lefebvre's conceptions of state space and territorialization in the context of late nineteenth-century India, reminds us,

> The colonial state performed its rule over space and society through a spectacular display of its authoritative presence, from the staging of elaborate political rituals and events to the construction of a vast network of dazzling "state works," the visible, material embodiments of its authority and "civilizing" modernity.

The broadening of footpaths into carriage roads in the early nineteenth century might not seem as extravagant or performative as the larger-scale infrastructural projects of the late nineteenth-century Raj, but this project served a similar purpose of demonstrating the strength of a government that was still not totally established nor normalized in the formerly autonomous interior.

22 *Pluriversal sovereignty and the state*

This was the political education of the early colonized youth who would be the adults of the next generation resisting colonial rule, and whose children would subsequently become those fluent enough in colonial governance and schooling in the late nineteenth century to begin organizing within the institutions of the state to take over, rather than dismantle, the colonial state. When words spoken by "natives," be they elite or non-elite, were translated into English-language newspapers, military court martials, or government documentation, terms like "pretender to the throne" were used. When colonial administrators and their assistants tasked with preparing reports, letters, and despatches created documents ostensibly for the purpose of objectively recording events, these documents were already steeped in discursive representational power. The very terminology of naming a rebel leader a "pretender" implied a legitimate sovereign entity (King George of England) and an imposter sovereign, whose success in swaying public opinion was always taken to be evidence of the "pre-political" or "backward" character of a pre-modern population that was not qualified to differentiate truth from fiction. As Marisol de la Cadena (2015: 13) describes it, the "historical ontology of modern knowledge both enables its own questions, answers, and understandings and disables as unnecessary or unreal the questions, answers, and understandings that fall outside of its purview or are excessive of it".

The question of translation of meaning is thus a central problem, though not one that I am qualified to deal with, as I am not fluent in Sinhalese or Tamil. Methodologically, however, de la Cadena's point speaks to the importance of not treating the archive as an objective stockpile of "facts" from which one might piece together different narratives. The reification of a universal or objective past that can be explained 'as it was' is an expression of colonizing epistemology (Boldt, 2014; Weckowicz, 1988).

As Dipesh Chakrabarty (2000: 27) observes, the challenge of writing history is in breaking the cycle of writing European history in different parts of the globe:

> It is that insofar as the academic discourse of history – that is "history" as a discourse produced at the institutional site of the university – "Europe" remains the sovereign political object of

Introduction: total territorial rule 23

all histories, including the ones we call "Indian," "Chinese," "Kenyan," and so on.

Chakrabarty is referring to the structure in which the historical narrative takes place. For scholars who have tried to do postcolonial or decolonial historical research using colonial archives, there is a constant need to resist the unacknowledged biases and implicit claims to universal knowledge that allow "experts" working from within a Eurocentric intellectual and ontological frame of reference to document the struggles, progress, and problems of subject peoples in what is assumed to be (in the most generous of terms) a slow and coerced march to eventual civilization. As Julian Crawquill (1839: 17), a British resident living in Ceylon and writing in the *Colombo Magazine* in 1839, opined:

> And why can England alone of the many nations of the earth, point with pride to her flourishing colonies? Because she has followed out wise and well-matured plans in a Christian-like spirit. She has endeavoured to conciliate and to enlighten wherever she has gone. She has made those amongst whom she settled partakers of her laws, of her arts and of her religion. She carried with her and disseminated, the seeds of Christianity and Civilization, and she has reaped the fruits of prosperity.

Crawquill's statements were obviously ideological and are easy to identify. He was writing at a time when missionary pressure was mounting to convince the British colonial government to sever its institutional, financial, and legal relationship with the Buddhist tradition (Hardy, 1841). While there may not have been such a clearly stated or acknowledged civilizing project in the documents of colonial administrators, many of whom often laid claim to trying to "keep the peace" or doing what was in the objective best interest of the colony and its peoples, these claims rested on a certain *a priori* agreement about what progress was, who "lacked" it, and how best to resolve "problems." As a consequence, when the ordinary people of Ceylon are found in colonial archival accounts, they often appear as criminals or misled children incapable of understanding the error of their ways. Ordinary people and the importance of their political actions can only appear like ghosts within the limits of modernist historical accounts because, like a spectre, they are hard to perceive,

24   *Pluriversal sovereignty and the state*

terrifying to the powers that be, and glimpsed translucently as if from another world.

De la Cadena (2015: 14–15), drawing on Ranajit Guha's reading of Aristotle, reflects on the boundaries or limits of what fits within the modern:

> … And borrowing from Ranajit Guha, the limit would be "the first thing outside which there is *nothing* to be found and the first thing inside which everything is to be found" (Guha 2002: 7, emphasis added). Yet this "nothing" is in relation to what sees itself as "everything" and thus exceeds it – it is something. The limit reveals itself as an onto-epistemic practice, in this case, of the state and its disciplines, and therefore a political practice as well. Beyond the limit is excess, a real that is "nothing": not-a-thing accessible through culture or knowledge of nature as usual.

The idea that ordinary people were pre-modern and thus outside the limit of the modern lens is an onto-epistemic problem in the writing of official documents, but also in the narration of secondary histories prepared by Sri Lankan historians. In terms of the writing of colonialists themselves, for example, Governor Torrington (1847–1850) placed the blame for the disturbances associated with the 1848 Matale Rebellion largely on the shoulders of a physician-turned-newspaper-man of Irish origins, Christopher Elliott. Elliott was accused of importing Irish political radicalism into the local newspapers and urging the Kandyan-Sinhalese masses to rise in protest against government tax hikes without meaningful political representation; the possibility that "natives" would have their own political wherewithal was not part of Torrington's perception of reality (K. M. de Silva, 1965). Sir James Emerson Tennent, Colonial Secretary of Ceylon from 1845 to 1850, did not share the view common to the British public and governor that the press played a central role in inciting rebellion, and was questioned to this effect in the parliamentary proceedings investigating the events. In response to a direct question concerning the role of the press, he answered, "I cannot help thinking that perhaps too much importance has been attached in Ceylon to the direct influence of the press; but I cannot avoid the equal and even more strong conclusion, it did produce a mischievous and prejudicial effect at that

Introduction: total territorial rule 25

time" (Tennent, 1850: 167). Pressed further on the circulation of the seditious articles and their presence in the areas of Kandy in which rebellion ensued, he continued:

> copies reached those districts, and were publicly read in the temples, or to assemblages of the people on their arrival in the district; but I do not attach the same importance to those articles as many do; I believe they were mischievous in their effect; but to assign them as one of the leading causes of the rebellion, would be to attach much more weight to them than in my opinion they merit.
>
> (Tennent, 1850: 168)

For Tennent, the cause of the rebellion was not Elliott's vexing words so much as it was the geopolitical threat of France supporting Ceylonese rebels deported to the former French colony of Mauritius, working together to undermine the British (Tennent, 1850: 167). It is not ever, in the archival account, a question of the political agency of the Kandyans, because within a British worldview, there was an ontological "knowledge" that the Kandyans had been for too long isolated from the modern world to be capable of entering into real politics or history. It was this "knowledge," that they were not true political agents, that bled into modernist postcolonial accounts at times as well.

This has led to an uncomfortable problem that is as much political as it is methodological. Much of the early historical research done on Ceylon in this time period accepted the condition of the archive as a collection of facts about the past out of which new, better, nationalist histories could be written, but which had not gone through the process of decolonizing the ontological assumptions necessary to conceive of "pre-modern" people. This has produced a tension in postcolonial historical research and its entanglement in Western academia, which I have discussed elsewhere in the context of West Indian history (Parasram, 2020). On the one hand, postcolonial national elites have, as Chakrabarty notes, been quick to reject the Hegelian idea of "lack" and the Rousseauian idea that the masses must be properly educated in order to exercise political citizenship; yet at the same time, they hold onto Eurocentric ideas which have continued to structure the shape of histories since Ramram Basu's 1802 *Raja Pratapadiya-Charit*

26   *Pluriversal sovereignty and the state*

(Guha, 2002; Parasram, 2020). Consider the representation of what would prove to be the beginning of the Matale Rebellion in this dispatch to the Colonial Office in London sent from Governor Torrington in Colombo:

> In endeavouring to obtain a census of the population, a report was about that 30 new taxes were to be put on, and women and children were to be taxed and women's breasts measured. Proper means have been adopted to explain the intentions of government to the people and Tennent has gone to Kandy and will see the Chieftains there and at other places and point out the advantages they will derive. I am happy to say that the Headman and Chiefs have shown no symptoms of uneasiness – indeed the whole of the disturbance at Kandy was caused by a rascally Malabar[5] (who says he is going to be King) going amongst the ignorant villages, and perhaps a rather wicked tho[ugh] clever letter in the Observer Ceylon Papers which was published in Cingalese, and tho[ugh] it pretends to disagree with [us] it [is still] sufficiently ably put to mislead many. It is hardly worth taking up all your time with this, but I feel it necessary to watch all these matters, and use every precaution, and my Malabar king will be punished when caught [illegible] as a vagrant.
>
> (Torrington to Earl Grey, July 5, 1848,
> in K. M. de Silva, 1965)

In this quotation, the representation of collecting census data and educating the "ignorant" masses about how taxation for the state is in their best interests presumes a national interest that can or must be led from a centre capable of perceiving it. In this case, it is the British government that is positioned to offer this guidance, and though the native assembly was never intended in this period to be a government in waiting, one can see the presence of the idea of creating an "improved" class of natives based on their proximity to and familiarity with British ways, which might bring them closer to the direction of true, universal history.[6] Academically, the writing of scientific histories resulted in the production of nationalist histories in the late colonial and postcolonial period that drew from the colonial archives with meticulous empirical detail, but were often complacent in their representation of ordinary people as primitive, and this did not interfere with the project of writing nationalist, state-centric histories in the twentieth century. As Guha (2002: 5),

Introduction: total territorial rule 27

reflecting on the problem of Eurocentric statism and the impact it has had on the discipline of Indian history, observes:

> The statism so firmly entrenched in South Asian historiography is an outcome of this narratological revolution which has, by its very success, prevented us as historians from apprehending it as a problem. Incorporated in World-history, we owe our understanding of the Indian past, our craft, and our profession as academics to this very revolution. We work within the paradigm it has constructed for us and are therefore far too close and committed to it to realize the need for challenge and change. No wonder that our critique has to look elsewhere, over the fence so to say, to neighboring fields of knowledge for inspiration, and finds it in literature, which differs significantly from historiography in dealing with historicality.

The coloniality of archives is revisited most substantially in the fifth chapter of this book. I have spent only a fraction of the time in archives that the scholars and practitioners I critically engage in Chapter 5 have, and my criticism is not meant to denigrate their work in any way. I mean only to highlight the ways in which the coloniality of archives continues to texture the narrative of history, and how theory can help us begin decolonizing the ontological assumptions that lie dormant within the archives.

Chapter progression

In Chapter 1, "Colonial contamination and the postcolonial moment," I make the case that formal political independence cannot be understood as decolonization. This is not to mitigate the importance of British departure; rather, it is to establish the point that by the time of formal political independence, the territorial and political structure of the state had become the vehicle through which freedom would be achieved as opposed to an "alien" or "contaminated" structure. In making this case, I explore relevant concepts in decolonial international relations that are key to understanding how and why universality incubates colonial violence.

In Chapter 2, "Universal sovereignty: externalizing violence, relational state formation, and empire," I focus on the coloniality

28 *Pluriversal sovereignty and the state*

of key concepts such as territory, sovereignty, and empire to argue that despite being one of the most hotly discussed structures in social science, "the state" itself remains largely de-politicized at the ontological level. Re-politicizing the state and its core components requires coming to terms with how these normalized concepts prevent ontological engagements that can meaningfully destabilize the hegemony of the Eurocentric state.

In Chapter 3, "Universal gaze and pluriversal realities," I focus on how a universal, British, and Christian gaze operated in a way that rationalized the spiritual, political, and intellectual inferiority of non-Christians in the early nineteenth century through positioning the Kandyan kingdom as primitive, and then Buddhist and Hindus as far removed from the "truth" of Christian religion from the vantage point of missionaries. In focusing on colonial writing and archives, I seek to shed light on how the British understood their superiority in universalist terms; I juxtapose this with a critical reading that seeks to make visible the pluriversal lived realities of people in Ceylon who were long accustomed to navigating simultaneous cosmologies and their political implications. In this way, I aim to set the historical and conceptual ground for Chapter 4, which explores the 1815 Kandyan Convention directly and interprets it as a moment of ontological sovereign collision. To accomplish this, I offer a historical narrative of the events that set the stage for early nineteenth-century Kandy for readers who are unfamiliar with the Sri Lankan context, including a widely circulating myth concerning the pounding of children to death on the order of Sri Vikrama Rajasinha. Drawing on missionary archives, I discuss the religious politics and ontological conflict between Christian missionaries and the Buddhists they encountered. I outline the early relationship between education, evangelism, and colonisation, and dwell on how the inability to move beyond a universal ontological framework limited and undermined the ability of missionaries to actually understand the "natives" they sought to civilize.

Chapter 4, "Ontological collision and the Kandyan Convention of 1815," details the historical encounter between the Kandyan kingdom and the British, which gave rise to the Kandyan Convention, a single legal document which had different ontological meanings for the different signatories. Building on Chapter 1's description of plural

Introduction: total territorial rule   29

ontology, I make the case for thinking about sovereign encounters as a kind of "galactic" collision, using a metaphor based on how actual galaxies collide. Rather than bumping against one another, galaxies pass through one another, reformulating and disrupting each other in different ways, but ultimately producing something new from the violence of the encounter. Similarly, in the sovereign ontological collision between the British and the Kandyans, they passed through and transformed one another in critical ways, including changing the geography, political economy, and *raison d'etat*. I draw on S. J. Tambiah's work on the galactic *mandala* system of states in Buddhist South-East Asia to ground this cosmic metaphor in the political history of the mid nineteenth century.

Chapter 5 returns to the coloniality of the archives and emphasizes their political and historical limits. Seeking to "archive in relief," I reinterpret the 1820s–1840s as a period of simmering insurrection, breaking with most historical accounts with the important exception of that of Kumari Jayawardena (2010), who similarly reads this period as one of "perpetual ferment." I make a case that scholars writing Sri Lanka's history have taken the structure of the state-nation for granted, and in so doing are imbricated in perpetuating colonial ontological assumptions about human social, political, and economic development. My contention is that this has made possible a modernist reading of history in which "traditional" people were overwhelmed by a technologically superior British Empire; however, the book reads the same history in a way that places local (Kandyan, in my case) and foreign (British) sovereignties as equal but distinct ontological practices to create a more vibrant picture of simmering resistance. This resistance to the new mode of centralizing state eventually gave way, after the 1848 Matale Rebellion, to a mode and form of anti-colonial resistance that instead sought to inherit or take over the state apparatus rather than resist it. This was something that would happen a full generation later in neighbouring India after the Great Rebellion of 1857 and the rise of national consciousness in the late nineteenth century, but the process began earlier in Ceylon. The chapter concludes by looking forward to the rise of Protestant Buddhism and Hinduism in the late nineteenth century and the centralization of sites and spaces of protest in Colombo rather than Kandy.

30   *Pluriversal sovereignty and the state*

The conclusion of the book brings together the various threads of ontological collision, political economy, colonial contamination, and imperial transformation to complete a picture of how the process of colonial state formation established the territorial and conceptual space within which toxic forms of anti-colonial nationalism could later flourish at the domestic scale, and an international "space" in which the violence of colonial state formation became normalized and largely de-politicized by the formal end of colonial rule. Here we return to the present day, outlining research trajectories and decolonial possibilities for identifying historical sites of sovereign ontological "collisions" in order to study them pluriversally.

Notes

Acknowledgement: revised portions of this Introduction come from my article "Erasing Tamil Eelam: De/Re Territorialization in the Global War on Terror," *Geopolitics* 17/4 (2012): 903–925.

1 Though there is a general consensus that 1815 marked the beginning of total British rule because of the Kandyan Convention, some scholars also privilege the 1833 Colebrooke–Cameron Reforms, which marked a significant shift in governance approaches based on the liberal inclination of Commissioners Colebrooke and Cameron. David Scott and scholars working in the camp of "colonial governmentality" in particular follow this line of reasoning. While both are logical choices, because the focus of analysis in this book is on how the process of state formation universalizes a single understanding of sovereignty, I see both of these dates as important components of a longer process of colonial state formation and normalization. See D. Scott, 1999.
2 As Mendis (2005) argues, however, the motivation for the administrative changes came from the Colonial Office and not from the administrative headquarters in Ceylon. The legislative councils were not intended to introduce representative democracy so much as they were to serve as forms of checks and balances from the absolute authority of the governor.
3 The colonial emphasis on racial categorization and community-based representation and rights eventually transformed to universal and majority rights in the Donoughmore Report of 1928. In the 1871 census

Introduction: total territorial rule 31

there were twenty-four races and seventy-eight nationalities listed, and by 1881 only seven remained. Wickramasinghe is especially attuned to the historical processes of shifting racialization and "strategic ethnicity." See Wickramasinghe, 1995.

4 For the purposes of this study, the emphasis on representation of "natives" in nineteenth-century Ceylon is sufficient. However, as historians of Europe have long maintained, a similar problem of exclusion exists with the representation of peasants and women within Europe, giving rise to the project of "history from below" as a strategy to correct or mitigate the severity of these exclusions. See Thompson, 1966; Kranz, 1988; Hobsbaum, 1997; Federici, 2004.

5 In the nineteenth-century English-language accounts, "Malabar" is used interchangeably with "Tamil" even though the group described as Malabar in the Kandyan context included Telegu speakers as well, some of whom also married into Sinhalese royal families in the pre-colonial period. See Obeyesekere, 2006.

6 Benedict Anderson describes the process of the Anglicization of British India as an effort to create a national culture through bringing Indians closer to the ideal of Britishness. He cites a complaint by Bipin Chandra Pal, in which Pal laments the impossibility of being truly treated as an Englishman while being Indian. The same character is explored by Chatterjee to highlight the internally fractious nature of nationalism and the externally homogenous representation of the nation. See Anderson, 1983; Chatterjee, 1993.

1

Colonial contamination and the postcolonial moment

The postcolonial moment

One of the enduring fictions of modern statecraft is that colonialism ends when a foreign power leaves a political territory. In the context of 1940s and 1950s South Asia, newly independent governments, comprised of national elites groomed in subordinate advisory legislative councils to the former British government, took up the reins of government and embarked on "modernizing" projects in order to catch up with the colonial-turned-"developed" countries of the "first" world (Bhambra, 2014; Frank, 1966). The coloniality of these institutions and the norms and expectations of total territorial rule that underscore the form of international sovereignty inherited by national governments from their imperial predecessors remain under-interrogated in global studies more generally, and in Sri Lanka and South Asia as well. As Ananda Abeysekara (2002: 8) notes, often the postcolonial labour to decolonize institutions and knowledge risks reproducing and consolidating the very kinds of categories and boundaries of knowledge such as "native" and "colonial." Abeysekara calls attention to the presentism that can run unchecked in postcolonial historical work by reading modern colonial concepts such as "religion" into pre-colonial pasts. Doing so risks treating "religion" as it was experienced in the nineteenth and twentieth centuries as being relevant to the twelfth or thirteenth century, which is historically inaccurate (Abeysekara, 2002: 22–23). It is clear from accounts of early national leaders, such as D. S. Senanayake, John Kotelewala, G. G. Ponambalam, Jawaharlal Nehru, B. R. Ambedkhar, M. K. Gandhi, or Mohamed Ali Jinnah,

Colonial contamination 33

that all were confident that they could step into government, and the national movements for independence around the British Empire attest to this fact. While there were spirited disagreements between these South Asian postcolonial nationalists about issues – perhaps most importantly the accommodation of minorities under universal suffrage – there was no concern among the postcolonial elite that the legal and increasingly democratic institutions of the state itself might continue to incubate and replicate colonial violence in the absence of the physical presence of the British. Stated simply, colonial oppression was understood as residing with the presence of the British, but not with the presence of colonially contaminated institutions.

To be invested in a Eurocentric philosophical understanding of the world does not require one to be European; many scholars from the south are intellectually invested in the ontological and epistemic frameworks of Eurocentric philosophy, an issue I take up squarely in Chapter 5 (Parasram, 2020; Williams, 1964; James, 1938; Mendis, 2005). The reverse is true as well, as many scholars located in the north – especially Indigenous scholars, who shatter the construct of "north" and "south" – are not invested in Eurocentric philosophy alone (Coulthard, 2014; Coulthard and Simpson, 2016; M'sɨt No'kmaq et al., 2021; Bernard, 2017). The geographic distinction can be treated as a heuristic device to highlight the hegemonic influence of Eurocentric philosophy in the last half millennium (Mohanty, 2003). The importance of scholars' investment in the lens of universal modernity cannot be understated, however, as organizing pasts into statist histories reifies a conceptual lens that James C. Scott (2009) has aptly described as our collective hypnosis by the state. As Karena Shaw (2008: 26–34) reminds us, the structure of modern sovereignty today relies on a shared ontological foundation established in Thomas Hobbes's first book of *Leviathan*. This conception of state and territory has ordered modern time in a linear fashion, representing systems of organization that are ontologically different from the modern, colonial condition as "pre-political," and thus representing the colonization and transformation of diverse lands into modern states as inevitable, rather than highlighting the profound violence of that transformation. The necessity of being a state in charge of a bounded territory

34   *Pluriversal sovereignty and the state*

in contemporary international relations has created havoc across much of the formerly colonized and still colonized world, producing some of the most pernicious forms of ethno-nationalist violence in pursuit of total territorial rule in recent memory.

At the anti-colonial Bandung conference in 1955, leaders of the former colonies met to discuss the meaning of decolonization and freedom from colonial rule, as well as strategies for anti-colonial solidarity, for economic modernization, and for ensuring that re-colonization by Europe was preventable (Lee, 2010; Chakrabarty, 2010; Gupta, 1992). Formal possession of state sovereignty was understood to be a strategy that, when paired with nationalism, could lead to the rehabilitation of denigrated nations and races, while at the same time enacting bordering practices and international experiments like the Non-Aligned Movement that were designed to keep former colonizers out (Fanon, 2004; Gupta, 1992). Challenging the legitimacy of sovereignty, as constituted in the post-Second World War state system, was not part of the political project at Bandung, nor was it among the many struggles across the British Empire for freedom from colonialism. The postcolonial state, and the integration of formerly subject peoples into a liberal, modern/colonial legal and sovereign global order within the fledgling United Nations, were fundamental to asserting the vital components of internal sovereignty, characterized as autonomy within established borders, and external sovereignty, characterized by non-interference and mutual recognition in the international system (Giddens, 1987: 282). In pursuit of that essential material goal – that is, the institutional expulsion of direct British rule – the newly independent states could inhabit the state and go about "catching up" with the former colonial states that were beginning to shed the identity of colonial rulers in favour of "civilized" and "developed" states instead. As Fanon's (2004) work makes clear, inhabiting sovereignty and nationalism was seen as a politically useful strategy for the time, but it was not uniformly seen as an endpoint.

Loyalty to the nation and popular nationalism were important in achieving political independence, but elite-led nationalism was only one of many ways in which colonized South Asians resisted colonialism. Political independence, particularly in British South Asia, was accomplished through a variety of means, including direct

Colonial contamination 35

violent struggles, civil disobedience, and national mobilization, between the late nineteenth century and the mid twentieth century in particular. Importantly, South Asian revolutionary thinkers and activists were global thinkers, engaging with Western and Eastern philosophy and movements as well as identifying radical points of overlap through which their anti-colonial politics could be articulated and translated (Ramnath, 2011; Singh, 2007; Tagore, 1917).

Coloniality and the violence of universality

This universal state, conceived of as a "container" that possesses sovereignty, houses nations, and accumulates wealth and power, is at the heart of international relations and associated disciplines; it continues to limit the range of what appear to be viable political solutions to postcolonial crises of sovereignty in the twenty-first century (Taylor, 1994). It does so because it fails to draw upon the global range of ideas and possible solutions available, which have been violently punished, contaminated, and transformed through the modern state under the liberal justification that this pluriversal reality needed ordering, simplification, and conformity in order to realize the fruits of modern development, which continued much of the economic, political, and cosmological work of colonialism into the "post-colonial" age. As Nicholas Onuf (1991: 426) has argued, "Liberalism is modernity's core ideology, capitalism its paymaster, and the state its highest social realization, primary agent, and paramount problem." This is particularly important because in many ways, state sovereignty was meant to be a strategy to border and monopolize violence; as Shaw (2008: 37) describes it, sovereignty as represented in Hobbes

> constructs the space of the state as the space of identity and meaning. It sets up sovereignty as the answer to all that ails, an answer meant to minimize violence and enable men to pursue their desires. It sets the terrain for the rest of his thought.

To be sure, in the everyday world of international relations as constituted by the mid twentieth century, sovereignty was an important concept and tool, reflecting, as David Blaney (1996: 462–463)

36 *Pluriversal sovereignty and the state*

explains, "the value placed on autonomy in international society; it stands as a claim about the right of each political community (conventionally organized as a state) to rule itself and, concomitantly, a denial of any political authority above states." This conception demonstrates the centrality of normative analysis to sovereignty and its dynamic and evolving nature, and also to the multiple motivations for wielding sovereignty in the present day (Ruggie, 1986). The universal approach is challenged by bringing to light the decolonial notion of "coloniality," which, Ramón Grosfoguel (2007: 219) argues,

> allows us to understand the continuity of continued forms of domination after the end of colonial administrations, produced by colonial cultures in the modern/colonial capitalist/patriarchal world-system ... part of the Euro-centric myth is that we live in a so-called "post" colonial era and that the world and, in particular, metropolitan centres, are in no need of decolonization.

The colonial encounter was, as Walter Mignolo explains, the "flipside" of the modern encounter, and neither modernity nor coloniality is conceivable without the other. The rapid proliferation of state sovereignty in the nineteenth century, overlapping as it did with the age of late empire, can be explained only relationally rather than sequentially. When the colonies stopped being colonies, they became the "third world" and "developing" countries, the empirical details of which are well documented in World Systems Theory and Marxist accounts of neo-colonial capitalism (Frank, 1966; Wallerstein, 1974). Karl Marx himself reflected on the problem of South Asia's integration into the imperial economy and the violence of that colonial integration through the destruction of South Asia's productive capacity that resulted from the encounter with the British (Marx, 1853).[1]

When I speak here of the coloniality of the state, I invoke the systems of knowledge that have informed long histories of spatial organizations in different parts of the world, and specifically how these ways of being are ignored and denigrated under the lens of "universal" reason that is a defining characteristic of modernity (Parasram, 2014). In addition to the epistemic aspect, there are of course many material relations that demonstrate how the making

Colonial contamination   37

of European states was fundamentally linked to imperial and colonial expansion. People, knowledge, resources, and approaches to governance circulated in ways that make it impossible to conceive of modern Western Europe in general, and the United Kingdom in particular, outside modern, colonial co-constitution. As David Blaney (1996) observes, reflecting on the turn to post-development thinking in the 1990s, one key limitation to dependency theory's approach is its modernist terminology, which obfuscated the inherently relational production of both metropole and satellite through the logics of capitalism and sovereignty.

The violence of universality

As Aníbal Quijano (2007) maintains, there has been no greater genocidal violence in the known history of our planet than the one enacted upon the Aztec-Maya-Caribbean and the Tawantinsuyana (Inca) of Latin America with the coming of the conquistadors after 1492; sixty-five million people died as a result of microbial genocide and military and economic violence in less than half a century. Cristina Rojas (2016), working from Anthony Pagden and Karena Shaw, shows that the development of European concepts like "natural rights" was always fundamentally premised on the racial superiority of Europe, drawing on the work of John Locke, a co-author of the Carolina constitution. In particular, Rojas argues that Locke's work seeks to rationalize the enslavement of Africans as well as the theft of Indigenous land on the basis that the "failure" to cultivate that land and transform it into something economically productive signifies an inability to own or claim it.

Such interventions draw attention, though not explicitly, to what the Argentinian philosopher Enrique Dussel has named the "geopolitics of knowledge" (Mignolo, 2002). The geopolitics of knowledge describes the disproportionate and hegemonic influence of ideas that are situated and deeply grounded within a European epistemic and ontological context; however, as a consequence of this grounding and the empirical histories of colonial modernity, it has been presumed that Western intellectualism is universally valid, while societies that operate differently have been

38   *Pluriversal sovereignty and the state*

scripted as inferior through the colonial encounter by Europeans (Grosfoguel, 2007: 211). As Donna Haraway (1988: 581) has noted, the idea of a universal and objective perspective relies on an ideology of science that no real scientists believe is possible in practice. Advancing the ideas of "feminist objectivity" and "partial perspectives," Haraway argues that the only objective point of view is a partial one, because a universal view is an illusion or "god trick" (Haraway, 1988: 581). This geopolitical, epistemological grounding of European thought takes on material meaning because the influential philosophies that have informed the modern period exist within a system of knowledge in which it is deemed both possible and desirable to make abstract generalizations about universal experiences, using intellectual and empirical points of reference of relevance to Europe, to explain the rest of the world.

As a revolutionary intellectual and political project within Europe, European political thought and philosophy with their "degovernmentalization of the cosmos" and corresponding invention of *raison d'état* and European scientific reason attempted to assert themselves as secular, universal alternatives to the universalizing worldviews of Christian theologies in the context of the scientific revolution and age of Enlightenment (Foucault, 2009). With reference only to Europe, we can see the project of modernity and Enlightenment in the familiar way in which it is represented in the Western academy: a period of intellectual emancipation, where ideas grounded in rationality, progress, and objective evidence offered a *new* universalizing lens through which to experience and study the one reality that existed. As both Mary Louise Pratt (2008) and Enrique Dussel (1995) have argued, the emancipatory intellectual discursive appeal to scientific exploration and discovery has long hidden the underlying violence of conquest. Gurminder Bhambra (2014: 40–44) argues that one of the founding myths of European modernity has been the belief that important events like the Renaissance, the French Revolution, and the Industrial Revolution were somehow endogenous to Europe, without regard for the inherent interdependences that demand a global understanding of modernity from the onset (Go, 2013). Dussel has described the totalization of European knowledge as "eurocentrism," which, according to Rojas (2016: 375),

Colonial contamination 39

halts the possibility of an exchange of knowledges. Moreover, this myth [of modernity] hides the other side of history: Europe's centrality was built upon a colonial project premised upon conquest of the Americas (and, of course, Africa and parts of Asia). Accordingly, there is no modernity without coloniality.

Part of the blindness of Western epistemology is its investment in the "'ego politics of knowledge' over the 'geopolitics of knowledge' and the 'body-politics of knowledge'" (Grosfoguel, 2013: 76; see also Maldonado-Torres, 2006).

In the context of outlining the significance of coloniality for this chapter, however, it is most relevant here to return to the "post-colonial" twentieth century, and the discourse of development and modernization. In this context, post-colonial states were understood to be on a socialist or capitalist path towards arriving as equals on the international stage, yet United States capitalism and Soviet socialism shared universal and totalizing views of the world predicated on the inevitability of linear progress. Both saw the existence of ways of organizing life that existed prior to the European encounter as "pre-modern" or "traditional." As Indigenous scholars and scholars concerned with the ontological dimensions of colonial encounters have noted, other-than-modern peoples have organized themselves on the basis of different ontological starting points in relation to the world and their contexts within it, such as through relational ontologies or unified material and cosmological realms (Coulthard, 2014; L. Simpson, 2017; Deloria, 1973; Gehl, 2014; Shilliam, 2015; de la Cadena, 2015). The historicization of the "state" with attention to colonial entanglements helps to show how the territorialization of the state-nation has been relationally determined on unequal terms, weaving violence into the fabric of the state in more than material ways alone. The coloniality of the state speaks to the ways in which the structure of the state has been largely removed as an object of intellectual and cosmological concern in order to "accept" a rational and physical notion of state territoriality. This notion, in turn, has inadequately described the many layers of intersecting forms of violence that universalized an understanding of sovereignty and territoriality that serves the stability of the system of states and the imperial interests within them.

40   *Pluriversal sovereignty and the state*

By the time freedom-seeking subjects of the British Empire succeeded in ending British rule in Asia, Africa, and the Caribbean in the mid to late twentieth century, the practice of *being* modern/colonial satellite states that were plugged into the formal imperial political economy worked to normalize the institutional structure of the state as a natural, or at least inevitable, spatial arrangement with universal legitimacy. Possession of the state, the institutional, social "Leviathan" through which one could "be," was the primary political mandate of independence movements in Ceylon and South Asia more generally. Conversely, one could not "be" within an international fraternity of states unless one was organized as a state.

The process of social, economic, and political territorial transformation that produced modern states depended on the violent denial and active dismantling of alternative methods of organizing social, economic, and political life that took on particular characteristics depending on Indigenous groups and colonial powers, the territories in question, and the time period in which the encounters between colonial and anti-colonial parties occurred. Following Rojas's work on the violence of representation, the presentation of the state as the universal way to exist in the modern/colonial world can be understood through the lens of a "regime of representation," which Rojas (1995: 196) explains "extends in time and space through the construction of meanings that are relatively fixed and distinct, so that the present can be differentiated from the past, and the self-differentiated from the other." Rojas's (1995; 2002) studies of post-colonial nineteenth-century Colombia demonstrate the importance of the "will to civilization" as the hegemonic lens through which liberal and conservative reformers contested how to go about civilizing Colombian artisans, and Indigenous and Afro-descendent peoples, either through the liberal push for laissez-faire individualism or through the conservative push for strong state management. Through this lens, we can see that the violence of state formation is much more than the material politics of what was physically done in the nineteenth century to produce states (i.e. road construction, expansion of administrative bureaucracy, integration into imperial political economy, etc.); it very centrally extends to the ontological conflicts and epistemic violence of what counts as knowledge and viable political options for a world that is

Colonial contamination

always changing (Blaser, 2013). While the literature on state formation varies in terms of when, and by which means, state sovereignty emerges, it is more or less in agreement that the state is principally a European model, infused with a particular genealogy of thought that includes key European philosophers extending all the way back to the ancient Greeks.[2]

The violence of universality, in terms of the representation of the state as the only viable means of political organization, speaks to the research interest of the Modernity/Colonialty/Decoloniality (MCD) research group, which seeks to prioritize "an-other way of thinking" based on the dual strategies of "de-linking" and "epistemic disobedience" in order to fracture the hegemonic intellectual influence of Eurocentric scholarship and broaden the intellectual starting point for scholarly research (Rojas, 2016; Mignolo, 2007). This is a shared political project with some variants of postcolonial theory, as Bhambra explains. Following Homi Bhabha's call for interrupting Western discourses of modernity with narratives of subalternized and otherwise excluded perspectives and experiences, Bhambra (2014: 116) argues that "The issue is more about re-inscribing 'other' cultural traditions into narratives of modernity and thus transforming those narratives – both in historical terms and theoretical ones – rather than simply re-naming or re-evaluating the content of these other 'inheritances.'" The postcolonial objective can be thought of as broadening the limited range of Eurocentric modernity – seeking to provincialize the "insufficient but indispensable" place of European and Eurocentric philosophy – but it remains firmly grounded in the idea of a single modern existence that needs to be pluralized (Chakrabarty, 2000; 2009; Parasram and Tilley, 2018). This overlaps with what Rojas has critiqued as the epistemic orientation of the MCD group, in terms of outlining an intellectual project through which "other" ideas are integrated into the modern framework in order to improve that framework. As she explains, "Notwithstanding its progress in decolonizing knowledges and making visible alternative ways of knowing and thinking, the MCD program still privileges knowledge over practice and over worlds-otherwise" (Rojas, 2016: 376). Similar to critiques of South Asian subaltern studies, the issue here is the privileging of ideas and thinkers that are squarely part of modern, Western,

42   *Pluriversal sovereignty and the state*

systems of knowledge; this includes intellectuals from the Global South but only those who are working within the confines of the (post)modern academe. In the language of decolonial thinking, this is Dussel's geopolitics of knowledge; in the language of South Asian subaltern studies and its critics, it is the problem of using abstract continental European philosophy to understand a Global South that remains an empirical testing ground for Western scholars, who remain the chief producers of knowledge (Lal, 2001). In both cases, the heart of the matter is an under-problematized intellectual investment in the broader applicability of philosophy that is grounded in a Eurocentric, universal philosophy, its application to the rest of the world, and the ways in which this kind of commitment silences other possibilities.

This can give rise to two important kinds of problem: the first is the emphasizing of post-structural and post-modern Eurocentric theorizing as the main tool used by scholars from the Global South to chip away at the hegemony of Eurocentricity within the modern academe (as in the South Asian and Latin American schools of "subaltern studies"),[3] and the second is what the Aymara sociologist Silvia Rivera Cusicanqui calls the "political economy of knowledge" through which ideas that originate outside the modern framework are "exported as raw material returning regurgitated in a grandiose mix as a final product" (in Rojas, 2016: 377). Thus, even when MCD scholars seek to use Indigenous concepts in their academic writing, it is assumed that the difficult work of "translation" is credibly done by the academic professional who applies the concept within a modern academic framework. This is, to some degree, an unavoidable complication, but it draws attention to the incompleteness and impossibility of "pure" translation of ideas between pluriversal "worlds."

The violence of universality, then, is something that is not at all unique to colonial thinkers of the fifteenth to nineteenth centuries; it continues as the coloniality of knowledge production in the academe. The epistemic work of subaltern studies, postcolonial studies, and the MCD has done a considerable job of exposing the exclusionary nature of modern academia. However, in outlining the distinction between universal and pluriversal thinking, it is important to note that highlighting the "lack" of Eurocentric

Colonial contamination 43

modernity as an attempt to arrive at a single story is insufficient for pluriversal politics.[4] In the context of colonial state formation, to consider the diverse options that have informed social and political life requires both epistemic and ontological disobedience, as historical accounts and archival collections cannot be understood as objective records that are separate from the ideology of those who formed and informed records and collections. By "fracturing the modern episteme," decolonial approaches that are committed to understanding ontological difference and putting those differences into practice – and through practice, which is necessarily much deeper than scholarly writing – open up new possibilities for enacting a pluriverse of possibilities (Rojas, 2016). The fracturing has led to many tributaries, some favouring epistemic manoeuvres that contest the singularity of "modernity" with the call for multiple modernities or "our" modernity, and others informing the "ontological turn" in which the project of rethinking modernity requires putting into practice ontological starting points that are not situated within the scope of modern thought (Chatterjee, 1997; Eisenstadt, 2000; Escobar, 2015; Coulthard, 2014; Blaser, 2013). The violence of universality, within the regime of representation through which the modern nation state has been imagined as an emancipatory end unto itself, is precisely the reason why fetishizing "total territorial rule" remains central to postcolonial conflicts today.

When coloniality is examined as the constitutive flipside of modernity, the intertwining of deeply entrenched Eurocentric ideas about the linear movement of human history and spatial developments with the modern nation state as a "natural" end becomes clear. The power of this pervasive statist discourse, I argue, has blocked formerly colonized peoples from charting pluriversal decolonial pathways that challenge the universal singularity of the Eurocentric, territorial nation state as the only game in town. While critical theory rightly identifies the ways in which capitalism in the Global South has served neo-colonial interests, I contend that in addition to capitalism, both the state and the system of states in which we are embedded are symptoms of the broader problem of colonial modernity. In the time and place of the 1940s and 1950s, especially in light of the nationalist movements and institutional

44 *Pluriversal sovereignty and the state*

organizing that had created the conditions through which independence was brokered in Ceylon, self-rule was indeed the logical starting point of decolonization. Ceylon is a fine example, however, of a country that, by this time, was seen by the international community to be a model example for modern post-colonial leadership because of good economic fundamentals and the elite-level cooperation of different ethnic groups within the country. Even when the first government of D. S. Senanayake passed legislation to disenfranchise a subset of the island's Tamil population – the descendants of the migrant labourers from the rise of coffee plantations in the Kandyan interior – the Tamil leaders in the north accepted it, on the basis that these migrant labourers were understood to be outside the body politic or fledgling Ceylonese national identity (Jegathesan, 2019; Parasram, 2012; 2014).

Conclusion

What, then, is the significance of colonial contamination for the critical postcolonial moment of sovereign handover? The failure to recognize the inherent structural, colonial violence associated with *becoming* modern nation states works to naturalize the ahistorical assumption that "the state" describes merely an apparatus of power that is driven by the political objectives of those who rule alone. Interpreting it as such is complicit with the broader colonial discourses of development and gradual improvement that continue to try to sanitize the history of the foundational role of colonial violence in the transformation of many worlds into a universal mould of state sovereignty. It is not that "the state" in an abstract sense was created through empire; it is that the particular territorial state, which would go on to house nations, became a global institution and requirement in the nineteenth century within which to act on the perceived collective will of "its" people. The contamination of pluriversal sovereign arrangements has been the gradual process through which seizing the state can be seen as enough. It has certainly been treated in this way by postcolonial national elites, and we hear it echoing through Mahinda Rajapaksa's "the writ of the state now runs across every inch of our territory"

Colonial contamination 45

("No Mention of Prabhakaran in Rajapaksa's Victory Speech," 2009) in May 2009.

By this I do not mean that all states are identical, but that the modern nation state as a concept relies on ontological assumptions that may have resonance in the European genealogy of thought, but that have been enforced through the modern/colonial encounter as being "universally" applicable around the world. Social science has largely dealt with the fissures arising from the ontological distinctions by relegating to the realm of "culture" or "mythology" the practices that have given and continue to give territory meaning in different parts of the world as lacking in truth or validity (Shilliam, 2015: 128–129). Put another way by Walter Mignolo (2011: 239),

> Modernity has its own internal critics (psychoanalysis, Marxism, postmodernism), but in the Third World the problems are not the same as in the First, and therefore to transplant both the problems and methods from the First to the Third World is no less a colonial operation than transplanting armies or factories to satisfy the needs of the First World.

While I disagree with Mignolo about the equivalences of military and intellectual projects in practice – Cortez with a quill would probably not have been as destructive as Cortez with arms – there is good sense in differentiating between intellectual attacks from "within" modernity and those from "outside" modernity (Ahluwalia, 2005). With the context of coloniality, pluriversality, and universality in mind, I turn now to the literatures on state formation to examine their contributions and limitations in terms of the book's emphasis on colonial state formation. With the political postcolonial "moment" interpreted through epistemic-postcolonial and ontological-decolonial sensibilities now in mind, I proceed to think through core concepts like territory and sovereignty while focusing on the imperially driven interdependent creation of modern state formation.

Notes

1 Marx and his contemporaries refer to "India," but the cities and areas that he names in his writings on India speak to contemporary South

46   *Pluriversal sovereignty and the state*

Asia more broadly. Colonial-era writing and archives often do not distinguish between "Ceylon" and "India" in terms of ethnic, social, religious, and political categories. Some of this, particularly in the early nineteenth century, reflects the fact that the Madras Presidency in southern (contemporary) India "controlled" the island of Ceylon remotely from 1796 to 1802, but culturally and socially, European missionaries, planters, and bureaucrats routinely conflated Ceylon, India, Buddhism, Hinduism, and even Malay people into interchangeable terms.

2 Stuart Elden usefully identifies the importance of genealogy in tracing the development of territory, stipulating that his 2013 book should be understood as one that is particular to the European development of territory and not easily or advisably transplanted to other regions of the world. See Elden, 2013. Other scholars see the process of state formation as a process that "refracts" from the colonies onto Europe, with B. Anderson (1983) seeing this through nationalism and J. Branch (2011) seeing the process as inherently territorial through cartography. But in both cartographic or national rendering, the genealogy of thought remains Eurocentric.

3 I do not mean to imply that post-positivist (to use the categorization from international relations) research more generally is somehow free from colonial intellectual investments, but rather only to say that within the academe, critical approaches offer more intellectual space. As Pal Ahluwalia has forcefully argued, post-modernism and post-structuralism are counter-discourses emerging from within the boundaries of modernism itself, whereas post-colonialism is a counter-discourse seeking to destabilize Western cultural hegemony. Although Said's *Orientalism* (1978) is widely regarded as the academic launch of post-colonialism, Ahluwalia notes that Said quickly moved beyond his investments in French post-structural theory. Following Ahluwalia, understanding post-structuralism requires addressing post-structuralism's silence on the question of French colonialism. See Ahluwalia, 2005.

4 Robbie Shilliam, for example, has attempted to counter the violence of universality by taking the process of "delinking" from modern expectations of academic scholarship further, and putting other-than-modern concepts grounded in their own genealogical traditions (specifically the Māori *whakapapa* and the Rastafarai *grounation* as methods of discovering deep relations and history-sharing between peoples and cultures) into practice to reject what he calls "colonial science" in favour of "decolonial science." Following Shilliam, decolonial science seeks to turn over

Colonial contamination

47

and engage with "pasts" using other-than-modern frames of reference. It is possible to critique the modern/colonial practices of history and science, but also to engage in the *reconstructive* work of decolonial politics by putting into practice what is reclaimed and relearned through the process. See Shilliam, 2015, 1–11, 43–58, 167–181.

2

Universal sovereignty: externalizing violence, relational state formation, and empire

This chapter offers a pluriversal reading of key concepts within social science, such as territory, empire, and sovereignty, with a specific view to advancing an ontological critique of the Eurocentric and universalized state. In a meditation on common concepts like territory, sovereignty, and empire, the importance of pluriversal sovereignty becomes apparent: failure to account for multiple ontological starting points makes these concepts irredeemably colonial in nature. The work of exposing the coloniality of these terms does not "decolonize" either the term or the institutions and regimes that are described by them. On the contrary, it reveals that there is no scientific or universal basis upon which these concepts firmly stand; rather, they are indebted to multi-scalar processes of colonization that developed locally, regionally, and internationally as a form of colonial global social theory and politics. In showing the extent of this debt, I seek to prime readers trained in the Eurocentric academe (like myself) to recognize that Eurocentric sovereignty is as much bound up in cosmology and ideology as it ever was in any accurate account of territory and, in so doing, to open a space within which we may do the more important work of resuscitating and building anew. Put another way, with the knowledge of how linear developmentalist readings of colonized societies have been used as a means of separating an "enlightened" Europe from an under-developed world not far removed from the thralldom of the imaginary state of nature, part of this chapter's work is to demonstrate that Eurocentric sovereignty is as heavily invested in religious and cosmological assumptions as anyone else. This fact seems obvious at one level, and yet the experience of history and

Universal sovereignty

the colonial present which we all inhabit demonstrates that the radical equality of human societies and their worldviews is far from generally accepted.

Scholars of state formation are divided about the origins and most significant causes of the rise and spread of the modern nation state, but generally speaking, this tends to be placed some time during the lead-up to the Peace Treaties of Westphalia in the 1640s, the transformation of property relations and rise of Britain as the first modern state, and the rise of the nineteenth-century balance of power marking the alleged 100 years of peace between the fall of Napoleon and the rise of the First World War (Branch, 2011; Teschke, 2002; Elden, 2013; Taylor, 1994). The modern, colonial state is a particularly important formulation of modern, colonial power. The violence of universal thinking that made possible the rise of the state as a universal container, however, is of older vintage. As Antony Anghie observes, writing on the colonial origins of international law in the work of the fifteenth-to-sixteenth-century legal theorist Francisco de Vitoria, the seemingly progressive granting of rational human status to Indigenous peoples in the Western Hemisphere perversely legitimized Spanish aggression against them by integrating the "Indian" into a system of natural law that insisted on a common ontological configuration of land and territory. Anghie (1996: 325) writes,

> The universal divine law administered by the Pope is replaced by the universal natural law system of *jus gentium* whose rules may be ascertained by the use of reason. As a result, it is precisely *because* the Indians possess reason that they are bound by *jus gentium*.

Drawing on Anghie and Pagden, Rojas (2016) argues that in recognizing Indigenous people as equal to the Spanish but doing so only through Spanish cultural, spiritual, and legal knowledge, the Spanish forced an ontology of land that reflected Spanish and Christian worldviews onto territory where such notions were alien. The effect of this was perversely a *de facto* justification of the genocidal politics of the colonial encounter; the failure of the "Indians" to recognize the universal validity of Spanish values was evidence, for the Spanish, of racial inferiority (Rojas, 2016: 371–372). Vitoria's assertion of universal reason thus denies the

50 *Pluriversal sovereignty and the state*

distinctiveness of Indigenous ontologies of "sovereignty," and through integrating Indigenous peoples into a legal framework that developed genealogically within Europe (but always with reference to an "outside"), it could justify the dispossession of Indigenous peoples while extending the European imaginary that its ideas carried universal validity (Shaw, 2008).

The violence of universality is not always so obvious, however. As Bhambra (2016) has argued, seminal work on state formation within comparative historical sociology has ignored the imperial context, relationality, and transnationality inherent to state formation. This exclusion thus mitigates the methodological utility and influence of "ideal types" of states that can be compared across historical and geographical contexts. This is not a problem of left- or right-leaning intellectuals; rather, it is part and parcel of a commitment to a modern, scientific form of reasoning in the study of state formation, encoded in the canonical works on the subject by Max Weber, Karl Marx, or, more contemporarily, Charles Tilly or Anthony Giddens (Bhambra, 2016). Though she does not frame it as such, Bhambra appears to be in agreement with John Agnew's (1994) famous call to avoid the "territorial trap" which, in international relations in particular, is a ruse that has made possible an erasure of the complex sociologies and geographies that have given rise to the universal state. While Agnew does not necessarily disagree with Tilly's general approach (1985; 1990) on the triumph of the state model and its mobster-like use of strategic violence, or Stuart Elden's (2013) call for genealogical specificity in territorial formations where Europe is indeed but one site of inquiry, Bhambra's methodological critique outlines the impossibility of thinking about state territory in the postcolonial world in the absence of its direct relation to European empire, and vice versa (Bhambra, 2016). Though Bhambra's concern is with the methodological implications of this problem for comparative historical sociology, her intervention highlights the importance of thinking about state formation in the colonial world as a fundamentally global, or at least imperial, project, which helps to expose the violence of universality in scholarship that does not engage with the colonial question in seeking explanations for socio-political developments in Europe. This is a point that Benedict Anderson (1983) has spoken

Universal sovereignty

to in the context of "nation" formation rather than state formation, referring specifically to the origins of the European "nation" in Latin American nationalism and postcolonialism in the nineteenth century. Anderson also shows the relationality of modern nationalism and empire in his distinction between popular grassroots nationalism and "official" nationalism, to whose rise it is a dialectical response and which is thus an elite attempt to consolidate sovereign authority in the state. This approach, as Anderson demonstrates, was not unique to Europe, and Japanese nationalism took on a particularly modern and imperial structure.

In addition to the empirical and methodological point that Bhambra's article draws attention to, she also demonstrates the way insightful research invested in modern thinking can often be blind to what ought to be obvious points, as they relate to the colonial encounter. For example, Anthony Giddens's (1987) thoughtful work on the relationship of violence and the modern nation state nevertheless obscures the two-way relationship through which state formation influenced both Europe and the colonies. He uses the term "nation-states" to refer to European states and flips the concept to "state-nations" to describe post-colonial states with special reference to those emerging from the British imperial system. I agree with Giddens's categorization of "state-nations" in identifying the fact that the normalization of the "state" predates the tenuous nation in British South Asia, but he overstates the discreteness with which states formed.[1] Giddens fits into the methodological critique that Bhambra offers of presenting ideal types that miss the inherent relationality of state formation, as his study clearly positions the birth of states in an "original, i.e., Western habitat" (Giddens, 1987: 5).

Building on Foucault, Giddens (1987: 187–191) advances the idea that a defining characteristic of modern nation states in Europe has been the gradual diminishing of the use of violence as a means of coercion within the boundaries of the state. Acknowledging that the degree and effectiveness of internal pacification varied throughout Europe and that its success in Britain was remarkably quick, he explains that the development of industrial capitalism played a decisive role in altering the use of force within European states. Building on Marx, Giddens (1987: 191) argues that "'dull economic

52   *Pluriversal sovereignty and the state*

compulsion,' plus the surveillance made possible by the concentration of labour within the capitalist work-place replaces the direct possibility of coercion by the use of force." Thus, the internalized disorder that preceded the rise of industrial society in Europe was one that relied on the blunt application and threat of force, in which rogues and robbers ruled the highways, and the application of force and the threat to take life were the only guarantees of safety. Demilitarization of the state is an essential component of coercion by commercial means for Giddens, and this view echoes the views of early nineteenth-century writers like Benjamin Constant, who argued that commerce and capitalism marked a separation between a pre-modern past of violence and war, and a modern present of "civilized" conduct through which the incentive structures of commercial society would render war anachronistic (Pagden, 2005).

I will return to Constant through Anthony Pagden's discussion of "divided sovereignty" later in this chapter, but for now, the point to draw attention to is that the claim that capitalist development led to pacification within Europe fails to account for the fact that this relative peace was paid for by the *externalization* of European violence in the colonies. Colonial capitalist and administrative reforms did not demonstrate a diminished use of force; rather, they were predicated on the necessity of dismantling ontologically distinct ways of organizing life and replacing them with a satellite commercial relationship to other hubs of the imperial economy. Siba Grovogui (2002) masterfully demonstrates how any internal conditions of peace within Europe in the nineteenth century were predicated on applying the rules of international relations differently. Grovogui notes that through the colonial encounter, African sovereigns were downgraded from being seen as equal to Christian-European rulers to being regarded as necessarily inferior, and this presented "failed" African states under the nineteenth-century balance of power as raw fodder upon which "failed" European states like Belgium could thrive through expropriation. An obscure state like Belgium, following Grovogui, was viable only because of the tacit agreement of the so-called Great Powers that Belgium ought to be allowed to externalize the violence of state-building to the people and land of the Congo, exemplifying the inherent racism of global primitive accumulation.

Sovereignty and territory

There are no easily acceptable definitions of "sovereignty," though few would contest that the most conventional use of the term reflects its pairing with the structure of the "state," specifically referring to the absolute autonomy of the state to do as it will within the confines of its borders. Following Max Weber (1919: 4), the state can be defined as a "human community that (successfully) claims the monopoly of the legitimate use of physical force within a given territory." There are many universal assumptions within this formulation of the state, including the presumption that territory and people are discrete entities, that human communities are the logical point of departure for organizing life, and that violence is a legitimate means of achieving order. Here I seek to outline the epistemological and ontological aspects of historical research on sovereignty and territory, situating them within a European genealogy that became globalized through the age of empire(s). By bringing a pluriversal lens to bear on this literature, I aim to bring into focus the need to understand sovereignty and territory as pluriversal notions with histories in different parts of the world which came into contact with each other through the externalization of violence in the modern, colonial encounter.

The common account of sovereignty in much twentieth-century structural international relations scholarship emphasized the critical significance that the signing of the Peace Treaties at Westphalia in 1648 had for wedding sovereignty to internally and externally recognized territorial boundaries, as well as the philosophical importance of Grotius, Bodin, Hobbes, and Rousseau in particular (Elden, 2013; Onuf, 1991; Maritain, 1969; Walker and Mendlovitz, 1990). Many international relations scholars argue that 1648 has been seen as a time of exaggerated significance, perhaps even giving rise to a "myth" of the Westphalian argument sketched together long after the fact and then read backwards into history (Osiander, 2001; Kayaoglu, 2010). John Ruggie (1993) reminds us that while systems of rule have always been about the organization of power, systems of rule have not always been territorially fixed and exclusive, and at times, they have not been territorial at all. When, and where, then, do territory and sovereignty fuse together?

54   *Pluriversal sovereignty and the state*

Following Onuf (1991), the "standard" international relations definition of sovereignty refers not to a political community so much as it does to a defined territory. The eminent classical realist Hans Morgenthau (1948) dates sovereignty to the end of the Thirty Years War in 1648, defining sovereignty as a political "fact" of supreme power. This implies an implicit internal and external dimension of sovereignty. In his genealogical account of sovereignty, however, Jens Bartelson (1995: 24) argues that it is important to avoid the ontological and historical mistake of tying sovereignty and anarchy together:

> the ontological primacy accorded to the state in international political theory implies the *givenness of sovereignty* as its defining property; sovereignty signifies what is inside the state, either constituted by the fall from a primordial unity or simply taken for granted at the level of definition. In either case, sovereignty is constituted as a primitive presence from which all theorizing necessarily must depart, if it is to remain international political theorizing.

Assuming dividing lines between internal and external sovereignty exemplifies a form of presentism through which a late modern and Eurocentric understanding is projected into the past, removing from inquiry the ways in which these notions of internal and external sovereignty took root (Bartelson, 1995: 60).The fact that "final authority" within a given territory has always, in practice if not in theory, been challenged throughout the history of the state system provides evidence of the problematic nature of the common assumption (Krasner, 1988: 88; Armitage, 2013: 215). Belief in the durability of Westphalian sovereignty persists, argues Krasner (1999: 9), notwithstanding its constant violations. The assumption of sovereignty meaning absolute rule over a given territory is well rehearsed and persistent, but as Ruggie (1986) in particular has argued, tied up with this assumption is a necessarily static understanding of sovereignty, which in turn is both a historical and a conceptual fallacy (see also Bartelson, 1995; Lake, 2003). Such a fixed conception of sovereignty, argues Onuf (1991: 432), presents "internal sovereignty" as something that "enables modernity to fulfil its many possibilities within states. Meanwhile, 'external sovereignty' denies the possibility of any such change in the relations

Universal sovereignty 55

of states." In his conceptual history of sovereignty, Onuf (1991: 434) argues that state sovereignty is a modern phenomenon and conceptual innovation made possible by the decline of the Roman church in the temporal sphere, alongside a decline in nominal empire, a rise in the autonomy of principalities, and, importantly, the international relations and diplomacy between these small units, which was unhindered by the larger-scale authority of either church or empire. For Onuf, sovereignty's antecedents include the Latin *majestas*, *imperium*, and a sense of the "populace." In the modern age, "nationalism gave rise to the principle that every nation needs and deserves the protective shell of a sovereign state in order to fulfil its potential" (Onuf, 1991: 439).

The political philosopher and theologian Jacques Maritain (1969) argues that sovereignty cannot be divorced from the spiritual context out of which the concept emerges. Applying sovereignty to an embodied leader, group of people, or territorially bounded political institutions is, he argues, a philosophical misconception based on a misunderstanding of the genealogy of the term itself. Maritain discusses the problems arising from imprecise translation of Greek words in Western philosophy, which has given rise to what he sees as the "original sin" that enabled philosophers like Hobbes and Rousseau to appropriate the concept of sovereignty and apply it to an embodied leader or a general population. Maritain takes issue with the translation of the Greek *civitas* as the English "state," arguing that the word should more appropriately be understood as "commonwealth" or "body politic." Similarly, "the words *pincipatus* and *suprema potestas* are often translated with "sovereignty," the words *kurios* or *princeps* ("ruler") with "sovereign" (Maritain, 1969: 43, n. 9). Critiquing Hobbes's application of sovereignty to the body of the "Mortal God" within *Leviathan*, as well as Rousseau's grafting of sovereign power onto the people in the general will, Maritain strives to show how both attempts forget that the etymology of "sovereign" implies the transference of power and authority from the people to a transcendent sovereign who is necessarily separate from the people. Hobbes introduces a conception of "the state of nature" as a way to describe the arbitrary violence that prevails in the absence of order, arguing that rational men will seek to leave that state of nature and secure protection through the

56   *Pluriversal sovereignty and the state*

willing sacrifice of their liberty to a sovereign in exchange for living within the sovereign territory (Carnoy, 1984). While the immediate context of the Thirty Years War in Europe was clearly on Hobbes's mind when he penned *Leviathan*, it is worth noting the considerable irony of Hobbes's view that brutish violence was a characteristic of "uncivilized" societies in light of the European-led genocides and attempted genocides of Indigenous peoples that resulted from early contact with Europeans in the 150-plus years leading up to the publication of *Leviathan* (Moloney, 2011). From a pluriversal perspective, an ontological assumption of a relationship between territory and sovereignty presupposes that all people relate to territory in the same way, which as Karena Shaw (2008: 32) argues in her reading of Hobbes, creates not only a natural division between an inside and an outside, but an outside within which there is an absence of order, lawfulness, or justice.

> The "outside" is awful. Life "there" is not pleasant. But it is also more than that: it is brutish. There is no account of time, no way to give one's life meaning, no way to change one's condition, no way to create or relate to a collective, a community. There is no progress. Thus sovereignty is marked not only by peace, but by an entire – quite specific – attitude towards time, history, meaning.

The very premise of a state of nature that is "outside" political order reserves for Europe alone the ability to possess and inhabit order. The ontological point to emphasize here is not whether Hobbes was right or wrong; rather, it is that the metaphor he developed has been further developed and has emerged within a context of Indigenous dispossession and active attempts by European colonizers to dismantle ways of being without ever understanding the ontological basis of different notions of territory and cosmology (Coulthard, 2014; Mackey, 2016; A. Simpson, 2014; Parasram, 2018).

The political and spiritual context of European "sovereignty" at the time when Hobbes was writing was an imperial one grounded in a secular (temporal) emperor and a spiritual emperor in the form of the Pope within the Holy Roman Empire. It was a conception of sovereignty that is absolutist in essence, which, Maritain contends, is a contradiction because a power that is absolute cannot be territorially bounded. Territory in Europe, however, was not yet a

Universal sovereignty   57

requirement for sovereignty, which is a point developed by Stuart Elden (2009) in his genealogical account of the concept. Political geographers in particular have drawn attention to the way in which social science has used the term "territory" to mean various different things such as land or terrain, which has created the illusion that territory could be seen to be a "passive spatial recipient" of the state (Brighenti, 2010; Agnew, 2010). The resulting "trap" of territory has interestingly not been that scholars have ignored the centrality of place and space in the formation of territory; rather, as Agnew argues (1995: 379–380), "social science has been *too* geographical and not sufficiently historical, in the sense that geographical assumptions have trapped considerations of social and political-economic processes into geographical structures and containers that defy historical change."

Stuart Elden (2013: 323) clearly links territory to history and power, arguing that "Territory comprises techniques for measuring land and controlling terrain. Measure and control – the technical and the legal – need to be thought alongside land and terrain." A historical and political analysis of territory, then, becomes very centrally related to the state; however, Elden's specific definition of the term is not uniformly accepted. For example, Saskia Sassen (2015) argues that Elden's definition of territory is overly limited, and thus gives meaning to territory only truly through the state, when territory perhaps could and should be more abstractly defined to help explain configurations of social power *prior* to the rise of the state. Sassen's critique of Elden's conception of territory is important in terms of challenging the universality of Eurocentric definitions of terms and the trade-off between specificity and ability to explain, as it opens up the possibility for pluriversal explanations grounded in history. In the Sri Lankan context, scholars like Qadri Ismail (1995) and Pradeep Jeganathan (1995) have sought to destabilize the post-colonial calcification of identities and histories by engaging textually and historically with how identities transformed across pre-colonial, colonial, and postcolonial time frames. Because identities and categories, particularly modern/colonial ones, can never truly be stable, investigating critical moments through which differences interact has become crucially important for understanding our contemporary condition (Abeysekara 2002;

58   *Pluriversal sovereignty and the state*

Jeganathan 1995). I seek to apply this to the context of sovereignty in Chapter 4's discussion of the encounter between Kandyan-Buddhist sovereignty and British/Christian sovereignty.

Maritain's claims about the absolute meaning of sovereignty are not unprecedented, but they do fall victim to Ruggie's criticism that sovereignty is held to be static when it should be understood as an evolving concept – one which, as Onuf suggests, takes on its full meaning only in the modern (colonial) world. Thinking pluriversally about the development of "sovereignty" not as a static term but, rather, as a way of organizing life related to different notions of territory, I would suggest that Maritain correctly identifies and traces an understanding of sovereignty that emerged out of the Christian European experience. As Bartelson (1995: 65) observes,

> We cannot demand, however, that the history of thought should supply us with solutions to our own problems ... we must learn from the past: the alien character of past beliefs is what constitutes their relevance to our present, since our own concepts nevertheless evolved out of them.

I agree with Bartelson, but also insist that the genealogies of "sovereignty" are evidence of a pluriverse of multiple ontologies and ways of relating, within which the Eurocentric understanding of territory, religion, and authority is just one among many others. This is more than "provincializing Europe" in the subaltern tradition, because to render Europe a province within a world already geographically constituted by provinces is akin to having a redistribution of power in a federal election; if the problem is the universal state, demoting a single province that has been disproportionately elevated could not undo the violence of universality woven into the state system.

Sovereignty, if it is to be understood historically, cannot be divorced from its geographic, cosmological, and historical configuration in all places, not merely Europe. The "standard account" and the preponderant understanding of what this means reflect the violence of universal state formation in the nineteenth century, as this was the period of imperial expansion through which Europe sought most actively to dismantle (either through direct violence of war or through indirect violence of civilization and development) other ways of organizing life within a given region, using techniques

Universal sovereignty 59

grounded in Eurocentric ontologies of land. "Territory" then, needs to be separated from its Eurocentric roots if we are to be able to study the process through which one form of territory was made to resemble another form of territory through nineteenth-century empire. Sassen (2015: 115) offers a more general description of territory, saying it should be seen as a

> complex capability with embedded logics of power (which in our western modernity found its most accomplished form in the modern state) and embedded logics of claim-making (which again, in our western modernity found its most accomplished form in today's understanding of citizenship).

Following Sassen, territory is untethered from its Eurocentric origins, and as we will see in Chapter 4, a more expansive understanding of territory opens pluriversal space in which the ontological diversity informing distinct notions of territory and spatial organizations become visible.

Sassen's point does not, however, undermine the importance of Elden's emphasis on understanding the historical significance of the evolution of territory within Europe. This is precisely the point of looking at the historical and ontological context associated with the development of notions of sovereignty in different parts of the world. As Pat Moloney (2011) has argued, Hobbes's assumptions that "savages" live in a state of nature presuppose that there are no other manifestations of sovereignty, and that so-called savages live in anarchy, which we know to be historically incorrect. According to Elden, an important and understated aspect of Hobbes's contribution to the development of territory and sovereignty is the specific referencing of boundedness within his writing. The context of sovereignty before Hobbes was one in which sovereignty, as Maritain reminds us, was limitless, universal, and vested in the spiritual realm. According to Elden (2013: 301), Hobbes was

> still trying to work with an earlier model: his aim is for absolute sovereignty – that is, sovereignty without limits – which is what we previously understood as temporal power but without a counterbalance of spiritual power. Yet in other respects his arguments break new ground. The notion of the empowered sovereign being constituted from the individuals who authorized it is a powerful notion.

60 *Pluriversal sovereignty and the state*

As Hobbes suggests, "The Multitude so united in one Person, is called a COMMON-WEALTH, in latine CIVITAS. This is the Generation of that great LEVIATHAN."

The point is that in forming the great Leviathan as a literal body politic, the sovereign surveyed a bounded Christian territory as represented in the famous illustration on the front cover of the book. This is a critical break in Eurocentric political theory in which the centrality of territory to sovereignty became important. Reading Hobbes through his responses to Bellarime, Elden (2013: 301) argues that Hobbes "suggests that a plurality of Christian sovereigns had rights of sovereignty in their multiple territories, and that the pope does not have civil power except in the territories he directly controls." This fragmentation of universal sovereign power across all land vested in the Pope as Christ's representative on earth, and then further down to territorially bounded Christian monarchs, was a central component in the development of sovereign territory at the heart of the much later modern territorial state.

Empire

Although most accounts of the rise of sovereignty and its meaning of absolute rule over a bounded territory trace it to Westphalia or nineteenth-century imperialism, Anthony Pagden argues that it is a much older concept originating at least in the age of Cicero. For Pagden, classical and later notions of empire required a moral justification of defence to justify what is, in every case, a violent conquest as empire expands. When European powers were expanding overseas in the sixteenth and seventeenth centuries, Pagden (2005: 30) argues that there was

considerable anxiety as to what kind of rights, if any, they might have in the territories they occupied. The debates to which this anxiety gave rise turned inevitably on the question of how wars of occupation and dispossession could be presented as wars of defense.

The resolution of these questions, at least from the vantage point of debates in international law as described in Rojas's and Anghie's work on Vitoria, discussed above, saw the violence of universal thinking in forcing Indigenous people into Spanish categories that precluded their ability to engage in "just" war and justified Spanish violence against them. Sovereignty, from the time of the Spanish conquistadors onwards in the Eurocentric understanding of the term, had neo-Aristotelian roots, meaning "perfect community," which implied undividedness (Pagden, 2005: 32; Anghie, 1996: 329).

This indivisibility was not a constant for empire, however, and Pagden argues that it was precisely the change in thinking of sovereignty as something that *was* divisible, particularly in the aftermath of Napoleon's attempt to build empire from within continental Europe in the late eighteenth and early nineteenth centuries, that permitted a shift into a second period of modern colonial "empire" – what Pagden calls "empire 2." In the first period of modern empire, which ended between 1776 and 1830, sovereignty followed a logic of indivisibility. In the late eighteenth and early nineteenth centuries in particular, the differences and overlap between the nature of settler-colonial empires in contemporary North America and those parts of the British Empire like South Asia which were not settler-colonies created internal imperial debates on the asymmetric treatment of the two. The application of singular sovereignty meant, for late eighteenth-century thinkers like Adam Smith and Edmund Burke, that empire ought to mean a single sovereign state across disparate territories in which everyone was a citizen (Pagden, 2005). Burke was very critical of the British East India Company in particular because, clearly, company rule in India did not offer subjects and citizens equal rights. Pagden marks this period as ushering in a new generation of colonial officials who saw reformation and liberal-colonial, forms of inclusion as the ultimate goal of the British in India; they were not yet present in Ceylon. This cohort of reformers were informed by the more classical Orientalist scholarship of their British East India Company predecessors who sought to translate and integrate Hindu, Muslim, and British legal traditions. Creating a universal law out of the pluriversal legal tradition within India ultimately failed because Hindu codes, Islamic *Shari'a*, and English codes could not be reconciled. As Pagden (2005: 35) writes:

62   *Pluriversal sovereignty and the state*

> But for all his enthusiasm and Jones's genuine and deep respect for (at least ancient) Indian culture, the distances between, on the one hand, a code based on custom sanctioned by usage, as was the common law, and on the other, those based on the supposed utterances of gods, as were both the various "Hindu" codes and the *Shari'a*, were irreconcilable. Ultimately, if non-Europeans were to be "citizens" of the empires that had engulfed them and not merely their subjects, they could only become so by accepting the undivided legislative authority of their distant sovereign.

This is important for a number of reasons. First is the point that when Sir William Jones was faced with the irreconcilability of ontologically distinct legal systems, the result of that irreconcilability remains the need to universalize a single system, understood to be a superior one. Rather than living with diversity, disciplining and erasing that legal diversity was perceived to be the only logical course of action from the colonial vantage point. Second, it demonstrates a clear break in the nature of empire by the early nineteenth century if we are to accept Pagden's date range. Third, we see a moral demarcation between an older "empire 1" and an "empire 2" in which Napoleonic forces were in decline. Drawing on Benjamin Constant, a critic of Napoleon, Pagden (2005: 36–37) shows that in Constant's view, the "modern" world of the nineteenth century was one ruled by commerce, which made men "gentle" in their actions.

> What the invention of commerce had achieved, entirely despite itself, was a radical change in the calculation of interest. "War, then, comes before commerce," he wrote. "The former is all savage impulse, the latter civilized calculation." And in the new world of calculation trade had taken over from empire, since the "infinite and complex ramifications of commerce have placed the interest of [individual] societies beyond the frontiers of their own territories." Modernity, in other words, cannot be other than peaceful and global.

From a purely Eurocentric point of view, perhaps Constant was correct, until the assassination of Archduke Ferdinand in Sarajevo in 1914. As explained earlier, however, the internally pacifying nature of commerce was predicated on the externalization of violence, which took the form of attempting to destroy ways of relating to and with land that did not fit within the ontological

Universal sovereignty 63

assumptions of modern capitalism and the modern state across the other-than-European world. Within approaches that consider the role of empire spreading and universalizing sovereignty, this was the critical juncture after which rule by empire and commerce came together in the nineteenth century under a normative framework of internal (European) pacification, reliant on an externalization of violence of an ontological and material nature in the colonies, ostensibly in service to a changing rationality of liberal improvement by the early nineteenth century. In Pagden's "empire 2" differentiation and indirect rule were the method of achieving this form of control, and they came with the assumption that the ultimate goal of colonial rule was to give up rule to a graduated population of "less civilized" others who, under European tutelage, would learn the values of capitalism, development, and centralized governance. As Jordan Branch (2011: 6) maintains, it was only in the nineteenth century that "rule came to be defined exclusively in terms of territories with boundaries between homogenous spatial authority claims."

Relational state formation: imperial or transcendent sovereignty?

Elden believes that within international relations literature, broadly speaking, revisionists tend to undersell the importance of Westphalia and its legacy in the development of modern notions of both sovereignty and territory, but he agrees that traditional readings of Westphalia overstate its importance. According to Elden, Westphalia was the codification of an already existing internal European imperial logic rather than a radical redefinition of territory and sovereignty. The word "sovereignty" appears only in the English translation of the Treaty of Münster. The Latin version of the Osnabrück Treaty refers to "iure territorii et superioritatis" ("territorial right and superiority"), and Elden (2013: 313) notes that the rights defined in these foundational texts are articulated with reference to the Latin *statibus imperii* or "states within the empire." This seems consistent with Hobbes's characterization of Christian rulers: "Every Christian Soveraign [sic] be the Supreme Pastor of his own Subjects … in their own Dominions" (Hobbes,

64   *Pluriversal sovereignty and the state*

cited in Elden, 2013: 301). Although the terms of the Osnabrück and Münster treaties did enable member states of the treaties to raise standing armies, form diplomatic and military alliances, and raise taxes to support their endeavours, members were not permitted to form alliances against the empire. As Elden (2013: 314) explains,

> This is indeed the key point: the treaties codified and reinforced an already existing state of affairs rather than distributing a wider set of rights. The elements within the empire were not yet states, because these rights came with their status as constituent parts of the empire. Nonetheless, taken together, these two points can be seen as crucial stages in the assertion of the state as laying claim to the monopoly of physical violence, both within the polity and as the means by which it would exceed its borders.

Elden goes on to note that the German word within these treaties that has been translated into English to mean "territorial sovereignty" is *Landeshoheit*, which, following Andreas Osiander (2001: 272), ought to be considered to mean "territorial jurisdiction" instead. As Turan Kayaoglu (2010: 195) argues, the Westphalian centrality was something that took on its contemporary importance to international relations' understanding of state sovereignty only in the nineteenth century, when German historians drew out of the Peace at Westphalia the narrative of "mutual independence, political tolerance, and the balance of power" in the political context of Napoleonic imperialism within Europe. Importantly, as Kayaoglu (2010: 195) explains,

> Nineteenth-century jurists added an external dimension to the Westphalian narrative: lacking a Westphalia-like arrangement, non-European societies remained in political disorder and religious intolerance. When these societies "fulfilled" the so-called "standards of civilization" the European states then "admitted" them into "international society."

Kayaoglu's account draws attention to the historical construction of what Osiander (2001) has called the Westphalian "myth."

For Maritain (1969: 61), the political transformations of sovereignty do not free the concept from its essential meaning, and he proposes that a new concept altogether may be necessary.

Universal sovereignty

The confusion in the concept of sovereignty as something possessed by a state or a people is that such approaches (in Hobbes and Rousseau) imply that sovereignty either resides at the hierarchically ordered top of the political community, or else is entrusted to the body politic as it assembles to deliberate and decide. But to be true to its history, sovereignty means rising *above* the body to exercise the transcendent authority of sovereignty:

> Either Sovereignty means nothing, or it means supreme power *separate* and *transcendent* – not at the peak but *above* the peak ("par dessus tous les sujets)" – and ruling the entire body politic *from above*. That is why power is absolute (ab-solute, that is non-bound, separate), and consequently unlimited, in its extension as well as in its duration, and not accountable to anything on earth.
>
> (Maritain, 1969: 47)

Maritain's historical and philosophical intervention highlights the original context in which "sovereignty" entered Europe, but treated in this way, the concept lacks a dynamic quality and, as Pagden's views on empire from ancient to modern times demonstrate, involves considerable change in terms of sovereignty and territoriality.

What is compelling about Maritain's intervention is that he highlights the fractious nature of sovereignty, even within the European Christian or secular tradition. Nevertheless, it bears remembering that Hobbes, Locke, Mill, and other seminal European philosophers were still theorizing about Europe in a way that was fundamentally related to non-European parts of the world, though they rarely acknowledged this explicitly. The distinctions between and conflations of terms like "state," "sovereignty," and "territory" introduce important questions about the development of these concepts, but also about the political importance of applying territorial conceptions of sovereignty to bounded places globally. As Bhambra (2016: 341–342) notes, the extra-territorial extension of European sovereignty to the colonies in the context of the nineteenth and twentieth centuries relied on a largely assumed ethnic and racialized understanding of "nation" which, in turn, made imperialism a constitutive part of economic and political nationalism in Europe in the nineteenth and twentieth centuries:

66 *Pluriversal sovereignty and the state*

> The nation, for Weber, is defined in ethnic terms. It is defined against the Polish people who may have lived within the borders of the Prussian and then the German state for centuries and it is defined against all other nations. This understanding of the nation is simply naturalized – there is no recognition of the historical complexity or contemporary contradiction – and it is established as the fundamental value within which social science should operate ... I want to argue that it is perhaps better to reverse this formulation and, instead, see Weber's political value system as central to his conceptualization of the nation. It is only this reversal that enables us to account for his concept of the nation-state failing to take into consideration his commitment, otherwise, to Germany being a world power, that is, an imperial state. What we commonly understand as the nation – and as the concept of the nation bequeathed to us by Weber – was actually an imperial state. While Weber elides the concept of the nation with imperial power, what enables the concept to gain traction in its own terms is the omission of German imperialism from what are presented as "national" histories.

Using Germany as an example, Bhambra explains that the concept of "nation," and the importance of the national wellbeing as wedded to imperial expansion in the non-European parts of the world, are evidence that the organization of sovereignty and state had imperial foundations in the practice of state- and empire-making in the nineteenth century. Nations were united in shared political destinies, which extended to becoming global powers, scripting the colonial world as "backward" or "undeveloped" with people who were "civilizationally unfit" to understand universal concepts such as private property, statehood, or citizenship (Mackey, 2016; Parasram and Mannathukkaren, 2021). Whereas Hobbes's universal decree of the "state of nature" strips the world of its pluriversal practices of what we might crudely translate in English as "sovereignty," Weber opens up the possibility of incorporating these "savage" places into a national project as part of an internal Western struggle "to become a world power through overseas expansion" (Bhambra, 2016: 343). Following Pagden (2005; 1993) however, this imperial impulse is hardly new, for in ancient Rome, the expansion of territory for the purpose of glorifying, protecting, and growing the nation was very much a part of imperial

Universal sovereignty 67

calculation. From a territorial point of view, Bhambra's point is very important, as it demonstrates the inherent transnational function of nineteenth-century *European* state formation, and the centrality of colonialism to making that international system function. In short, the Eurocentric state system and the leading imperial European states could not exist without the externalization of violence coordinated by nineteenth-century global empire.

By the end of official, institutional colonialism, territorial borders that had been created to protect delicate imperial negotiations between warring European empire-states which had dragged the world into imperial and global warfare for a second time had at times been challenged (for example, by the partition of India and Pakistan), but the logic of total territorial rule over a bounded territory in a Weberian sense was, at this point, an accepted norm of global political existence at the elite level. This is not to suggest, however, that this perspective was universally shared among the people. It is not the case that the hegemony of the state meant the obliteration of alternatives to total territorial rule. The point here is that by the time of formal political independence, the many political possibilities for how to organize territory were already shrouded in darkness, leaving the modern nation state glimmering in the sun that never set on the British Empire, embedded within a system of states that embodied Eurocentric ontologies of territory and sovereignty made to fit over other-than-modern ontologies. The question that pluriversal sovereignty presents is not whether Indigenous ontologies of territory could better manage the contentious nature of the colonial present; the point is only that the force-fitting of Eurocentric understandings of territory and sovereignty creates a particular kind of modern, colonial constellation that defines and enforces contemporary territory in universal ways that are unsustainable. In force-fitting the diversity of human sovereign experience into the pressure-cooker that is the postcolonial state, it is not surprising that explosions, such as ethno-nationalist strife, have occurred as diverse peoples have competed to claim historical precedent over a colonial structure and institution that has only a thin history. Indigenous ontologies of land have also been fractious, resulting in conflicts, resolutions of conflicts, and the effective management of socio-political life in diverse ways, and why

68   *Pluriversal sovereignty and the state*

should it be any other way? For example, the galactic *mandala* system that underscored pre-colonial state operations in South and South-East Asia, and the Haudenosaunee Great Law of Peace which managed international relations on eastern Turtle Island for more than 800 years while informing the fledgling American constitution, were not perfect systems, but they were systems that reflected the genealogies and ontologies of territory and rule within the areas in which they arose (G. Hill, 2008; Grinde and Johansen, 1991). Part of the colonial violence of universality is in the denial – often through organized political violence – of other-than-modern ontologies and cosmologies. That denial of the centrality and importance of knowledge and experience that came before which is blanketed over as "pre-colonial" or "primitive" is denied conceptual and political space within the framework of universal and Eurocentric sovereignty, but it never actually goes away. The lack of acknowledgement exacerbates conflicts rather than avoids them, as can be clearly seen in the kinds of territorial and sovereign contestations that define Indigenous and settler-colonial conflicts across Turtle Island today (Parasram and Tilley, 2018; Coulthard, 2014; M'sɨt No'kmaq et al., 2021).

In standard and conventional historiography, the writing, co-opting, and knowing of a "scientifically" modernist model of the past are a reflection of the ideological power of narrating the past using territorial frames of reference that look like states. If social science is thought of as a telescope, that scope is calibrated with a view to Europe. As a consequence, it provides (perhaps) a clearer picture of the socio-political dynamics of Europe than of those elsewhere; however, when that scope is swiveled to the east or the west, the calibration no longer captures the most meaningful picture. Of course, history is always a narrative, which necessarily means that elements of a much more complex past are taken out in order to advance a particular master narrative. My point is not that an objective history is either possible or desirable, only that the process of writing history in modern social science is deeply invested in projecting a universal, Eurocentric understanding of "sovereignty" and "territory" that limits the scope of possible questions we might ask about how past organizations of "territory" might better inform decolonial futures.

Universal sovereignty

By the time of the famous meeting of recently independent states at Bandung in the 1950s, international relations and related fields of social science saw, through the lens of developing modernization theory, that there was not one inevitable path of "catching up," but two (Bhambra, 2014). The Soviet Union and its representation as *the* alternative path to capitalist modernization have further entrenched modernist reasoning, as the genealogy of Marxism emerged firmly out of a European philosophical and political tradition with a view to universalism, albeit of a somewhat different economic variety.[2] More than just political colonialism and the state are intertwined: the foundation of the capitalist system and Western epistemology is invested in this matrix as well. As Mignolo (2002: 59) explains,

> The expansion of Western capitalism implied the expansion of Western epistemology in all its ramifications, from the instrumental reason that went along with capitalism and the industrial revolution, to the theories of the state, to the criticism of both capitalism and the state.

Efforts to justify these processes were philosophically linked to the intellectual project of modernism and the Enlightenment, which has had lasting structural effects across the social sciences, empowering discursively produced notions of the rational, European self over the "profane" Oriental other (Munro and Shilliam, 2011). As Robbie Shilliam (2011: 2–3) notes,

> It is within this context that European scholars of the comparative tradition could assume a universal standard of civilization modeled upon an idealized Western Europe to define modernity *tout court*, and thus relegate all other peoples and cultures in the world to an object of inquiry rather than as thinking subjects of and on modernity.

While efforts to "provincialize" Europe have been pursued in postcolonial studies, provincialization within a framework of container-states, imbued with what are Eurocentric understandings of sovereignty and territory represented as universal characteristics of human social organization, still misses the violence of universality encoded in the proliferation of the modern state-nation (Chakrabarty, 2007). Giorgio Shani draws attention to the fact that

70   *Pluriversal sovereignty and the state*

the inter-state system cannot be understood as free from the structural reverberations of the colonial encounter. In an essay concerning the future of international relations theory, Shani (2008: 723) argues that "the ontological premises of western IRT [international relations theory] need to be *rethought* not merely 'enriched by the addition of new voices' from the global South" (emphasis in original). Like Agnew's (1994) warning to avoid the "territorial trap," Shani's point warns of the importance of working through a "coloniality trap" within the inter-state system. Failure to decolonize the ontological assumptions that hide the co-constitution of modernity and coloniality limits our ability to engage the past, and to build better futures.

Conclusion

In this chapter, I have sought to expose the hidden "coloniality" of the state structure, and to make a case for a pluriversal approach to re-engaging with pasts in order to better understand the processes that worked to artificially universalize Eurocentic notions of territory, sovereignty, state, and history.[3] If, as I have argued, the universal territorial state is indeed a manifestation of coloniality, then the ability of Eurocentric concepts to become universally accepted norms speaks to the de-politicization of "state," "territory," and "sovereignty." By "de-politicized" I mean the naturalization of these concepts as universally applicable to the colonial world, and of their specific use to better understand the process of state formation in colonial Ceylon, which is the subject of the remaining chapters of the book. I am not arguing that the methods of mass mobilization and nationalism used to articulate a state-centric anti-colonialism in the nineteenth and twentieth centuries were not "political"; rather, I am arguing that by the time national movements claiming to represent the total territorial "writ" of the island of Ceylon began mobilizing in the latter half of the nineteenth century, the terms of the struggle for sovereignty, state, and territory had already been forfeited to a Eurocentric, universal view of what these terms ought to mean in the modern world. In other words, the process of colonial state formation was predicated on

Universal sovereignty 71

the violent erasure, or attempted erasure, of other-than-modern ways of life. This does not mean that a discrete European understanding of sovereignty destroyed Indigenous notions of sovereignty; it is precisely the ongoing conflict of differing ontologies and cosmologies of "territory" and "sovereignty" that comprises the colonial assemblage of the modern territorial state in Ceylon/ Sri Lanka, and by extension to the international system of states as well. Thus, it is not just that the state of Sri Lanka is an expression of coloniality; the international system that developed relationally with states itself encompasses the universalizing colonial violence of state-formation as well.

Pluriversal politics and a decolonial agenda are thus necessarily a global project: the "West," broadly speaking, is also in need of decolonization precisely because of the fact that the modern state and state system are inconceivable without imperial and colonial encounters. Understanding modernity and coloniality as being two sides of the same coin intellectually and practically means that the colonial matrix is, as Mignolo (2011: 66–67) says, "a structure not only of management and control of the non-Euro-American world, but of the making of Europe itself and of defining the terms of the conversations in which the non-Euro-American world was brought in." This line of reasoning implies that the development of European territory and nation states was not separate from, prior to, or dialectically related to the colonized places of the world; rather, the constitution of metropolitan-colonial and colonized territory or place was simultaneously linked in practice (Grovogui, 1996; Bhambra, 2016). Thinking about the state in pluriversal terms means thinking decolonially about the development of the state as a multi-scalar project unfolding locally, imperially, and globally. Emphasizing the colonial side of modern territory brings to light the centrality of slavery, genocide, coerced migration, and disruptive geographical transformations of Indigenous places into extractive plantations that were plugged into the world capitalist economy as servicing satellites to more advanced industrial states (Williams, 1964). Europe, especially the territorial units of Spain, England, France, Holland, and Portugal, is inconceivable without reference to genocide, slavery, coerced migration, and state geographing over Indigenous spatial systems. These processes have

72   *Pluriversal sovereignty and the state*

given institutional shape to the post-independence territories across the Global South that have been incorporated into the global system of states. Re-politicizing territory necessitates moving outside modern/colonial pathways, engaging with other-than-modern ideas about state, territory, and sovereignty, and bringing these ideas into conversation with European ideas. In this way, there is clear overlap in the core motivations of the postcolonial and decolonial projects as I have explained them above, though the radical potential of re-politicizing territory cannot be done using the language and conceptual limitations of modern social science alone.

As rain falls and water moves along a particular trajectory, the earth surrounding the moving water erodes, creating grooves, drains, tributaries, and even canyons. Over time, it can be difficult to imagine that water ever ran another way, especially from the temporal scale of reference of a human being who does not experience this historical process completely. Like the natural movement of water, rivers and streams change form and direction over time. But, unlike moving water, the statist "grooves" in which we find ourselves constricted are not the products of "natural" human development; they are, rather, more closely likened to a colonial damming of free-flowing water. These dams have disciplined movement in a way that has provoked an understanding of the state from today's temporal standpoint as being *the* natural way to exist as a human collectivity, but in the *longue durée*, that which appears static is far more fluid.

Re-politicizing territory means destroying the colonial dams and releasing the decolonial waters, allowing them to find their many ways to exist. This will be a turbulent and violent process, just as the destruction of a dam will necessarily be a turbulent and violent process because creatures embedded in a system respond to the cues of that system. If towns have been built on stolen land around a dammed river, for example, those towns may need to be swept away. There is no theorizing in the abstract alone; as Indigenous scholars on Turtle Island working in the Indigenous resurgence tradition have long noted, decolonization is a profoundly material process that is grounded to land (Coulthard, 2014; M'sit No'kmaq et al., 2021; L. Simpson, 2008, 2013; Alfred, 1999; Lawrence and Anderson, 2005; Lawrence and Dua, 2005; Hunt, 2013). It is a

Universal sovereignty

radical project, so attempts to integrate "decolonization" into liberal projects, including the United Nations, and/or attempts at truth and reconciliation in different colonial contexts remain toothless if they do not mean significant transformation of systemic privilege and dismantling of the "universe" of Eurocentric understandings of the world (Matsunaga, 2016).

The impact of a few hundred years of colonial modernity has also universalized a particular reading of "history" – a point that has been well criticized in postcolonial and decolonial studies in particular. The universalization of history has led to the exclusion of intellectuals who ought to have been engaged as equals, but has also colonized the territorial frameworks upon which philosophical and political debates can occur. This is the value of pluriversal politics: different ontologies are always interacting and transforming, though the violence of universality continues to miss great opportunities as a result. The remainder of this book picks up on one particular manifestation of colonial violence in the multifaceted norm of "total territorial rule" in the nineteenth century. The contemporary significance of modernity/coloniality, then, is truly a global problem that exists not only in history, but in the unquestioned ways in which institutions of colonially administered modernity continue to dictate the limits of what is and is not seen as politically possible. The success of colonial domination over subject peoples is being able to convince us all that our freedom ultimately rests in our ability to control the systems of government that were used to establish and normalize universal modernity in the first place. As Fanon (2004: 236) observed, "how could we fail to understand that we have better things to do than follow in that Europe's footsteps?"

Notes

1 Here, Partha Chatterjee's distinction between an externally performed or represented homogenous nationalism towards the rest of the world and an internally fragmentary and contested understanding of nationalism for "insiders" is useful. See Chatterjee, 1993: 1–15.

74 *Pluriversal sovereignty and the state*

2 It is important to acknowledge that anarchism also emerged out of a European genealogy of thought, especially as I have proposed South Asian engagements with philosophical anarchism as a possible avenue for charting alternatives to the state earlier in this chapter. As Ramnath (2011) argues, there is a difference between the local lived experiences of organizing society outside the structure of the state, broadly defined, and this "small 'a' anarchism" cannot be wedded to a single intellectual tradition. James C. Scott (2009) makes a similar argument in his work on South-East Asian peoples actively seeking to live beyond the limits of the state in uphill South-East Asia.

3 Parts of this conclusion come from my article "Postcolonial Territory and the Coloniality of the State" (Parasram, 2014).

3

Universal gaze and pluriversal realities

The same day we dined with our Baptist friends and in the evening saw the Governor come in from the Kandian country, where he had been to organize the newly-acquired territory. You will have heard of the overthrow of that system of tyranny and cruel despotism which has for so many years prevented European intercourse with the interior of this island. God understood the cause, and gave their cruel King into the hands of the Governor, together with all his territory, without the loss of any of our troops. Now the way is open for the Gospel into the interior.

> Elizabeth Harvard of the Wesleyan Methodist Missionary
> Society, in a letter to her parents from Colombo,
> March 26, 1815 (Harvard, 1833: 49)

The Religion of Boodhoo [sic] professed by the Chiefs and inhabitants of these Provinces is declared inviolable, and its Rites, Ministers and Places of worship are to be maintained and protected.

> Clause 5 of the Kandyan Convention ("The Kandyan
> Convention Proclamation," 1815)

The diary of Elizabeth Harvard, missionary of the Wesleyan Methodist Church, captures the cognitive dissonance of the early British colonial project in Ceylon. From the first of the quotations above, one might expect evidence of Christ Himself riding into battle to protect the noble British crusaders in their mission to cleanse the frontier of the scourge of idolatry and false belief. Harvard was just the latest in a longer chain of Christian crusaders invested spiritually in cleansing the island. Indeed, according to Nira Wickramasinghe (2006: 20–22), the coming of the Catholic Church as the ideological apparatus of Portuguese colonization was

76 *Pluriversal sovereignty and the state*

so destructive in its aggression against Buddhism and Hinduism that it ushered in a "dark age," out of which the distinctions between "Buddhists" and "Hindus" began to take on modern significance. It came as a surprise to the early Christian missionaries that Kandyan Buddhist priests had historically offered shelter and protection to Catholics fleeing persecution by Dutch Protestants in the maritime regions (S. G. Perera, 1944: 144). A colonial diary can tell us only what was believed to be true from one standpoint, and from Harvard's diary, it appears clear that the British governor Sir Robert Brownrigg gave her cause to believe that evangelism had a role to play in the early consolidation of colonial territory. The problem, which is fundamentally part of the story of colonial state formation, was that "organizing the newly acquired territory" meant entering into the Kandyan Convention earlier that month in a lavishly performative ceremony of sovereign handover, in which King George of England, protector of the Anglican faith, simultaneously became a *bodhisattva* king and protector of the Buddhist faith. I return to this in Chapter 5's conclusion in a comparison with the Royal Proclamation of November 1, 1858 in India.

There are many layers of rich contradictions that could be explored between these two statements, but for the purpose of this chapter, I focus on the pluriversal significance of the conflict between what we might crudely describe as British-Christian worldviews and Kandyan-Buddhist ones. There is no shortage of literature on Buddhism in Sri Lanka, and some of the more influential English-language works tend to highlight the ways in which Buddhism interacted with the state in the late colonial and postcolonial context on the one hand, and how Buddhism developed independently of European "discovery" on the other (Gombrich and Obeyesekere, 1988; Jeganathan and Ismail, 1995; Tambiah, 1992). Ananda Abeysekara (2002) rightly cautions against the tendency in postcolonial studies of Buddhism to establish or reinforce the representation of a binary of Buddhist and other-than-Buddhist worlds, which also echoes concerns in research within the field of political ontology. I agree with Abeysekara that the partisan and political context of the late colonial period saw a particular institutionalization of political Buddhism in Sri Lanka. As Nihal Perera's (2002) work on late nineteenth-century Colombo shows,

Universal gaze and pluriversal realities 77

"indigenizing" the colonial capital of Colombo partly involved shifting organizations and buildings to Colombo, and the ways in which organized political interests would be geographically compelled to make their case in the capital played a subtle but important role in legitimizing the state. By focusing on the critical juncture of the Kandyan Convention and the pluriversal nature of sovereignty I do not mean to suggest that Kandyan Buddhism and British Christianity somehow operated in isolation; global history cannot be compartmentalized so neatly. This chapter focuses on the universal orientation of the missionary gaze in misunderstanding the pluriversal lived realities of the people the missionaries sought to convert in early to mid-nineteenth-century Ceylon. My small contribution to this vast literature on Buddhism and the state in Sri Lanka is only to say that the ontological meeting point of Kandyan-Buddhist and British-Christian understandings of the state *together* produced the state we observe in history and today, albeit not on equal terms.

Most historical accounts date the beginning of British "total territorial rule" to March 2, 1815, the day the Kandyan Convention was proclaimed, though as Obeyesekere (2017: 225) maintains, the document was signed only on March 10. To the British elites, the Kandyan Convention meant ousting the reigning monarch of this large native kingdom in the centre of the island, thus ending nearly two decades of simmering warfare. To influential parts of the Kandyan aristocracy, it meant a temporary alignment with yet another European power to supplant a dynasty with roots in South India.[1] From a Kandyan point of view, there was every reason to believe that the British would do what the Dutch and the Portuguese before them had done – arrive in the central highland areas, burn some villages, and then retreat to the coast. The British had recently lost two wars with the Kandyans, the last of which led to the massacre of an entire British regiment, and although the kingdom had been bled economically since the Dutch were able to cut off its access to the sea in the eighteenth century, one can understand why the Kandyans saw themselves as holding a position of strength.

Unlike previous waves of foreigners to the island, the British period saw the first *de jure* as well as eventual *de facto* establishment of a central political administration in the south-west, made

78   *Pluriversal sovereignty and the state*

possible in part by bringing the hitherto "foreign" interior territories into legible, recognizable British space (N. Perera, 1998: 185–195). Whereas in India, where British officials were able to learn about the functioning of the Mughal imperial state system through first-hand knowledge, the case of Ceylon was considerably different. As Bernard Cohn (1996: 60–61) observes, concerning the first fifteen years of Governor General Warren Hastings's career:

> he was stationed up-country near the court of the last of the effective nawabs of Bengal. There he acquired first-hand knowledge of how an Indian state functioned and could not totally share the prevalent British ideas that Indian rulers were despotic, corrupt, and extortionate. He believed that Indian knowledge and experience as embodied in the varied textual traditions of the Hindus and Muslims were relevant for developing British administrative institutions.

Following a 1772 act of the British parliament, Hastings was appointed to the new position of Governor General and set about blending his knowledge of Indian and British statecraft. As Cohn (1996) rightly maintains, one cannot study British and Indian modern state formation separately, as the techniques and practices affected each other and were applied in both directions. Moreover, the idea of British state outside the parameters of "empire" is inconceivable, not only because the unification of 1707 made the invention of Britain a project of imperial state formation, but also because the lessons of statecraft moved in all directions (Bhambra, 2022; Anderson, 1983; Cohn, 1996). This pre-existing Orientalist knowledge of India from the late eighteenth century would have brought only confusion; one, I argue, that stemmed from the ontological distinctiveness of the *rajamandala* system and its genealogy, which I take up more directly in Chapter 5. As Wickremeratne (2006) has argued, there is nothing unique about combinations of religion and violence, and often it is the Western Orientalist caricature of "Buddhism" that seeks to apply the same Eurocentric relationship of state and church and is then surprised that a "peaceful" religion could endorse such acts of state violence that we see in what we understand to be Buddhist states like Sri Lanka or Myanmar. The Kandyan Convention, prepared in English and

Universal gaze and pluriversal realities 79

Sinhalese, was the legal basis on which the British believed they exercised "total territorial rule," yet the differing genealogies of sovereignty that had been normalized in the British tradition as opposed to the Kandyan tradition meant that this document had different meanings for each party. What would eventually, over the course of the nineteenth century, develop into a unitary sovereign colonial satellite state off the coast of the expansive British Raj on the subcontinent did not materialize in the way either contracting party thought it would. The dynamics of religious politics and the ontological meaning of sovereignty in the Kandyan-Buddhist and British-Christian traditions produced a clash of ideas that spurred the Uva Rebellion of 1817–1818, and though the next major rebellion would not break out until 1848, a simmering fear of attempts to drive the British out of Ceylon remained during the thirty years between the two.[2]

In this chapter, I focus on how a universal, British and Christian gaze operated in a way that rationalized the spiritual and intellectual inferiority of non-Christians in the early nineteenth century. In focusing on colonial writing and archives, I seek to shed light on how the British rationalized and understood their superiority in universalist terms, and I juxtapose this with a critical reading that seeks to make visible the pluriversal lived realities of people in Ceylon who were long accustomed to navigating simultaneous cosmologies and their political implications. In this way, I aim to set the historical and conceptual ground for Chapter 4, "Ontological collision and the Kandyan Convention of 1815," which explores the 1815 Kandyan Convention directly and interprets it as a moment of ontological sovereign collision. To accomplish this, I offer a historical narrative of the events that set the stage in early nineteenth-century Kandy for readers who are unfamiliar with the Sri Lankan context. Through drawing on missionary archives, I discuss the religious politics and the ontological conflict between Christian missionaries and the Buddhists they encountered. I outline the early relationship between education, evangelism, and colonization, and dwell on how the inability to move beyond a universal ontological framework limited and undermined the ability of missionaries to actually understand the "natives" they sought to civilize.

Modernity and coloniality: a historical sketch

The island's written history spans thousands of years in which spatial orders rose, fell, converged, and adapted (Duncan, 1990; Wickramasinghe, 2006). The Bay of Bengal has been a region of trade, migration, and politics for thousands of years. Europe joined in by the early sixteenth century, becoming a domineering player by the mid to late eighteenth century in the regional geopolitics of South Asian ocean space. After the British took the Dutch Maritime Provinces of Ceylon in 1796, they administered them out of their Madras Presidency in the south of modern-day "India" until 1802.[3] As Nihal Perera (1998: 30) argues, the institutional politics of Ceylon would have followed a very different trajectory had the 1802 Treaty of Amiens contained different terms, as the Dutch then sought to have Ceylon returned to them and incorporated into the short-lived Batavian Republic. In colonial geographic terms, Ceylon could have been incorporated into what would become British India to the north, or into what would become Indonesia far to the east. Much colonial correspondence between missionaries and their organizations and families back home during this era and well into the nineteenth century made no consistent distinction between India and Ceylon. The early missionaries usually came to Ceylon via India, and from their point of view there was little reason to think the native populations of "idolatrous Oriental heathens" (Hardy, 1841) were significantly different; Ceylon and India were equidistant from "true religion." European scholarship on South Asian cosmologies at the time demonstrated some familiarity with selective readings of Hinduism, but there was a paucity of European knowledge of Buddhism, complicated by the many characteristics shared between the two religions. For those coming from an Abrahamic ontology, grasping the Hindu notion of *jiv-atma* and *param-atma* (transcendental soul and divine essence) or the Buddhist disinterest in the existence of a single creator-God was difficult, particularly because of the presumed universality and superiority of Christianity in this time period.[4] The development of European knowledge of South Asian cosmopolitan practices that are now disciplined by the boundaries of modern "religion" was

Universal gaze and pluriversal realities   81

rocky, moving through waves of shock, rage, secularization, and patronizing sympathy throughout the nineteenth century. During this period, missionaries believed at times that Ceylon was either the key to converting the entire subcontinent to Christianity, or a necessary obstacle to overcome in service to this goal (Harris, 2006; Lynch, 1808–1858). Even without European interference, it is conceivable that the island might have been incorporated into a spatial organization involving parts of Dravidian South Asia; the reality of this has always been a major source of postcolonial insecurity for ethnic Sinhala, who comprise a majority on the island but are very much a minority in relation to the Tamil population in neighbouring continental South India. The significance of these possible sovereign configurations is that one should not see physical geography as a natural bordering process or a limitation to political possibilities. Territorial formulations are historically, geographically, and philosophically specific (Elden, 2010a; 2010b; 2013).

Although South Asian sovereigns have historically and symbolically laid claim to the entire island in the past, none in over a thousand years has ever materially done so. As scholars of the island have established, the historical imaginaries projected by modern political actors, be they Sinhala or Tamil, tend to read the contemporary unitary state ahistorically into the past (Wijeyeratne, 2011: 309; Korf, 2009). The spatial organization of power on the island prior to British rule was not centralized; at the time when the Portuguese arrived in 1505, there were three overlapping areas of political control based on a northern Tamil kingdom in the Jaffna region and two Sinhala kingdoms in Kandy and Kotte. In 1521, the once-powerful Kotte fractured into three territories, Kotte, Rayigama, and Sitavacam, with Kotte becoming a client state of Portugal (Duncan, 1990: 31). Although Portuguese rule was unable to extend far behind any coastal region, its influence in Kotte was significant enough that the King of Kotte converted to Catholicism and bequeathed the kingdom to the King of Portugal. This marked the first time a Sinhala king of Lanka had not been Buddhist since the conversion of King Devanampiyatissa in 250 BCE, and the outrage in neighbouring kingdoms forced Kotte's king to seek refuge in the Portuguese fort of Colombo from his rival, the King of Sitavaca (Duncan, 1990). The perceived

82 *Pluriversal sovereignty and the state*

political opportunities offered by alliance with Christianity reached even into Kandy, where the reigning kings in the 1560s–1580s converted to Christianity (Harris, 2012: 270; Obeyesekere, 2020). Part of the complexity of South Asian polities was that exact boundaries were not clearly defined, and Kandy was a relatively recent independent kingdom that had left Kotte in the fifteenth century. Neither the Portuguese nor the Dutch were able to centralize their rule over the island.

The short-lived Treaty of Amiens in 1802 settled the territorial dispute from the perspective of the Dutch and the British, but neither possessed any deep knowledge of the island's interior at this time. Not only did the British know little of Ceylon and the regional dynamics and migrations that textured its global history, but there is little evidence to suggest that they cared to know much about it in the early days; they were not wedded to keeping the maritime territories or to controlling the entire island (Harris, 2006). European geopolitics was the primary motivation for acquiring the territory and using the harbour in Trincomalee as a way of fortifying the Madras Presidency on the mainland from incursion by Napoleon's France (Powell, 1973: 180–181). This geopolitical vantage point was crucial to British interest in the region, "the real key by possession of which alone you can hold the naval superiority of India," in the words of Britain's second governor, Sir Thomas Maitland (cited in Jeffries, 1962: 14). Dispatches from the Colonial Office to Maitland and his predecessor, Fredrick North, clearly outlined that London had no ambition to pursue total territorial rule in the early days. There was disconnecting policy between the Colonial Office and Governor North, however, who actively pursued military expeditions into the interior with consistently negative outcomes. North's orders upon taking office granted him authority to disarm and deport people aiding the enemies of the British crown, as well as giving him the ability to act militarily in defence of the colony, but these orders explicitly (clause 24) forbade him from declaring war without London's approval (Mendis, 1957; Powell, 1973). When in 1805 North was removed (at his own request) from the post of governor, the Colonial Office communicated to Maitland that efforts to centralize political rule should not be pursued:

Universal gaze and pluriversal realities 83

> Abstracted from every principle of Justice, there does not appear any principle of Policy which ought to induce Great Britain to wish the entire subjugation of that Island, as the advantages derivable from such a Possession could not be commensurate to the Expense of maintaining it; but when the Principles of Justice are combined with those of Policy (and on all occasions they ought to be inseparable), I feel satisfied that there is no ground for our desiring greatly to extend the territory we acquired by just Rights from the Dutch …
>
> (Colonial Office to Maitland, 1805, cited in Powell, 1973: 179)

The policy should not be confused with benevolence, as it was the outcome of several botched military attempts and considerable paid espionage to destabilize the Kandyan kingdom since the British had come to Ceylon in 1796 (Powell, 1973).

To the British, Kandyan territories were a frontier; they described what British territory was not, and when the British crossed into that frontier, there was always a lurking threat from the tropical jungle itself as well as locals skilled in guerilla warfare (Duncan, 2007). While maps from this era illustrate the shifting territorial boundaries of control, according to Simon Casie Chitty (1972), the physical territorial claims of British "Ceylon" and Kandy prior to the 1815 Kandyan Accord were 10,520 and 14,144 square miles respectively, making Kandy the majority of the island, encircled by British Ceylon (Chitty, cited in N. Perera, 1998: 41, n. 23). Kandy was presumed in colonial writings to be a kingdom with a tyrannical and savage king at the helm, an idea which served to legitimize the British "intervention" on behalf of the Kandyan people in 1815 as well as to fuel contemporary Buddhist-Sinhala nationalism concerning the corrupting influence of the Nayaka Tamil dynasty that brought about the end of the independent Kandyan kingdom (*A Narrative of Events*, 1815). Recent Sri Lankan scholarship on the Nayakas, and in particular on Vikrama Rajasinha, has forcefully argued that much more work needs to be done to excavate the historical realities of the last days of Kandy not only from the colonial gaze, but also from competing contemporary national gazes (Obeyesekere, 2017). Perceptions of inherent native inferiority clouded the fact that Britain had not been able to hold any territory conquered in military expeditions, in large part because of an active

84   *Pluriversal sovereignty and the state*

anti-road politics pursued by the Kandyans which prevented the easy movement of British troops and equipment into the interior.[5] To the Kandyans, the terrain itself represented an important line of defence against external aggression. The jungle, mountains, cliffs, and rivers in the rainy season enabled Kandyan soldiers to integrate the land into their military planning, forcing invading armies into passes so narrow that they would need to move in single file (Mendis, 2005: 29). As Governor Thomas Maitland, Ceylon's second governor, wrote in a dispatch to the Colonial Office on October 19, 1808, "I shall not enter into any foolish expeditions; I will not throw away the Lives of His Majesty's Subjects by Disease in burning and destroying the defenceless Huts of the innocent Natives" (cited in Powell, 1973: 184). In the colonial writing that would follow the eventual surrender of Kandy in 1815, the event is historicized as a major military achievement that again shows the shortsightedness of the colonial gaze, for the oft-touted fact that the British succeeded without suffering casualties in 1815 was attributed to the people of Kandy's desire for British governance rather than the strategic diplomacy of the Sinhalese aristocracy seeking to oust their king. The bloodshed that quickly followed the Kandyan Convention and the subsequent insurrections in the decades following speak to the importance of Kandyan agency in these international relations.

The reigning monarch of Kandy in the British period was Sri Vikrama Rajasingha, fourth and last in a dynasty of kings with roots in southern India who had been localized and integrated into Kandyan society through marriage and ritual. It had been a practice of the Sinhalese kings of Kandy to marry South Indian women, and when the last Sinhalese king neared death without a male heir from his main wife, he decreed that his son by a subordinate Malabar wife would succeed to the throne. The period of consolidating the dynasty was not without difficulty, and it involved careful attention to the rituals and symbolism of Buddhist sovereignty by the Malabar rulers. Vikrama engaged in lavish beautification projects of the capital, many of which remain to this day, but this was a time when the economic pressure of being cut off from marine trade routes by the British led to considerable strain and inflation within the kingdom. He accomplished these projects by extending the

Universal gaze and pluriversal realities 85

reach of *rajakariya*, the king-service owed by the general population, which had historically been used for irrigation and agricultural work, to include beautification, a measure which proved unpopular (Banderage, 1983; Jayawardena, 2010).

Vikrama grew increasingly distrustful of the Kandyan Sinhalese aristocracy with good reason: Pilimatalava, his long-time advisor who had been instrumental in installing him on the throne in 1798 and who served as his *Maha Adikar* (Prime Minister), was plotting against him with the British governor Frederick North. Pilimatalava sought to leverage a British deal to oust Vikrama – the eighteen-year-old nephew of the former king, Sri Rajadhi Rajasinha – and in 1800 convinced North to send an emissary to Kandy to negotiate making the kingdom a protectorate of Britain. North obliged and sent General MacDowall to accomplish the task, but Vikrama, who was not convinced that allowing a garrison of British troops into Kandy would ultimately serve his interests, dismissed him (Mendis, 2005: 17–19). Nevertheless, MacDowall returned with useful intelligence that would inform the British military strategy in future military episodes (K. M. de Silva, 1981: 224–226). In 1803, North gave the order (without clear consent from the Colonial Office) for General MacDowall to send an expeditionary force to Kandy. The Kandyans had seen this coming, evacuated the capital, and embarked on a campaign of guerilla warfare against the invaders. The British installed a puppet king for a short time, but as K. M. de Silva (1981: 225) explains,

> When the monsoon set in, the elements, combined with disease, brought about the destruction of the British troops in the Kandyan kingdom. With the loyalty of the Malay troops suspect and the lascarins deserting in droves, the British forces attempted to evacuate the capital they had occupied.

MacDowall himself had to retreat early to Colombo because illness, leaving command to Major Davies who, in turn, retreated before the order to do so came from North in Colombo. As the remaining British troops sought to evacuate the capital, the Kandyan forces intercepted them on June 24, 1803 on the banks at Vatapuluva. The puppet king was swiftly executed, along with nearly all of the British forces, save Davies and three others. K. M. de Silva (1981)

86   *Pluriversal sovereignty and the state*

notes that Pilimatalava's biased intelligence may have led the British to underestimate the fact that the people of Kandy supported their king. As will be explained in Chapter 4's discussion of galactic sovereignty as ontology, Vikrama held considerable *symbolic* power, but material power tended to remain in the Sinhalese aristocracy, whose loyalty to the young king was openly disputed. Part of Vikrama's internal strategy to weaken the position of the Kandyan elites was to appoint junior branches of Sinhalese aristocratic families to vacant posts, punishing chiefs who were being oppressive to the people under their jurisdiction and reintroducing taxes on the chiefs. These internal policy changes within the Kandyan kingdom in the early nineteenth century were operating within the expectations of caste order, but were clearly subverting the desires and power of the chiefs, whom Vikrama saw increasingly as plotting against him. He encircled himself with his own Nayaka relatives and began to alter the geographic districts, which, for generations, had been under the material jurisdiction of the chiefs. Long before the arrival of Governor Brownrigg and the eventual fall of Kandy, then, the galactic sovereign order was already beginning to fall out of its delicate balance (Mendis, 2005: 19–21). In response, Pilimatalava conspired with a *Muhandiram* (headman from the lower country) and some sixty Malay bodyguards to assassinate Vikrama, while simultaneously raising a rebellion with the help of headmen in Udunuvara and Yatinuvara in 1808. The timing was poor, however, leading to a premature uprising that was quelled before the bodyguards could kill the king. Vikrama stripped Pilimatalava of his titles and authority and, following confession to the charges of treason, he and other conspirators were executed in or around June 1812 (Colvin R. de Silva, 1953: 130–131).[6]

Vikrama appointed Pilimatalava's nephew Ahelepola to the post of *Maha Adikar,* probably in an attempt to keep his enemies under closer surveillance. Like his uncle, Ahelepola hailed from the southern Kandyan province of Sabaragamuva, where the king's influence was weaker than in the core central regions. The balance of spiritual power and material power that had developed over more than three hundred years of Kandyan sovereign practice was disturbed when Vikrama extended his material powers to punish the regions of his kingdom outside the centre. In Sabaragamuva,

Universal gaze and pluriversal realities 87

Ahelepola had long been in correspondence with John D'Oyly, chief translator of the British government in Colombo, who had held the post under Governors North, Maitland, and Brownrigg. In letters shared between Ahelepola, Brownrigg, and D'Oyly, it is clear that the destabilization of Vikrama's Kandy came as rather unexpected news in Colombo.

Governor Brownrigg in Colombo took seriously his orders from the Colonial Office not to overtly seek to interfere with the politics of the interior. Nevertheless, he simultaneously sought to ramp up his military resources in the event of conflict (Brownrigg to the Earl of Bathurst, June 28, 1814, in Vimalananda, 1984). In a dispatch dated March 29, 1812, Brownrigg explained to the Secretary of War and Colonies that since the capital punishment of Pilimatalava and some influential followers in the failed rebellion, all had appeared to be quiet in the territory. He assured the Colonial Office that D'Oyly was in regular correspondence with the new *Maha Adikar*, Ahelepola (Brownrigg to the Earl of Liverpool, March 29, 1812, in Vimalananda. 1984). The merging of Kandy and British territory in 1815, however, was the outcome of diplomacy conducted mostly between Ahelepola and Governor Brownrigg through the translations and diplomacy of John D'Oyly. When open hostilities between the aristocracy and the king broke out, Ahelepola refused to present himself upon royal demand in 1814 for what might well have been his own arrest and execution. Instead, he defected to the British and was followed by other chiefs, which resulted in Vikrama exerting an especially brutal punishment on Ahelepola's family in the capital. In popular accounts stemming from the narrative of a British person claiming to have been present during the Kandyan Convention of 1815, when the executioner came to seize the elder boy, the child clung to his mother. According to many sources, and in a moment memorialized to this day in Kandy, the younger son volunteered to be killed first, following which the children's mother was made to crush her own infant to death with a large mortar. The female relatives of Ahelepola were tied to stones and drowned in the Kandy Lake (*A Narrative of Events*, 1815). The accuracy of this story, or what Obeyesekere (2017: 197–209) has described as the "myth model," is highly suspect as it relies on accounts from people who could not have been present and who would have been

88 *Pluriversal sovereignty and the state*

drawing on previous accounts of violence – specifically the image of pounding children to death – that already existed as legends within Sinhalese folklore at the time. In his substantial engagement with the execution of Kumarihari (Ahelepola's wife) and her children, Obeyesekere reconstructs the execution as a more routine, albeit cruel, exercise of Kandyan law. It was lawful for the king to hold captive the family of a person accused of treason, as Ahelepola was, and to execute them should the accused not present themselves to the king. Ahelepola would have known this when he defected to the British, as his successor, Molligoda, also understood this and remained loyal to the king until such a time as he could relocate his own family to Colombo. The caricature of primitive cruelty, however, was repeated many times within colonial accounts and reported as truth, though it was never described in such brutal detail in official accounts by D'Oyly.

This public act of cruelty – real or imagined – was the opportunity Governor Brownrigg was waiting for, and on January 15, 1815 he issued an order in council defending the decision to wage war on Kandy to protect the Kandyans from their king:

> But it is not against the Kandian nation that the arms of His Majesty are directed; his Excellency proclaims hostility against that tyrannical power alone, which has provoked, by aggravated outrages and indignities, the just resentment of the British nation, which has cut off the most ancient and noble families in his kingdom, deluged the land with the blood of his subjects, and, by the violation of every religious and moral law, became an object of abhorrence to mankind.
>
> (cited in *A Narrative of Events*, 1815)

By the time the British began their invasion, Ahelepola's replacement, Molligoda,[7] along with most of the remaining aristocracy, had already defected and the Kandyans mounted no defence (Jayawardena, 2010). The next generation of colonial writing about this military "victory" would laud the achievements of Brownrigg and D'Oyly, each of whom was rewarded with a baronetcy. The emphasizing of Brownrigg and D'Oyly over and above the contribution of Ahelepola in the sacking of Kandy also highlights the loss in studying "modernity" in the absence of "coloniality," as it was the diplomatic manoeuvres of the Kandyan aristocracy, and

Universal gaze and pluriversal realities 89

not British might, that made the victory possible. The "military victory" of Kandy that led to the *de jure* unification of the island under the British in the spectacle of the Kandyan Convention of 1815, then, was really more a story of long-term internal Kandyan court intrigue than it was about superior British military tactics. The dominant historical narrative as offered by the influential Sri Lankan historians G. C. Mendis (2005) and K. M. de Silva (1965) is in agreement that it was only a matter of time before the British occupied Kandy, thanks to the "medieval" characteristics of its governance. Instead of Kandy being seen as a "pre-modern" Indigenous kingdom that could not keep up with the times, the fall of Kandy should be seen as resulting from a confluence of forces that were mainly driven by the internal dynamics of an Indigenous spatial order beginning to fall apart as the symbolic relationship holding king, *adikars*, and territory fell out of orbit. One cannot theorize historical hypotheticals, but the epistemic investment in gradual development and technological advancement contaminates the past with modernist thinking, exaggerating what Shilliam (2015: 7) has described as the "fatal impact thesis" of colonial inevitability. In the next section, I turn to missionary writing to emphasize the distortive dimensions of the fatal impact thesis.

Christian subjects, but not only Christian subjects

While British Protestant missionaries were only just beginning to learn about what they would name "Buddhism," South Asians who would later be described and then self-identify as religious Buddhists and Hindus in Ceylon had a lengthy history of experiences with Catholics and Protestants. The Portuguese destruction of Hindu and Buddhist places of worship in the mid to late sixteenth century led to refugees taking shelter within, and then retaliating with support from, the Hindu and Buddhist independent kingdoms of Jaffnapatam and Kandy respectively (Harris, 2012: 270–272). By and large, however, Christian missionaries were confused by what they saw as a lack of direct resistance to their attempts to convert the masses to Christianity in the first half of the nineteenth century. This was at times pitied in missionary writing, where it was

90   *Pluriversal sovereignty and the state*

perceived as evidence of primitive development and a consequence of living in ignorance of universal, divine truth. In one account, the Wesleyan missionary William Bridgalle describes the Kandyan territories in which he was based in the 1820s as "spiritually barren." He continues to describe what he sees as a logical and gradual decline of Buddhism:

> It must surely be regarded as somewhat ominous of the rapid decline of Buddhism in the Kandian country to hear so many Kandian children, in the presence of several of their parents and friends, join in saying after the missionary, "I believe in God the Father, Almighty, Maker of heaven and earth. And in Jesus Christ His only Son our Lord."

> (Bridgalle, 1828)

What Bridgalle and his contemporaries were not able to perceive was that from a Buddhist or Hindu ontological starting point, the incorporation and regard of a new deity was not evidence of people "leaving" Buddhism or Hinduism. South Asians across the expansive reach of the British Empire practised "civic Christianity" as an effective way to navigate the material conditions of the colonial present of the time, as will be explored below.

By the late nineteenth century, it was clear that association with Christianity and knowledge of the English language offered material advantages in terms of government employment, which tended to favour coastal regions of the island that had had associations with Catholic Christianity since the early sixteenth century via the Portuguese (K. M. de Silva, 1984; 1965). Yet even in the early nineteenth century, these benefits were already present. At a congress of the Madras-based Wesleyan Methodist Missionary Society in 1822, the Rev. James Lynch offered a report on the progress of the mission to his brethren. In it, he noted that since 1816, some 2,500 children had been taught to read and to discuss Christianity in their own languages, with 300 of the brightest advancing to learn English. In Trincomalee (in the north-east), he noted that sermons were routinely offered in both Tamil and English, and that many young men who had already left their schools as of 1822, occupied important positions in the early colonial administration (Lynch, 1808–1858).

Universal gaze and pluriversal realities 91

At the ontological and cosmological level, there is no particular conflict from a Buddhist or Hindu point of view in being simultaneously Christian. As scholars of religion and Sri Lanka have long noted, Buddhists and Hindus understood the process of formally embracing Christianity as more a civic task than a spiritual one (Harris, 2012: 272). The simultaneous existence of other conceptions of cosmology was not an *ontological* problem within Buddhist and Hindu genealogies because to them the centrality of a god or many gods is not nearly as important as it is in monotheistic traditions. In contrast, Judaeo-Christian-Islamic genealogies of thought demand a universal adherence to monotheism: it is not sufficient to acknowledge and accept the existence of the Christian God to satisfy the missionary; one must *deny* the existence of multiple cosmologies. Within the universal gaze of the monotheist British missionary, it is not possible to recognize pluriversality, because evidence of the pluriverse is misunderstood to be "idolatry" or other such evidence of spiritual primitiveness. The colonial worldview of universalism is not capable of perceiving pluriversality. Colonialism, then, is also pedagogy, and its inculcation in the liberal-colonial era through schools and legal requirements of conversion for professional advancement produced structural incentives to at least perform Christianity if not genuinely to become Christian. Women missionaries in the nineteenth century enabled missionary schools for heathen girls to become common across Ceylon and India by the 1820s. As Kumari Jayawardena (1995: 27) explains, "The schools were class-based; some provided education only in the local languages to poorer sections of the population, while others gave an education in English to daughters of upper and middle-class families." Schools, in particular, were understood to be fundamental to "civilizing" natives, and this process occurred in a highly gendered way. In a letter of November 1817 to her sister, Elizabeth Harvard, one of the early Wesleyan missionaries in Ceylon, identified mothers as particularly recalcitrant sources of heathenism:

> The importance of educating the native girls is very considerable. By the blessing of God, a religious education will not only tend to the advancement of their own salvation, but the [sic] better qualify them to act as wives and mothers, should they be spared to fill those stations. *The heathen females are the main support of paganism.*

92　　Pluriversal sovereignty and the state

> Some of our native converts have repeatedly confessed that their almost unconquerable bias to idolatry arose from the example of their mothers, whose attachment to heathenish worship and ceremonies was such as to lead them to carry their children to the temples as soon as they were able to go out; and while infants, to put their little hands together and teach them to bow before their senseless images. If then we can succeed with the mothers of the next generation, how much of this will be prevented! They will teach their little dears to bow to Jesus instead of idols.
>
> (cited in Harvard, 1833: 84–85, emphasis in original)

Here, in the account of this Wesleyan who was based in the Colombo area in the earliest period of *de jure* British rule, mothers were identified as the reason why attempts to proliferate the universal Christian faith have been stymied. British missionaries were limited by their universal ontological framework, which prevented them from moving between Christian and Buddhist worlds. Consequently, they lashed out at those who, as a result of the multiplicity of their lived experiences, had some navigational tools to inhabit these worlds. As Malathi de Alwis (2002: 675) observes,

> it was bourgeois Ceylonese women's bodies, beliefs, and behavior that were produced as the repositories as well as signifiers of Ceylonese "culture" and "tradition" in the face of the onslaught of colonialism and modernity (which worked hand in glove) upon Ceylonese society.

The colonial and related anti-colonial nationalist targeting of women and essentializing them as domestic reproducers of nation and society had lasting impact and have continued well into the twenty-first century (Jayawardena and de Alwis, 1996; Hyndman and de Alwis, 2004; de Alwis, 1995).

The Wesleyans did not establish missionary centres in the Kandyan region, but the Anglicans did. In their accounts, one can see quite clearly the ontological irreconcilability of British-Christian cosmologies with Kandyan cosmologies. The Anglicans arrived in Ceylon shortly after the Wesleyans in 1818, following the Kandyan Convention (1815) and the Uva Rebellion (1817–1818). The interior, as Harvard notes in the introductory epigraph to this

Universal gaze and pluriversal realities 93

chapter, was "open for the Gospel," and by 1833, the Church Missionary Society had established centres in Kandy, Nellore, Badalgamma, and Cotta (Bailey, 1833). Speaking on the subject of obstacles to the propagation of Christianity, the Rev. John Bailey, secretary to the mission, noted that one of his greatest difficulties was the fact that Hindus appeared to make no separation between civil and religious matters:

> One of the most obvious difficulties to be encountered, in the dissemination of Christian Truth among the Hindoos, is the *exclusive and unsocial nature of their Institutions, both civil and religious.* These are blended together in all their endless ramifications; and they rest on the same authorities, viz., the shasters, remote antiquity, and universal practice.
>
> (Bailey, 1833: 30, emphasis in original)

Bailey continued to speak to the ontological difference in terms of understanding cosmology in reference to Hindu regions of the island by arguing that Hindus simply could not grasp the "truth" of one god:

> Another obstacle … [is] being obligated to employ terms which, from their heathenish use and application, necessarily convey to the mind of the hearer ideas different from those intended. Thus if God be spoken of, the Hindoo, unless he has long been under Christian instruction, will probably understand by it some one of his deities, who yields to the vilest passions, and allows his worshippers to do so too.
>
> (Bailey, 1833: 33, emphasis in original)

Education, then, was clearly seen by the missionaries as the path to correct thinking. Bailey argued that the local stories and perceptions of divinity were "monstrous" and, perhaps most importantly from the perspective of modern rationalism, identified as evidence of their primitiveness the lack of proof necessary in order for them to be convinced. "With a people so credulous," he wrote, "the evidence arising from real miracles has little weight" (Bailey, 1833: 31). That he saw no complication in knowing how to correctly perceive "real miracles" on the basis of nothing more than the ontological assumption of his own universal cosmology draws attention to the limiting lens of universality; perhaps it also highlights a fracturing within Western-Christian universalist theology and the rapidly expanding

94 *Pluriversal sovereignty and the state*

project of scientific positivism in the nineteenth century and its Enlightenment antecedents. Scientific thinking, following Thomas Metcalf, extended logically from British self-perceptions. The British never learned the lessons of ontological difference that were being offered as described above but, rather, continued throughout the nineteenth century to graft a pseudo-science of racial and developmental superiority onto their initial assumptions of their own inherently superior cosmology that took the form of education. As Metcalf (1998: 67) observes of the Victorian era, a generation after the period under study in this book:

> No longer a product of mere assertion, in the manner of James Mill, Western pre-eminence was now demonstrated, or, more properly, assumed, as it underlay the scientific structures that grew up around it. Victorian science, like its historicism, thus necessarily if not always consciously fitted India into a hierarchical relationship with Europe and provided the firm footing of legitimacy which the British sought for their Raj.

A generation earlier, one can see a similar logic unfolding in Ceylon.

Modern/colonial religious education

Aside from launching into ignorant misreadings and misrepresentations of Hindu and Buddhist texts, Bailey more empirically observed that while Christian education could offer a way out of incorrect beliefs, parents themselves remained obstacles to their children's betterment.[8] While some locals across the geographic spread of their missions were willing to accept missionaries as friends and part of the community, adults remained irritatingly disinterested in their messages about "true" and "correct" religion. Bailey noted that particularly in Kandy, attendance in school was highly irregular. Parents kept children

> at home frequently without any good reasons; and always when they can make any use of them. In harvest-time, and at other seasons when the assistance of the children is of importance to the parents, no objection is made to their being absent from school.
>
> (Bailey, 1833: 9)

Universal gaze and pluriversal realities 95

Where missionaries were not able to convince people to adhere to their universal precepts, Bailey (1833: 9) hoped to have a longer generational impact through schooling, requiring that pupils memorize scripture: "the minds of a great many of them have become imbued with the doctrines and precepts of Christianity, which, by the Divine blessing, may in after life be found of incalculable advantage." Missionaries of all stripes took schooling very seriously, and the Anglicans of the 1830s filed daily reports from all of their schools, which were systematically analysed in advance of weekly meetings in which superintendents would advise teachers individually and collectively. In some unpublished papers prepared for a book on the Wesleyan mission in Ceylon, the authors noted that "civil Christians" were a sufficiently large population that the missionaries referred to them as the "Government Christians" (Wesleyan Methodist Missionary Society, 1950). Missionary reports and diaries show the missionaries' constant swings between feelings of optimism that the whole of Ceylon would embrace Christ in the near future, and angry, desperate frustration associated with what they saw as insincere or bad Christianity.

This confusion arose out of the ontological irreconcilability of universal thinking with pluriversal lived realities. The well-documented confusion on the part of Christian missionaries in Ceylon in the nineteenth century is understandable on account of the fact that belief in "a true god" takes on meaning in monotheistic traditions in ways that do not compare with reverence or meaning within Buddhist or Hindu genealogies; the existence or non-existence of god(s) is simply not a central question (Gogerly, 1863; Harvard, 1833). We should recall that within Europe, the dominant religions that vied to monopolize the administration of grace were all monotheistic traditions that at least shared the Hebrew Bible in common: Catholicism, Protestantism, and, to a lesser degree by the nineteenth century, Islam and Judaism. These religious traditions were accustomed to making their claims against one another within a discourse that could at least agree on the necessity of one true god, while disagreeing on particular interpretations or on where to draw the line concerning new developments in how to interpret scripture or receive "prophetic" or messianic influences. Jesus was a messianic figure for Christians who emerged as a fissure *within* the

96   *Pluriversal sovereignty and the state*

Jewish tradition after the fact. Mohammed was a prophet spoken to by God via the angel Gabriel and meant to update and correct the tradition in his time and place. Islam, in turn, splinters on questions of whether divine authority ends with Mohammed or continues to his nephew Ali and Ali's descendants. Christians splinter on the question of whether the church is the ultimate mediator of the divinity on earth, or whether the Bible ought to be engaged with directly. The brutality of internal monotheistic battles gave rise to perceived needs to "cleanse" Christian territory of Muslims and Jews on the one hand, but also to the influential traditions of scientific rationalism and secularism in response to this history grounded in the particular time and place of "Europe" as the continent and its developing political geographies were taking modern/colonial form. Despite the many important differences within and across the monotheistic traditions of Christianity, Judaism, and Islam, they all share a common (albeit distant) genealogy based on a belief in a God separate from the earth who, in the book of Genesis, creates the world and humanankind separately, with the former to serve the latter. This absolutism and the cosmological separation of humankind, land, and God have been essential to the development of "sovereignty" in the European context.

The birth of "religion" as a modern category capable of engaging with liberal-colonial states is beyond the scope of this chapter, but it will be sufficient for the purposes of this book to point to the ways in which the Christian-monotheistic ontology tried to fit existing cosmologies into the category of "religion" for ease of understanding and control.[9] It is not the case that monotheistic traditions were alien to South Asia. Islam had a robust history in the region and was the major imperial presence prior to the East India Company, and the subsequent British Raj, on the subcontinent. However, the methods of spatial organization in the Mughal Islamic tradition are distinct from European projects of colonialism; my point is not to argue that cosmological distinctness *determined* the outcome of political ontology in early British Ceylon, just that in the particular time and place, the ontologies of "sovereignty" of the major actors (Kandyan and British alike) were informed by differing cosmologies and a differing balance between civil and cosmological relations, as will be discussed in the next chapter.

Universal gaze and pluriversal realities 97

In order to rationalize South Asian cosmologies into a form that was more comprehensible to nineteenth-century European minds, British missionaries and scholars worked to force-fit local customs and traditions into "religions" as they expected to find them, based on one or many gods and philosophical propositions that could be rationally refuted by what they saw as universally "true" religion. Even secularism, as it developed in the Enlightenment, articulated its grievance with theism on the basis of a replacement of universal religious truth by universal "scientific" rationality. Within cosmologies that are other than European, the historical and political problems that gave rise to the need for a "secular" division (or attempted division) between "church" and "state" did not happen, and there is no basis upon which to conceive of such a break. "Church" is not a place-holder for the institution of religion, though in the parlance of twentieth- and twenty-first-century Western social science it often is; both the concept of "church" and the concept of "state" are historically produced institutions that reflect particular cosmologies and ontological starting points. Just as it is incorrect to graft the modern territorial state onto places that had their own spatial systems without accounting for the historical processes that enabled the universalization of "state," so too is it a colonial manoeuvre to graft the concept of "church" onto systems grounded in cosmology that have developed along their own trajectories.

Conclusion

What makes the colonial encounter so important from the standpoint of the politics of "religion" or, more accurately, the ontological clash of cosmologies, is not the meeting of different ontologies; this has happened throughout history. Islamic and Brahmanical cosmologies met and interacted across South Asia and the Indian Ocean region more generally long before the arrival of the British. Before the arrival of Islam there were historical cosmological meetings between various South Asian traditions and various Persian and Greco-Roman traditions as well. For the purposes of understanding the significance of colonial state formation

98   *Pluriversal sovereignty and the state*

in nineteenth-century Ceylon, however, what is significant is the meeting of different ontologies within a historical and political context in which one (the British-Christian), in order to fulfil its internal requirements and expectations, had to dominate the other, enlisting the nineteenth-century institutions of state and developing civilizing mission in its service. Aimé Césaire has elegantly exposed the parasitic ways in which the relations of colonizing nations with the rest of the world have unfolded. Aside from identifying at the onset the hypocrisy of identifying Christianity with civilization and an all-encompassing "paganism" with "savagery," he also offers a more subtle critique in drawing attention to museums:

> And the museums of which M. Caillois is so proud, not for one minute does it cross his mind that, all things considered, it would have been better not to have needed them; that Europe would have done better to tolerate the non-European civilizations at its side, leaving them alive, dynamic, and prosperous, whole and not muti-lated; that it would have been better to let them develop and fulfill themselves than to present for admiration, duly labeled, their dead and scattered parts; that anyway, the museum by itself is nothing; that it means nothing, that it can say nothing, when smug self-satisfaction rots the eyes, when a secret contempt for others withers the heart, when racism, admitted or not, dries up sympathy; that it means nothing if its only purpose is to feed the delights of vanity; that after all, the honest contemporary of Saint Louis, who fought Islam but respected it, had a better chance of *knowing* it than do our contemporaries (even if they have a smattering of ethnographic literature), who despise it.
>
> (Césaire, 2000: 20–21)

Césaire's point that the enemy that respects its foe better under-stands the other than the one who condescends is notable. As will be discussed in the next chapter, it was precisely the oscillating balance between symbolic and material "galactic" sovereignty that defined pre-European Kandy. The term *agama*, which missionaries would translate as "religion" as understood in Europe, and the mul-tiple ways in which Buddhism is referred to in early Christian and colonial writings in Ceylon attest to the confusion. British admin-istrators and missionaries would at times describe "the religion of the Boodoo," and at other times understood Buddhism as being

Universal gaze and pluriversal realities 99

part of Hinduism, as well as engaging in debates about the possible divinity of the Siddharta Gautama himself (D. Scott, 1999: 57). In a Buddhist or Hindu genealogy, there is no contradiction in multiple simultaneous expressions of divinity. Indeed, in some Buddhist sutras, the Buddha converses with Hindu gods, including Brahma, the god of creation (Bodhi, 2000).

All this is not to suggest that all converts to Christianity were employing "weapons of the weak" (J. C. Scott, 1987) in order to subvert European control. There are many reasons why Christianity and its cosmology were genuinely appealing. Elizabeth Harvard describes what appears to be a Buddhist priest's very genuine conversion to Christianity, noting:

> it never occurred to him that there was any great Creator; but he imagined that all things came into existence by mere chance. Now he sees that it is only "the foolish" who think, in their hearts, "there is no God." May he more fully know Him whom to know is life eternal, and become, to his benighted countrymen, a useful minister of the Lord Jesus.
>
> (Elizabeth Harvard, letter to her parents, August 26, 1816, in Harvard, 1833: 63–64)

Similarly, the fact that two *bhikkhus* agreed to travel to England and give up their privileges in Ceylon was taken, for instance in an account by "Philoyvenues" (1817), as evidence of the ultimate victory for Christian worldviews over heathenism and idolatry at the time. This account notes that the two priests, upon reaching England, communicated in broken Portuguese and ultimately came to master English and "improve" their knowledge of religion. The author proclaims that they did not know anything about writing because they merely wrote on leaves in Ceylon, and expresses amazement at the speed with which they were able to master astronomy, geography, and religious precepts ("Philoyenues," 1817). My point in introducing this example is not to suggest that the *bhikkhus* did or did not genuinely become Christian; the more important point is how within a universalizing view of modern/colonial British Christianity, the highly skilled Buddhist scholars and priests were not already seen as the equals of Christians in intellect, and the confusion surrounding their abilities emerged from the

100 *Pluriversal sovereignty and the state*

failure to recognize the pluriversality of cosmologies that made the encounter possible in the first place.

Though the details of internal cleavages within Christianity in Europe are well beyond the scope of this chapter, it is worthwhile to note that in this time and place, the monastic traditions that had given rise to Western philosophy and science were seen by the British missionaries as being inherently "truer" than the systems of knowledge cultivated in Ceylon and throughout Buddhist South-East Asia more generally. In the missionaries' understanding, the priests were uneducated, illiterate, and spiritually backward only in the universe of modernity; they were highly educated people, but educated *otherwise*. As Elizabeth Harris's work on Buddhist–Christian relations shows, it was Buddhist monks who taught Christian missionaries how to read Pali and to write in Sinhalese. When missionaries like Gogerly and Spence Hardy, who owed their knowledge of Buddhism to monks who worked with them, turned around to publish influential pamphlets such as *The British Government and the Idolatry of Ceylon* (Hardy, 1841) and the Sinhalese-language *Kristiyāni Prajñapti* ("The Evidence of Christianity"), the aggressive dogma of these denunciations was offensive. As Harris (2012: 298) writes,

> To some members of the Sangha, it would have appeared that the Law of Kamma was being turned on its head, since the fruit of generosity should have been generosity. Instead, the fruit was a representation of Buddhism that amounted to a threat to the dhamma, demanding defence, if the monastic Sangha was to be true to its traditional role.

The ontological importance of Buddhism for sovereignty is the subject of the next chapter, but for our purposes here, it is important to note that British-Christian ambivalence or hostility towards Buddhism failed to appreciate the relationship between *dhamma* and sovereignty. In the latter half of the nineteenth century, many of the consequences of this hostility would begin to take shape as public debates between Buddhism and Christianity took on anticolonial and increasingly nationalist importance. While that period of history is extremely important, it is already well studied and lies outside this book's emphasis on state formation. In the late nineteenth and early twentieth centuries, the "state" was already

Universal gaze and pluriversal realities   101

mostly naturalized, and Buddhists began shifting their political projects away from Kandy and towards the capital, Colombo (N. Perera, 2002).

Notes

1 Although the Nayakas are seen as South Indian in origin, scripting them as such is rife with problems. The Nayakas had a long history in Kandy that predated the dynasty because Sinhalese kings had a tradition of marrying Nayaka women and relying on allegiances with Nayaka soldiers. Thus long before the establishment of the Nayaka dynasty, their cultural and political presence was integrated into the very centre of Kandyan court life. See Obeyesekere, 2017.
2 There were attempted rebellions in 1817–1818, 1823, 1824, 1834, 1843, and 1848. See Chapter 5 for details, as well as Jayawardena, 2010.
3 I place "India" within quotation marks because at this time, "India" did not truly exist. There were many sovereign native Hindu and Muslim kingdoms, centres of European power around the coast (Dutch, Portuguese, French, and British), and enormous areas of *adivasi* territories that were not meaningfully part of any of these. Though the Moghul empire did centralize much of the administration of the territory between the sixteenth and eighteenth centuries, "India" as we know it today is a geographical imaginary that was negotiated with diplomatic and coercive force in the mid twentieth century and is constantly being renegotiated on the basis of internal and regional political pressure.
4 In an imperial context of Western Orientalism and missionary education, Buddhist children with Westernized educations began to take public space in the latter portion of the nineteenth century through public debates between Buddhism and Christianity. See Gombrich and Obeyesekere, 1988; Harris, 2006; Jayawardena, 1995.
5 Thomas Metcalf offers a compelling explanation of British self-perception in the eighteenth and nineteenth centuries, particularly in terms of how their liberal colonialism fuelled ideological conceptions of what British rule in South Asia offered to subjects. See Metcalf, 1998.
6 Colvin R. de Silva argued in 1953 that Vikrama ultimately put Pilimatalava to death, but in more recent readings of the period from Kumari Jayawardena (2010), Pilimatalava is named as a conspirator along with Keppitipola in the 1817–1818 Uva Rebellion and is said to

102　*Pluriversal sovereignty and the state*

have ultimately been exiled. Gananath Obeyesekere (2017) discusses different vignettes and accounts of the early nineteenth-century intrigues and notes that there was also a Pilimatalava Jr, who may have been the figure allied with Keppitipola years after Pilimatalava Sr was executed by Vikrama Rajasinha.

7 Molligoda is a surname, and confusingly, at least three relatives sharing this name were involved at the upper echelons of the Kandyan kingdom at this period; it is not known specifically which one became *adikar* in this moment. See Obeyesekere, 2017.

8 Parents were more broadly understood as an obstacle to overcome later in the nineteenth century when upper-class non-Christian families sought access to Westernized education without religious indoctrination in the form of education for girls in the home. See Jayawardena, 1995.

9 Sanjay Seth makes a similar point about the overlapping similarities that make it possible to conceive of a broad concept such as "modern Western knowledge" by virtue of shared background assumptions. See Seth, 2007.

4

Ontological collision and the Kandyan Convention of 1815

In this chapter, I draw on S. J. Tambiah's conceptual approach to understanding Buddhist South and South-East Asian states through the galactic *mandala* system in order to reinterpret the significance of the 1815 Kandyan Convention. I argue that the signing of the Kandyan Convention in March 1815 needs to be reconsidered as a moment of sovereignty ontological collision instead of an actual transfer of sovereign power. In this moment, two genealogies of sovereignty came into conflict, and the many conflicts in the generation that followed created the context within which the logic of total territorial rule emerges.

In this chapter, I first sketch out the historical development of "galactic sovereignty" and the role of "Buddhification" as a means of integrating foreigners in pre-European Ceylon. Drawing again on Tambiah but also on Gananath Obeyesekere and Roshan de Silva Wijeyeratne, this section highlights the important place-based practices that played a central role in defining what sovereignty meant in the Kandyan region. This was not, I argue, merely a function of the kingdom's isolation as influential historical accounts describe it (see Mendis, 2005; K. M. de Silva, 1965; 1981); rather, it was a pulsating spatial politics that was capable of integrating external influences and addressing social, political, and economic affairs with close attention to balancing both cosmological and material realms of existence. In the next section I draw upon the work of Mario Blaser to explain the concept of ontological conflict, a position that cannot be adequately studied through the lens of "universality" as explained in Chapter 1. In this section, I lay out the conceptual tools necessary to show the value of a pluriversal framework, one

104   *Pluriversal sovereignty and the state*

that considers multiple ontologies, in exposing the fundamental disagreements grounded in cosmologies that are historically distinct. Finally, I apply the pluriversal framework of ontological conflict to reinterpret archival materials and secondary literature on the Kandyan Convention. I argue that Kandyan-Buddhist and British-Christian understandings of sovereignty conflicted, in large part because of the latter's inability to reconcile the realities of pluriversality within the universal orientation of British-Christian understandings of sovereignty. I elaborate on the significance of this religious politics, drawing on archival reports and diaries from missionaries and colonial officials present in the period and at the Convention itself to highlight the ontological conflicts that defined the early nineteenth-century encounter with the British in Ceylon.

Galactic sovereignty

With an understanding of the historical and political context within which British and Kandyan sovereignties would collide in 1815, this section describes sovereignty within a galactic *mandala* system in order to better appreciate the pluriversality of nineteenth-century sovereignties. The power dynamics between the centre and the periphery of Kandy depended on the balancing of symbolic and administrative duties; sovereignty invested in the centre was largely a virtual practice, in that the king's power was vested in his role of maintaining cosmological and material balance throughout the territory (Wijeyeratne, 2014; Seneviratne, 1977).

Tambiah's work on South-East Asian Buddhist polities (Tambiah 1976; 1977; 2013) includes Kandy as a key case study. He elaborates upon his adaptation of the *rajamandala* (circle of kings) model of sovereignty that had its classical political philosophical origins in the continental Mauryan Empire from the fourth to second centuries BCE. Its key characteristic was its simultaneous centralizing and decentralizing tendencies, which defined the spatial organization of power. Thus in the Kandyan kingdom, the central capital city was encircled by nine small *rata* (districts), which were functionally controlled by officials. Collectively, these districts comprised the central domain. Around this central area were twelve provinces of varying

Ontological collision 105

sizes, divided between the first and second *adikars* in the south and north. The provinces further from the centre experienced the least influence of the king, and also brought the Kandyan territories into more contact with non-Kandyans. Further outward, the centre's gravitational influence waned and the relative gravitational pull of the *adikars* increased over the smaller agents within their sphere of influence. Just as the Sun's gravity animates the celestial bodies of our solar system yet in turn orbits the galactic core of the Milky Way, the adjective "galactic" can be used to describe this practice of sovereignty.

At the outer limits of the kingdom in particular, strategies of accommodation and integration were developed such that foreigners could be brought into the local Kandyan order. Contrary to contemporary ethno-nationalist ideas that developed from the late nineteenth century onwards, the incorporation of outsiders was a crucial component of galactic sovereignty. Muslim traders, non-Kandyan Sinhala, and Tamils were incorporated through a differentiation of work and caste relations within the Kandyan galactic order. In practice and in ceremony, this was related to work owed to the king (*rajakariya*) based on caste and status. As Tambiah (1992: 174–175) explains,

> They elaborated the division of labor, and provided niches for immigrant groups, or stranger groups of different "ethnic" origins and different "religions," and assigned special functions, such as serving as mercenaries, conducting overland trade, or making luxury artifacts ... The mandala pattern of devolution and replication could and did solicit and tolerate, positively place and mutually benefit from the presence of and engagement with satellite principalities, specialized minorities and sectarian or heterodox communities, waves of immigrants, and groups of war captives all given niches and incorporated within the larger cosmological and politicoeconomic framework. Indeed, it was this galactic blueprint that positively enabled the Sinhalization and Buddhicization of south Indian peoples and gods to continue uncoerced.

Galactic sovereignty was as much about fluidity in its incorporation of outsiders as it was about rigid attention to ceremonies bridging the spiritual and manifest domains, the significance of which will be explained below.

106   *Pluriversal sovereignty and the state*

For Tambiah, there was nothing in any of the classical Anuradhapura and Polonnaruwa kingdoms that could adequately be described as a "state" in the modern sense of the word. Drawing on South Asian sources of political theory, such as the *Arthashastra, Agganna Sutta* ("The Discourse on What is Primary") and the *Cakkavatti Sinhanada Sutta* ("The Lion's Roar of the Wheel-Turning Emperor"), Tambiah (1992: 172) describes territory in flux, organized as "pulsating galactic polities":

> The polities modelled on mandala-type patterning had central royal domains surrounded by satellite principalities and provinces replicating the centre on a smaller scale and at the margins had even more autonomous tributary principalities. The effective political arena extends beyond any single "kingdom"; it is multicentric, with rival "kingdoms" jostling each other, changing their margins, expanding and contracting, according to the fortunes of wars, skirmishes, raids, and diplomacy.

The local political spatial constellation was structured in an orbital fashion rather than a ladder-like fashion. This does not mean there were no hierarchies; the point I am drawing attention to is that the force holding the polities in balance was animated more gravitationally than through specific kinds of top-down accountability (Seneviratne, 1977). Caste relations, for example, played an important role in Sinhala-Buddhist society, though, according to Chandra R. de Silva (1987: 50–52), caste did not occupy the same role nor have religious centrality as it did in Hindu India upon its introduction to the island during the Anuradhapura period (377 BCE–1017 CE). Nevertheless, caste identity did play an organizing role in the exploitation of labour as well as determining the severity of punishments for transgressions. This kind of structured and embodied privilege, enjoyed by and taken advantage of by upper-caste chiefs in particular, was not a central part of the new British administration in Kandy. Caste determined a person's role in society to a large extent, and the lack of respect for it in official terms was socially disruptive to the old order (Mendis, 2005: 20–22). In part because the British relied on Dutch archival sources for much of their early knowledge of maritime Ceylon and the Kandyan interior, they misunderstood the dual meanings of "Sinhala" wherein

Ontological collision   107

a person could be culturally Sinhalese, or politically Sinhalese, or both. When the Dutch discovered in the eighteenth century, for example, that South Indian, occasionally Tamil-speaking, Nayaka-caste kings were ruling over Kandy, they (unsuccessfully) attempted to use this as an example of "outside" rule to ferment disunity within the Randala nobility (a subgroup of the Goyigama caste) to press their interests in Kandy. The Dutch, and the British who followed them, did not understand the dual meaning and purpose of Sinhala-ness, and the fact that belonging to a cultural Sinhalese identity did not have to be more important than a Sinhala political and economic identity, which caste relations make clear. Upper-caste elites would have greater reason than lower-caste workers to relate to other upper-caste elites, regardless of a cultural Sinhalese identity, so long as the political Sinhala-Buddhist relationships were held in balance (Rogers, 2004; Gunawardana, 2004: 49–59).

Sovereignty in Ceylon was often a contested terrain in which a European power occupying a small patch of coastal land would proclaim dominance, while the inhabitants of that area would continue their allegiance to another power, not dissimilar to the multiple spiritual allegiances that confused Christian missionaries (Wickramasinghe, 2006). In the pre-colonial Vanni region, for example, a region of mixed ancestry of Sinhala, Tamil, and Vedda (Indigenous) peoples at the outer limits of Kandy's control (to the south) and Jaffna's control (to the north), the sovereign boundaries fluctuated – but more importantly, they were understood to be in flux. As Nira Wickramasinghe (2006: 9) describes it, "Some of the Vanniar chieftains, in the Vanni region in the East of the island, appear to have recognised the overlordship of the Kotte and Jaffna kingdoms equally and at times acknowledged both simultaneously." The ontological understanding of sovereignty in its Buddhist conception was certainly structured and hierarchical, but it was not characterized by centralized or unitary rule. In contrast to a European hierarchical feudal model, Kandyan sovereignty was based on devolving the practical aspects of governance to the periphery rather than concentrating them in the centre, which was meant to mirror the spiritual centre of the kingdom. Importantly, within South Asian spatial forms of organization such as that of Ceylon, the norm of "total rule" existed in the symbolic

108   *Pluriversal sovereignty and the state*

and spiritual realm but was not manifested bureaucratically and politically. This is significant, because the galactic sovereign order was already breaking down prior to the consolidation of *de jure* British rule over the island in 1815, with the longer-simmering tensions between the Sinhalese aristocracy and the Nayaka king leading to tensions within the balance of power and order (Mendis, 2005; Jayawardena, 2010). It is within this Kandyan sovereign context that the interventions of the British should be understood.

As James Duncan (1990: 117) notes, the city of Kandy was meant to be "a heaven to the kingdom as a whole." The king, who symbolically represented the authority of Buddha, did not engage in the details of administration, which was conducted by his *adikars*. In the spiritual domain, power was centralized, while in the physical, day-to-day world of running the state, power tended to be decentralized instead. The legitimacy and enforceability of policy did not come from the king but from the *adikars*, who would approve and enforce policy and thus played a crucial role in the practical devolution of sovereignty. *Adikars* exercised judiciary and military powers, served as go-betweens for the king and subjects, supervised the system of public works labour (*rajakariya*), and signed state documents (Wijeyeratne, 2014). There was thus an important system of checks and balances in the Buddhist system of sovereignty that gave unlimited symbolic and ritualistic power to the king, but severely limited the king's ability to act materially without the consent of the aristocracy. In contrast to the European tradition, Buddhist priests did not jockey for political power with the king, nor did they offer a mirrored or alternative governance structure; the monastic tradition worked as part of the Buddhist polity with autonomy rather than competition (Abeysekara, 2002). This spatial order, and Sri Vikrama's falling-out with the Kandyan aristocracy in the final decade of his rule, were what ensured the fall of Kandy, not any military or technological advantage held by Governor Brownrigg or his predecessors.

Symbolism and ritual have always been important legitimizing components of "sovereignty," and Ceylon and Buddhist South-East Asia more generally are no exception to this. As Wijeyeratne (2014: 575) explains,

Ontological collision 109

The rituals of State were not only an intrinsic part of the symbolic glue that contrived a form of *virtual* unity to a disparate and decentralised *galactic* polity but also refracted the spatial division of the cosmic order within the order of ritual.

It was not so much that Buddhist sovereignty in the Theravada tradition *required* that the spiritual and material realms be connected; rather, it was that within this ontology of sovereignty, there was never a rupture that might artificially separate them. There were several key ontological starting points for the organization of sovereign rule that marked the South Asian practice of sovereignty as distinct from European sovereignty. The first, discussed above, was the pulsating expansion and contraction of rule in the *rajamandala* or galactic model. Rather than being organized through vertical differentiation of increasingly local duties, the practice of sovereignty was based on replication of the "galactic core." In a way, this is similar to a fractal relationship in that a fractal represents the schematic of the whole, even within a small part. The next and related point was the practice of sovereignty playing out at local levels, in which lesser kings replicated the spiritual and practical obligations of the sovereign in their smaller kingdoms. Among the duties of those enacting sovereignty was careful attention to the spiritual and manifest domain, which were held together in practice. This process was what enabled the Kandyan kingdom to view the coastal Dutch government as administering territory on its behalf through much of the eighteenth century. Since symbolism was central to the practice of sovereignty, it was possible for the Dutch and the Kandyans to each see the other as subordinate; the decentralized and autonomous nature of politics allowed contradicting virtual power relations to exist simultaneously in ways they could not under a centralized polity. Finally, from the point of view of Buddhist sovereign ontologies within a galactic model, there was no contradiction in a distant subordinate satellite territory exercising considerable autonomy as explained above, nor was there any fundamental problem with a person being a Christian, or a Hindu, or a Jain, so long as they fulfilled the ritual requirements of sovereignty alongside the material requirements. The greater the distance from the galactic centre, the greater the level of material and political

110 *Pluriversal sovereignty and the state*

autonomy that was practised. This spatial characteristic of organizing political power was what enabled Ahelepola, and his uncle Pilimatalava before him, to plot with relative autonomy against Vikrama Rajasinha, as they both hailed from Sabaragamuva, far from the centre and close to the British coastal territories. By the time of European arrival in the sixteenth century, over a thousand years of political history had already defined the spatial parameters of sovereignty and the ebb and flow of power between territorial units on the island.

Becoming Kandyan through "Buddhification"

The urban geography of the city of Kandy illustrates the importance of symbolism to the practice of sovereignty. Kandy was constructed and ordered to physically represent hierarchies of moral order in which the connection between the king-as-*bodhisattva* was connected as closely as possible to the Buddha in the spiritual realm in the east, while the secular areas were further to the west (Duncan, 1990). Urban beautification and emphasis on symbols of sovereignty were especially important to the last dynasty of Kandyan kings, the Nayakas, because their patrilineal lines connected them to the Indian subcontinent and thus demonstration of their Buddhist credentials was especially important. In effect, the continental Nayakas had to "become Kandyan" through demonstrating their ability to perform the tasks of a Buddhist sovereign as well as their additional identity and family association with Hindu southern India. At the same time, they were not truly foreigners when the first Nayaka king was consecrated in the eighteenth century, for Nayaka regiments had supported the Sinhalese kings of Kandy since the first consecrated King of Kandy, Vimaladharmasuriya I, in 1591 (Obeyesekere, 2017: 30). Vimaladharmasuriya I's ascent to the throne exemplifies the cosmopolitan influences within the region at this early stage. Before he claimed the throne, his father was murdered by a rival, leading him to flee south to Kotte, where he converted to Catholicism. Volunteering to lead a Portuguese regiment into Kandy, he then betrayed the Portuguese, claimed the throne of Kandy, and reverted to Buddhism, taking the name

Ontological collision

Vimaladharmasuriya (Obeyesekere, 2020). The *mandala* system's ability to incorporate outsiders reflects an ontology in which many cosmologies might coexist in a way that would be very problematic within a universal understanding of "sovereignty" as it developed in the British-Christian tradition. Incorporation of foreigners, and especially of Dravidian foreigners, was an important part of Kandyan politics. Although since the formal independence of Sri Lanka, Kandy has been imagined as a place of pristine Sinhalese anti-foreign influence, even rich accounts of the late stages of the independent kingdom written by Sinhalese nobles make no particular mention of Tamils or Malabars being a problem within the kingdom.[1] Following the capture and exile of Sri Vikrama Rajasinha, the Uva Rebellion of 1817–1818 was led in part by a Nayaka Malabar relative of Vikrama named Wilbawe, who commanded considerable loyalty among the Sinhala aristocracy, as is evident in transcripts of the interrogation of Kohukumbra Ratteralle, a Kandyan chief.[2]

Ceremony was essential to the legitimization of territorial rule in the Kandyan tradition, and was part of the process of what Tambiah describes as the "Buddhification" of South Indian sovereigns who rose to power. When the Sinhalese king Narendrasinha died in 1739 without a male heir, his queen's brother, Sri Vijaya Rajasinha, was crowned king and began the Nayaka dynasty. Though it had been a tradition since the reign of King Rajasinha II (r. 1635–1687) for Sinhalese kings to marry South Indian women of Nayaka lineage based in Madurai, Sri Vijaya's identity as a South Indian ascending to the throne and his subsequent marriage to a Nayaka women established a "foreign" dynasty of South Indians to the Kandyan throne, which offended some of the Sinhala chiefs and aristocracy.[3] Vijaya Rajasinha, having no male heirs of his own, was succeeded by his Nayaka queen's brother, Kirti Sri Rajasinha (r. 1747–1782), who was in turn succeeded by Rajadhi Rajasinha (r. 1782–1798), who died of fever in 1798 and was also childless. There was considerable intrigue in the Kandyan court as to who would succeed Rajasinha; following K. M. de Silva's account, the most powerful person at court was Pilimatalava, the *Maha Adikar*. Muttusami, a brother-in-law of the recently deceased king, claimed that he had been named by the king as successor, and was jailed by Pilimatalava

112   *Pluriversal sovereignty and the state*

along with his sisters. An eighteen-year-old Nayaka protégé of Pilimatalava was ultimately crowned as Vikrama Rajasinha (r. 1798–1815), and according to de Silva, it was the intention of Pilimatalava to control Rajasinha indirectly rather than attempt to supplant him and re-establish Sinhalese rule in Kandy. This is an important point, as de Silva notes that generations of practice had "indigenized" the Nayakas to the point where there was no political will among the population to supplant them (K. M. de Silva, 1981: 221–222). The Nayakas embraced the Buddhism of their new home and, especially under Kirti Sri Rajasinha and Rajadhi Rajasinha, "identified [themselves] with the Kandyan national interest and blended the Nayaka personality into the Kandyan background with consummate skill" (K. M. de Silva, 1981: 221–222).[4] Although this did not sit well with the Sinhala aristocracy, ordinary Kandyans accepted the Nayakas without noticeable concern. Indeed, the first major attempt to re-establish a Sinhalese dynasty came only in 1798, when *Maha Adikar* Pilimatalava installed the eighteen-year-old Sri Vikrama, against whom he would later unsuccessfully rebel (K. M. de Silva, 1981: 132). Following Wijeyeratne's reasoning, by the time of Vikrama Rajasinha's coronation, the contradiction of the galactic *mandala* model of spatial organization of de-centralizing sovereign authority outwards had already left the king powerless in relation to the distant provinces. As Wijeyeratne (2014: 591) explains,

> Symbolic of the overwhelming power of the nobles who controlled the administrative bureaucracy of the kingdom, in 1798 Pilima Talauvē "combined in himself sixteen offices" of state. The king was the *galactic sovereign* par excellence himself encompassed by the provincial bureaucracy, the *galactic* centre turning into the *galactic* margin. Such was the multicentric nature of the Kandyan polity that it was the king who in the absence of a developed monetary economy remained dependent on the "loyalty of the disavas."

The ritual of sovereign practice is the galactic mass that held together the fluctuating centre, periphery, and semi-periphery of the Kandyan state (Wijeyeratne, 2014: 591). By the fourteenth century, the fertility ceremony of the *Äsala Perahera* had developed into an important spectacle of sovereignty. This procession was a powerful ritual through which sovereignty was annually reaffirmed

Ontological collision 113

and performed for all to see; it dramatized state power and further naturalized and entrenched a Buddhist ontology of how Kandy's core replicated cosmic balance and thus social order.

Part of the Nayaka contribution to the development of the *Äsala Perahera* consisted of making the *dalada* (tooth) relic the centrepiece of the *Perahera* (Tambiah, 1992: 162; Wijeyeratne, 2014: 593). The relic further reinforced the balancing of cosmology and materiality, as it was said to have come from the Buddha's funeral pyre and was taken to symbolize the legitimacy of sovereign rule, a subject of much controversy among Christian missionaries and British administrators in the decades to follow. The *Perahera*, with the *dalada* front and centre, reinforced the king's symbolic function as a *bodhisattva* for his people, and ceremonially demonstrated the centrality of the city of Kandy for the galactic kingdom. The procession ordered the entire galactic polity. A state officer in charge of the register of land title led the procession, which solidified how land was managed within the kingdom, and also the centrality of the Goyigama caste within the procession. The second and third parts of the procession, as well as sections 23–28, represented the central government, such as the elephant department and the military. Sections 16–21 represented the religious functionaries of the state (Wijeyeratne, 2014: 593–594). Although the material day-to-day operations of the state in practice empowered the *adikars* and represented de-centralizing political tendencies, the overall legitimacy of sovereignty was publicly rehearsed and performed through its mirroring of the spiritual realm, and the two were united in the urban geography of the city of Kandy (N. Perera, 1998). Despite the material autonomy of the periphery, the *disavas* (officials) in the periphery could not miss the *Perahera*, along with other rituals of the state that held the *mandala* together.

During the period of British rule, the *Äsala Perahera* was substantially discouraged, and this worked to highlight how foreign the British government truly was from the conventions and expectations of Kandyan sovereignty. British distaste for the *Perahera* came partly from its unwillingness to contribute funds towards the event, but also was periodically influenced by Christian evangelical pressure, depending on who was in the governor's chair at the time. As H. L. Seneviratne (1977) argues, when the British took

114　　　*Pluriversal sovereignty and the state*

over governance in the Kandyan region, they understood that they could not simply end the *Äsala Perahera*, and instead handed responsibility for it to the *Diyavadana Nilame*, or "Water-Bearing Official," who was in charge of the Dalada Temple, as well as the two chief monks of the Asgirya and Malwatta monasteries. The Water-Bearing Official was obliged to take financial responsibility for the *Perahera* and have personal insurance in order for it to proceed, so that he could bear the cost of any damages that it incurred (Seneviratne, 1977: 67). While missionary pressure to disassociate the colonial government from Ceylon grew through the nineteenth century, the British approach to both the *dalada* relic and the *Äsala Perahera* in this period represented a kind of slow-bleeding support intended to discourage the historical *Perahera* without legislating against it directly. As Seneviratne (1977: 73) observes, this greatly contributed to the postcolonial importance of the *Äsala Perahera* and how it has been adopted by Buddhist nationalists whose roots are not necessarily Kandyan, but coastal and with significant historical interaction with missionaries and the British government. The British promise to maintain the unity of Buddhism and state was clearly insincere, and the unwillingness or inability of the British to perform their duties as other foreigners had historically done has played a critical role in postcolonial nationalist claims to the state.

Obeyesekere (2006) has also written about processes of "Buddhification," drawing on historical texts as well as folk dramas. He maintains that historical records would not include most migrants who entered Ceylon peacefully and integrated into local societies, but folk traditions can also help to explain these processes. Obeyesekere (2006: 152) describes ritual dramas in which two performers play the role of Buddhist guardian deities at the gates of Lanka, blocking aliens who are attempting to enter:

> These aliens speak a funny kind of Sinhala with a strong Tamil accent and they constantly utter malapropisms, unintended puns, and spoonerisms. In their ignorance they make insulting remarks about the gods at the barrier, they know not Sinhala and Buddhist customs and the audience has a lot of fun at their expense. Gradually, the alien visitors recognize their errors of speech and custom; they learn to speak properly; they begin to properly worship the deities and

Ontological collision 115

acknowledge the superiority of the Buddha. Then the gods open the barrier and these aliens enter Sri Lanka.

This process mirrors the more formal process of Buddhification at the regal level in the case of the Nayaka dynasty. Obeyesekere argues that prior to European colonization, beginning with the Portuguese in 1505, there was an understanding that at the village level, where people were long accustomed to receiving southern Indian immigrants, understanding integration into the social fabric as a process of Buddhification made sense, as did the lack of differentiation between "Buddhist" and "Sinhala." While there would certainly have been individuals who would have seen southern Indian immigrants as "Others," the deference to Buddhism and respect for the genealogy of sovereign practice did not make their Otherness more significant than the Otherness of Europeans, who exhibited far less tact for 310 years before the Kandyan Convention of 1815. As Obeyesekere (2006: 156) explains, "The universalizing of the unconditional identity, Sinhala=Buddhist, with the primary emphasis on the first part of that duality, namely being Sinhala, is the product of the colonial period."

Political ontology and the pluriverse

In India, Orientalist scholars committed considerable energy towards studying Sanskrit, and through their studies they learned about the Asokan era and began to discover the connections between ancient India and ancient Greece (Metcalf, 1998: 80–81). As Thomas Metcalf explains, this was an Enlightenment-inspired effort, aimed at understanding all cultures, and this ideology influenced the creation of the Asiatic Society of Bengal in 1784. Under Governor General Warren Hasting's patronage, this organization was a hub of scholarly learning, emphasizing translations from local languages into English and the publication of the "uniquely influential journal, *Asiatic Researches*" (Metcalf, 1998: 80–81). As subaltern studies scholars have long emphasized, the British East India Company administration and its emphasis on bringing India into "worldhistory" through recasting seemingly disordered narratives

116   *Pluriversal sovereignty and the state*

into statist narratives were central to the making of modern, colonial India (Guha, 1997: 182). The modern state, instead of the written language, became a symbol of modern civilization and played the role of providing "evidence" of Indigenous "lack" to legitimize the domination of "pre-historic" people, land, and cosmology, ostensibly for the benefit, improvement, and development of "natives" themselves. What was different in the nineteenth century was that it was not only alleged civilizational inferiority and divine providence that justified colonialism, but an aligning of ideas and interests emerging into a "science" of racial inferiority, as well as linear, universal temporality in which the structural presence of the state marked the border between civilization and those lacking it (Metcalf, 1998: 80–92).

The ontological differences between initial assumptions have been outlined thus far; what remain to be considered are the consequences of ontological *conflict* and its importance for understanding colonial state formation, beginning with the Kandyan Convention. Mario Blaser, working mostly in the area of Indigenous studies in Latin and North America, offers a compelling example through which to understand the politics of ontology, and I lean on his work to explain this point. Blaser offers the example of the Mowachat/Muchalaht First Nation in what is commonly called British Columbia, Canada, to illustrate the contemporary importance of ontological collision. When Canada's Department of Fisheries and Oceans tried to launch a plan to relocate a young orca whale in 2012, the Mowachat/Muchalaht intervened on the basis that the whale was their recently deceased chief, Ambrose Maquinna, who had promised to return to his people in the form of a whale (Watson, 2004). The whale's presence, they said, represented the chief's desire to remain with the people and should be respected, and as Blaser (2013: 548) states,

> This was not a conflict between two different perspectives on an animal but rather a conflict over whether the "animal" of scientists, bureaucrats, and environmentalists was all that was there. Ontological conflicts thus involve conflicting stories about "what is there" and how they constitute realities in power-charged fields.

As Blaser's example shows, the conflict is not a question of either A or B, but rather a question of whether A is part of B, but not all

Ontological collision 117

of it. It is not that the Mowachat/Muchalaht deny that the whale in question is a whale; rather, they point to the fact that the whale observed and categorized in Western science is only part of what is actually there. While the empirical ways in which ontological conflict plays out in particular places are very distinct, there is nothing particularly unique about the conflicts that arise when different ontologies come into contact. In the context of colonial state formation in Ceylon, Blaser's notion of ontological conflict is instructive as it shows the violent implications of failing to understand that there are multiple realities interacting in the political connections between worlds that are ordered along different ontologies.

In the case of the British and the Kandyans, a belief in the universal meaning of what sovereignty and territory meant within distinct genealogies led to an ontological conflict, which was also essentially a *political* conflict. From a modernist, universal view, this has been historicized as mere duplicity on the part of entrepreneurial leaders within the Sinhalese-Kandyan aristocracy, and I do not dispute the fact that such political intrigue was central to the story. However, the more interesting problem is the enactment of politics associated with the meeting of different ontologies of "sovereignty" that inform what it means to exist and practise sovereignty. That the British and the Kandyans conceived of this differently brings to light the relational development and fragility of the concept of state sovereignty as it was developing in the early nineteenth century. When the Kandyans refused to act in a "proper" way as understood from the perspective of a Eurocentric, universal view of sovereignty, Kandy forced an opening between worlds of meaning. In the meeting of Kandyan and British ontologies of sovereignty, there are, to stretch the meaning of the concept, *two* status quos or established systems of order. This is the importance of pluriversal politics, because Kandyan sovereignty and British sovereignty each represent a world with a long history of sovereign development.

A pluriversal perspective on the meeting of different histories of sovereign practice highlights the enactment of pluriversal politics. Ontological conflict offers a destabilizing opportunity in which to see and put into practice "other" ways of knowing material and cosmological existence. At the ontological level, modernity demands that there can be only one sphere of being and experience,

118   *Pluriversal sovereignty and the state*

a *uni*verse, which has been projected and enforced throughout the colonial encounter as a political project of domination that has been manifested differently across time and place. How ontological conflicts are resolved is unpredictable and historically contingent, in large part because the existence of multiple ontologies does not preclude the mingling and interaction of ontologies which has been a facet of all human history. In the case of the British and the Kandyans, they had encountered one another many times, and the Kandyans, in particular, had a long history of military and diplomatic relations with European powers. It is relevant to reiterate that while the interaction with what I am calling British-Christian sovereignty in the Kandyan centre was new, Kandyans had long been acquainted with Christianity, and Catholicism in particular. Kandy was remarkably cosmopolitan in the eighteenth century: Queen Kusumasana Devi, also known as Dona Catherina (mother of Rajasinha II, wife of both Senerat and Vimaladharmasuriya I), was a devout Catholic and passed many of her traditions forward, alongside Buddhism (Obeyeskere, 2017: 30–33). Returning to Blaser's example of ontological conflict in twenty-first-century "Canada," we can see one possible outcome of conflicting ontology: a de-politicized, normalized, everyday application of modern, "scientific" universal thinking that cannot comprehend the Mowachat/Muchalaht position. As Blaser (2013: 554) describes it,

> the claim of the pluriverse (or multiple ontologies) is not concerned with presenting itself as a more "accurate" picture of how things are "in reality" (a sort of meta-ontology); it is concerned with the possibilities that this claim may open to address emergent (and urgent) intellectual/political problems. Central among these problems is the extent to which those of us (persons and institutions) who have been shaped by an ontology that postulates/performs a "one-world world" are ill prepared to grapple with its increasing implausibility.

The truest form of colonization is that which occurs ontologically and in which the worldviews and practices of the colonized are made to reflect those of the colonizer – the disciplining of the pluriverse into the universe. Such ontological colonial violence has many manifestations, one of which is the post-independence idea in South Asia that a strong central state must control "every inch

Ontological collision

of territory" in order to exist in a global system of states connected and constituted through hundreds of years of colonial violence (Parasram, 2014).

Multiple ontologies vs multiple modernities

Thinking about the politics of ontology is a useful way to reconsider the collision of sovereignties in the unification of Ceylon in 1815, because it draws attention to the different genealogies of sovereignty and their irreconcilability due to the developing rule of colonial difference. Seen in this light, colonial difference positioned South Asia as a place outside history, relative to a Europe in which progress was a defining characteristic that was divinely ordained. British scholars in the late nineteenth century went so far as to theorize that Rajput systems of organizing sovereignty, by virtue of resembling European ones more closely than other forms of sovereignty, were indicative of their Aryan racial blending. As Metcalf (1998: 74) explains, "A system of government that could be described by analogy with that of Europe, even the Europe of the Middle Ages, was by definition superior to a system which was purely 'Oriental' in character." Clearly the imagined universal ontology of race dating from the early nineteenth century had not given way in the late nineteenth century, but nonetheless, as a method of historical discovery, the politics of ontology can be a useful analytical tool with which to study the past differently. Political ontology, then, is about how to put into practice many "verses" of history and politics, a pluriversal rather than universal conception of ontology.

This is not to suggest that "modernity" is not a contested regime of knowledge, either within Europe or elsewhere in the world. There are political reasons why modernity is usually framed in terms of enlightened philosophy, human rights, and freedom from religious persecution rather than in terms of slavery, genocide, and the immiseration of global (including European) working classes. Yet there is an important distinction between "multiple modernities" and "multiple ontologies." The idea of multiple modernities draws attention to the fact that Eurocentric modernity offers an incomplete way of understanding the processes of industrialization,

120   *Pluriversal sovereignty and the state*

modernization, and development. This emerges in the work of Shmuel Eisenstadt (1974), who was an earlier scholar of modernization theory. Multiple modernity as a concept became more influential towards the end of the twentieth century (Bhambra, 2014; Eisenstadt, 1974). As Bhambra (201a: 32–34) observes, the case for multiple modernities was made to add a cultural dimension and inflection to the processes underscoring universal institutions such as the state and the market. This revision of earlier modernization theory thus sought to escape the charge of cultural relativism by keeping the institutional basis for a universal understanding of modernity, while resisting the European domination of modernity by emphasizing the cultural distinctions of how modernity unfolds in different places. Multiple modernity, then, still implies different perspectives on a materially objective and describable "reality," which, as Blaser's work makes clear, is not the same as multiple ontologies.

The difference between multiple ontologies and multiple modernities is the central feature of pluriversal politics, in which whole cosmologies, complete with ontological starting points and knowledge cultivated by means that may not be knowable from outside those worlds, interact. The use of political ontology as an analytical lens to understand colliding British and Kandyan sovereignties at an important moment of sovereign transformation allows us to focus on the multiple ontologies that conflicted and enacted a pluriversal conception of *politics* in which both Kandyan and British worlds were forced to transform, albeit not on equal terms. In light of the work of Chapter 1, we can see that focusing on pluriversal politics instead of universal politics means that our lens must de-link from the centrality of Europe, and this comes at a cost. As noted in Chapter 1, when a telescope is focused on a particular image, the complexity of the background is blurred. The choice to emphasize "coloniality" rather than "modernity" as the focal point of interest in this study means that the complexities and contestations *within* modernity are held artificially static. As I have strived to show throughout this book, the de-politicization through the violence of universality as it pertains to the histories of modern/colonial state formation relies on discursive power to normalize Eurocentric ontologies, epistemologies, and practices.

Ontological collision 121

Modernity requires an ontological *belief* in universality, whether it is through linear temporality or through a fundamental civilizational hierarchy of difference (Guha, 2002; Metcalf, 1998). However, the crucial component of this story is that the use of modernity as a mediator or lens through which to know the world is a colonizing master-narrative that has, through five hundred years of political practice, normalized its own universality as a standard by which all others must be evaluated; and this method of evaluation has been axiomatically proclaimed and has enforced its validity with coercive power as well as attempting to prove it. This has indeed been central to the colonial encounters of the past, but as the story of the Mowachat/Muchalaht shows, modernity *continues* to depend on the silencing of other worlds. Ontological conflict helps to explain the religious politics introduced earlier in this chapter between Christian and Buddhis worldviews. Christian worldviews informed the political and messianic motivations of British missionaries and administrators in the early nineteenth century just as they were starting to learn and produce knowledge about *buddhagama*, or what they would eventually name "Buddhism." With this history and this theoretical approach in mind, I turn now to the physical encounter between the British and Kandyan aristocracy in Kandy in 1815 to explore the political ontology of the Convention.

The Kandyan Convention as political ontology

Though it was not a *Perahera* that marked the ritual handover of sovereignty from the Kandyan aristocracy to General Brownrigg, the ceremony was spectacular, involving the ceremonial arrival in the king's palace of Governor Brownrigg alongside the current *Maha Adikar*, Molligoda, and the most recently deposed *Maha Adikar*, Ahelepola, whose defection to the British catalysed the course of events leading to the sovereign handover. The British troops assembled in the square in front of the Royal Palace at 3.00 p.m. and formed a lane from the outside into the King's Hall, where the sovereign of Kandy sat for official ceremonies. Governor Brownrigg, alongside the main chiefs, passed through this military flank into the King's Hall and took the king's place, sitting to the

122   *Pluriversal sovereignty and the state*

immediate right of the recently ousted *Maha Adikar* Ahelepola. Ahelepola's replacement, Molligoda, served the role of *Maha Adikar* and led the procession of approximately twenty *dessaves* (ministers) of the provinces and principal chiefs. Brownrigg rose to receive them, and he and Ahelepola, who had accepted the official title of "Friend of the British Government," remained standing for the rest of the ceremony.

As they entered the palace, a British ensign began raising the Royal Standard outside, but deep in the heart of the city of the *bodhisattva* king, attention to ceremony and due process was more important than strength of arms. A Buddhist priest, Wariyapola Sri Sumangala, intercepted the breach of protocol and

> pulled down the Union Jack, which he saw being hoisted by a British ensign, when Governor Sir Robert Brownrigg entered the Audience Hall at Kandy on March 2, 1815 and placing his foot on it shouted, "The treaty is not signed yet." A sword was drawn but it went back to its sheath. The Union Jack remained lowered until the ceremony was over.

> (Etipola, 1952)

The simmering tension associated with the drawn swords and flag-stomping speak to the tenuousness of this moment. Obeyesekere (2017: 226–238) cautions that it is unlikely that this event occurred, despite its being commonly accepted in the nationalist histories. He argues that it is unlikely that Sumangala would have been present for the signing on March 10, and also notes that the flag raised by Brownrigg would have been the Royal Standard and not the Union Jack, as the point of sovereign handover was to represent the British monarch. Even without this particular piece of drama, the spectacle and ritual of sovereign handover was significant both for the people of Kandy and for the British government. Blaser's work on political ontology helps us to see that the meaning of that ceremony was quite distinct. The point of contention between a Kandyan genealogy and practice of sovereignty and the Kandyans' British counterparts was not just a question of who would be sovereign, but was about what it meant to exercise sovereignty. From the perspective of the genealogy of Kandyan sovereignty, this required a pulsating galactic order whose legitimacy emerged out of local practices of

Ontological collision 123

cosmological and material balance, requiring foreigners to "become Kandyan" and perform the Buddhist obligations of sovereignty. Indeed, for more than a thousand years, the process of integrating foreigners more generally, never mind sovereigns, into the local political milieu was based on their Buddhification, but this was not ontologically possible for the British (Obeyesekere, 2006). To be sovereign in a galactic *mandala* system was to wield power, but it was also much more than the wielding of power.

The purpose of existing within the Kandyan sovereign system was not to escape a Hobbesian state of nature but, rather, to exist within a kingdom that balanced cosmological and material obligations (Tambiah, 2013). To the British, sovereignty was much more a question of material rule sanctified in a hierarchical organization of authority that placed the British sovereign at the top and endowed them with absolute authority, however problematic this might be (as outlined in Chapter 1). What was developing was an imperial and relational conception of modern sovereignty. Kandyans required a galactic centre – *Sri Menanti* – modelled on a Kandyan-Buddhist understanding of balance, but the British required a geographically fragmented and imperially mediated form of disassociated sovereignty that connected to a London centre and a Christian monarch via mediating centres far removed from the Kandyan galactic centre. That these differing ontologies of sovereignty would clash, in light of all that has been discussed so far in this chapter, should not seem surprising.

While Sumangala and the British ensign clashed outside the palace at Kandy in 1815 (or did not!), the spectacle and rituals of sovereign handover were continuing inside the hall. I quote at length an anonymous and self-described "gentleman on the spot," who was probably an officer in Brownrigg's army or a bureaucrat:[5]

A scene no less novel than interesting was here presented, in the state and costume of the Kandian Court, with an English Governor presiding, and the Hall lined on both sides with British officers.

The conference began with complimentary inquiries on the part of the Chiefs, which were graciously answered by the Governor, and mutual inquiries made. His Excellency then thanked the Dessaves for the attention shewn [sic] to the troops in their various routes through the country towards the capital; which gave occasion to the Chiefs

124   *Pluriversal sovereignty and the state*

to observe, that they considered them as protectors, and that by the arrival of His Excellency and the army they had been rescued from tyranny and oppression.

The Governor observed he was gratified in having been the means of their deliverance; he assured them of full protection, in their persons, their property, and all their rights; and added, that while he had the honour of holding the administration in the island, it would be his study to make them experience the blessings of His Majesty's benign government.

It was then intimated to the Chiefs, that a paper had been prepared expressive of the principles on which the participation of His Majesty's government was offered to their acceptance, and that it was about to be read; which they requested might be done.

The Treaty was then read in English by Mr Sutherland, Deputy Secretary to the government, and afterwards in Cingalese by the Modeliar of His Excellency's Gate, Abraham de Saram. This important document was listened to with profound and respectful attention by the Chiefs; and it was pleasing to observe in their looks, a marked expression of cordial assent, which was immediately declared with great earnestness ...

... After the Treaty was read in Cingalese, the Adigar Molligodde and the other Chiefs proceeded to the great door of the Hall, where the Mohottales, Coraals, Vidaans, and other subordinate headmen from the different provinces were attending, with a great concourse of the inhabitants; and the headmen being called on by the Adigar to range themselves in order according to their respective districts, the Treaty was again read by the Modeliar in Cingalese; at the conclusion of which the British Flag was hoisted, for the first time, in the town of Kandy, and a royal salute from the cannon of the city announced *His Majesty George the Third Sovereign of the whole Island of Ceylon.*

(*A Narrative of Events*, 1815: 44–49)

It was at this point that two distinct ontological understandings of political sovereignty collided, one representing a Western European Christian genealogy and another representing a South Asian Buddhist genealogical tradition. The British believed that with King George as "Sovereign of the whole Island of Ceylon," they were firmly in control, but to the Kandyans, to be "sovereign" required Buddhification and a galactic model of power in which disparate territories exercised considerable autonomy. This was the historical precedent; foreign sovereigns, like the Nayakas, went to

Ontological collision

great lengths to show deference to local traditions and history of the territory in order to normalize and sanctify the legitimacy of their rule, but to the British, this was not at all part of the plan.

At the most basic level, the British were rude! This is evident in what appears to be double-speak by Brownrigg when, a few weeks following this event, he led the Wesleyan missionaries to believe that the "centre was open to the gospel," a statement which is a far cry from Article 5 of the Kandyan Convention, which declares Buddhism to be inviolable. As is clear from the description of Obeyesekere's close engagement with the Convention in both Sinhalese and English, there were considerable differences in the texts, with some English words and passages not translated into Sinhalese and vice versa. Obeyesekere (2017: 226–227) translates an important part of the Sinhalese text that was not represented in English:

> The officials and the people resident in these provinces (*rataval*) who have faith in the *sasana* of the Buddha and the religion (agama) of the Devas can never be broken (*kadakalanohakiva*) and [their affairs] should be conducted properly; the duties (katayutu) of the aforesaid Sangha and their viharas and their residences and as well as the devales should be properly conducted and protected.

Outside the limits of the text itself, Brownrigg met with monks to affirm the centrality of Buddhism as a requirement for the Convention, even though he and his British contemporaries clearly could not apprehend its importance to sovereignty, let alone religion. For example, the year before this, Brownrigg hosted the missionaries at Government House, advised them on where to concentrate their resources as well as where Tamil- and Sinhalese-language skills would be necessary, and provided them with generous government stipends and grants of land so that they might evangelize more effectively (Ault, 1814). My point is not that the Kandyans believed in 1815 that the British were their subordinates, but that two understandings of what it meant to practise sovereignty collided, while simultaneously being articulated together in this document and the ceremony that sanctified it.

The Convention, written side by side in English and Sinhalese but with substantial differences, represented the formal legal transference of Kandyan sovereignty, embodied by the ranking chiefs, to Britain,

126   *Pluriversal sovereignty and the state*

embodied by Governor Robert Brownrigg. It recognizes two different readings of temporality, themselves evidence of different understandings of reality, as the text begins by noting the difference between the recorded years, 1815 in the Christian calendar and 1736 in the Sinhalese calendar. The first three clauses in English vilify the "cruelties and oppression of the Malabar ruler" and importantly, state that the ousted sovereign had habitually violated the "sacred duties of a Sovereign" ("The Kandyan Convention Proclamation," 1815). The Convention laid the problematic groundwork for how the British and Kandyans would relate to each other, promising extensive protection for Buddhism (clause 5), the preservation (but subjugation) of Kandyan laws, and the supremacy of British rule and domination over trade in particular (clauses 8–11). In clause 4, Kandy is hierarchically situated within the British Empire, and while Kandyan *adikars*, *dessaves*, and other positions of authority are recognized, they are subordinated in a legalistic, British/feudal way in clause 4:

> The dominion of the Kandyan provinces is vested in the Sovereign of the British Empire and to be exercised through the Governors or Lieutenant-Governors of Ceylon for the time being, and their accredited Agents, saving to the Adigars, Dessaves, Mohottales, Coraals, Vidaans, and all other subordinate native headmen, lawfully appointed by authority of the British Government, the rights, privileges, and powers of their respective offices and to all classes of the people the safety of their persons and property, with their civil rights and immunities, according to the laws, institutions, and customs established and in force amongst them.
>
>   ("The Kandyan Convention Proclamation," 1815)

Capital punishment was reserved for the British, which is significant in that it was the alleged abuse of capital punishment by Sri Vikrama Rajasinha, cited by Governor Brownrigg in a January 1815 proclamation, that offered the moral impetus for the invasion in the first place.

Galactic sovereign collision and political ontology

The political implications of this ontological collision were not immediately obvious, though the effects began to materialize soon

Ontological collision 127

afterwards. The meeting of ontologies of sovereignty between the South Asian galactic model and the European vertical model can be understood by analogy with what happens when galaxies themselves come into contact with one another. In the pluriverse, multiple ontologies have always coexisted, and the implication of this is that they do come into contact with each other, and also into conflict. When galaxies come into contact with one another, the fallout from that collision is not uniform throughout. Galaxies are, at one scale of abstraction, very porous and animated by gravity, and rather than bumping into each other, they pass through one another, reforming one another as they interact again and again.

Figure 4.1 shows a graphic interpretation of the moment of galactic collision between our Milky Way galaxy and our closest galactic neighbour, the Andromeda galaxy, based on predictions from NASA. The ontological conflict of British and Kandyan conceptions of "sovereignty" can be likened to this first moment of galactic collision because the implications of the collision are not immediately clear. The galaxies, and the ontologies of sovereignty,

Figure 4.1 Milky Way and Andromeda galaxies colliding (Time 1). NASA artistic prediction, May 31, 2012. Taken from https://www.nasa.gov/mission_pages/hubble/science/milky-way-collide.html (accessed May 23, 2023).

can "pass through" one another where sovereignty has been transferred from the Kandyan territories to the British, but the ontological question of what it means to wield and exercise sovereignty can be misunderstood by both parties.

In Figure 4.2, the galaxies have passed through one another, and this passing through has affected each of the galaxies. Over time, they will collide again and ultimately converge into something altogether new. Such repeated collisions and encounters can be likened to political processes between distinct ontologies of sovereignty throughout the subsequent four decades.

The ontological collision of sovereignty resulted in almost immediate problems, as the Kandyans believed the British would leave Kandy after the Convention, and Brownrigg instead left troops behind. The immediate difficulty and borderline impossibility for Christian British rulers of performing the ceremonial obligations of Kandyan sovereigns was apparent. While the British took possession of the sacred *dalada* relic, all that the relic meant to them was a "superstition": the relic needed to be guarded so as to trick a backward people

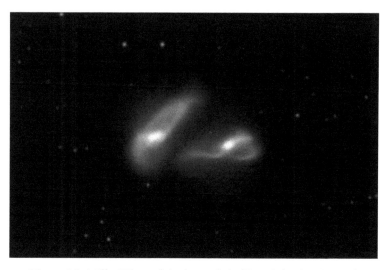

Figure 4.2 Milky Way and Andromeda in Time 2, having "passed through" each other. NASA artistic prediction, May 31, 2012. Taken from https://www.nasa.gov/mission_pages/hubble/science/milky-way-collide.html (accessed May 23, 2023).

Ontological collision 129

into obedience. Conversely, it was a necessary symbol of sovereign legitimacy in Kandy, developed over centuries and used as a deliberative and performative centrepiece by the Nayaka kings in particular. It took less than two years for the Uva Rebellion to break out, in which the Kandyan aristocracy, the Buddhist priests, and masses of people rose up to try to re-establish the old order; the details of these uprisings will be discussed in Chapter 5.

To the evangelically inclined among the British Christians, the association of the British government with the *dalada* relic was akin to aligning their Christian nation to idolatry. To the Kandyans in the rebellions and near-rebellions that followed (1817–1818, 1823, 1824, 1834, 1843, 1848), the *dalada* was a sought-after symbol of legitimacy and a rallying point. Sri Sumangala, whether or not he dramatically stomped on the Royal Standard in 1815, would later steal the *dalada* relic and give it to the anti-British rebellion, a treasonous crime for which he was eventually jailed. In the decades that followed the Convention, the British downplayed the significance of the tooth relic and constantly strove for "rational" explanations of why Governor Brownrigg would have agreed to such a commitment to Buddhism. A prime example of this comes from the writing of James Steuart (1850: 24), a colonial administrator in Ceylon for nearly forty years:

> When we reflect on the Christian character of Sir Robert Brownrigg and the sterling religious principles of his legal adviser, the late Sir Hardinge Gifford, then Advocate Fiscal, we are both surprised and concerned to find in the treaty of convention of 1815, that the Religion of Buddha professed by the Chiefs and Inhabitants of the Kandian Provinces is declared to be "inviolable and its rites, ministers and places of worship to be maintained and protected." But when we are told the Kandians believe that the security of the Government of their country depends on the possession of the "Dalada" or relic of Buddha, we may perceive the policy, which prompted the English to avail themselves of this popular superstition to keep down insurrection, by placing a guard of British soldiers over the principle Temple in which the imaginary tooth of Buddha is deposited, and henceforth to promise it British protection … the Kandian Priests of Buddha are indebted for the protection which their Idolatrous worship receives from the British Government.

130   *Pluriversal sovereignty and the state*

In Steuart's observation, thirty years after the signing of the Kandyan Convention, it is clear that the ontological dissonance of sovereignty has not lifted. He sees in the *dalada* relic only a strategic technology of colonial rule, not an objective charged with sovereign legitimacy and embraced by a legitimate Buddhist worldview that underscores the balance of political order. Within a British framework, it could be rationalized only in instrumental terms, as a technology of colonial rule, but within a Kandyan framework, there was never any confusion about the importance of it. Ontologically, the tooth symbolized a union of cosmological and political realms, rehearsed and practised in *peraheras*. That the British could not fully grasp the significance of this or reconcile it with their Christian sensibilities, which demanded that such objects be considered idolatry or demonic in essence, was a problem for the British, not the Kandyans. As with Blaser's example of the Mowachat/Muchalaht, the issue at hand was not whether the tooth relic was an idolatrous affront to Christianity. Rather, it was its importance to Buddhist sovereignty, which started from distinct ontological assumptions grounded in a long genealogy of practice that came into conflict with a British-Christian understanding of sovereignty in the spectacle and document of the Kandyan Convention. The universal perspective of sovereignty from a British-Christian cosmology could not comprehend the meaning of the Kandyan-Buddhist cosmology and the significance of the galactic model that Tambiah describes.

Four years after Steuart wrote the above reflection, the *dalada* was given back to the Kandyans and into the care of Giranegama Ratanajothi Thera, chief priest of the Danbulla Temple. Like Sri Sumangala before him, Ratanajothi would grant spiritual legitimacy to the Matale Rebellion led by Gongalegoda Banda by crowning Banda "Sri Wikrema Siddipathi," King of Kandy, in a treasonous ceremony in 1848 ("Heroes in the Struggle for Independence," 2012). Just a few months before the rebellion took off, on August 15, 1847, Governor George Byng, seventh Viscount Torrington, described the tooth relic in a dispatch of August 15, 1847 to the Colonial Office as "a mere bit of ivory, very brown in colour, and I should doubt very much as to the estimated value of the jewels" (in K. M. de Silva, 1965). The day before, on August 14, Torrington lamented a Colonial Office order to place

Ontological collision 131

the *dalada* relic in the hands of the locals, which had come as a result of a concerted effort on behalf of missionaries to disassociate the British government from "idolatry" between 1815 and 1848.[6] In this letter, Torrington suggested that a far better solution would have been to lie to the locals, telling them that Queen Victoria "has a splendid temple called the *British Museum* in which she would place it and take care of it for them" (in K. M. de Silva, 1965). In a twisted way, Torrington was perhaps correct, as it was the authority of the sovereign relic that helped grant ceremonial legitimacy to the crowning of Banda as king, or in British parlance "pretender" to the throne. Utterly ignorant of the importance of the Buddhist priesthood, Governor Torrington had the priest dragged out in his ceremonial robes and shot for treason, an event that he would later blame on the priest for not requesting to change his clothes prior to being executed. This act of executing the chief priest in his ceremonial robes would become a catalyst that brought about the end of Torrington's administration following a royal inquiry into the heavy-handed way he chose to deal with the uprisings of 1848 ("Copy of a Letter from Viscount Torrington," 1857; Forbes, 1850).

Conclusion

By examining contrasting ontologies of religion and sovereignty in the early nineteenth century, this chapter brings to light illustrative archival evidence to re-conceptualize the beginnings of modern territorial state formation in Ceylon. The narrative unfolds amid a hostile milieu of Christian evangelism, diplomatic intrigue, and a conflicted British administration bound by law via the Kandyan Convention to protect and uphold Buddhist ceremony, religion, and traditions, while unofficially supporting Christianization. The well-documented inability of successive generations of British missionaries, administrators, and planters to reconcile the cognitive dissonance of being a civilizing Christian empire and supporting what they understood as "idolatry" and "false religion" reflects an ontological inability to understand the importance of symbolism present in South Asian pre-colonial sovereign organization

132   *Pluriversal sovereignty and the state*

that relied on balancing, rather than differentiating, questions of cosmology and material politics.

The problem of Christian universalism was not just a problem for Kandyan–British relations. In important ontologically conflicting ways, the Kandyan Convention predicted the Royal Proclamation that brought India under the rule of Empress Victoria in 1858 following the First War of Independence or Sepoy Rebellion. The protection and privileging of Buddhism in the original Kandyan Convention was a source of ire for generations of missionaries and some evangelically inclined bureaucrats, and as noted above, this privilege was removed in the 1818 proclamation following the end of the Uva Rebellion. Forty years later in Allahabad, it would seem as though the British had learned something from their experiences in Ceylon. As Metcalf (1998) observes, the British simply could not or would not come to terms with the fact that their liberal-colonial reform agenda was not received by ordinary people in the way British administers imagined it to be. For example, in the Sepoy Rebellion, the British expected the Oudh peasantry to side with them against the rebels and failed to understand the many different reasons for and rationalizations of why they joined the rebellion against Britain. Though Victoria's proclamation affirmed the universal truth of Christianity, it also stated that all people regardless of their religious faith "shall enjoy the equal and impartial protection of the law." At the same time, the 1858 proclamation ("Proclamation by the Queen," 1858) acknowledged Indigenous ways of relating to land, but immediately subordinated to interests of the state:

> We know, and respect, the feelings of attachment with which the Natives of India regard the Lands inherited to them by their Ancestors; and We desire to Protect them in all Rights connected therewith, subject to the equitable demands of the State; and We will that generally in framing and Administering the Law due regard be paid to the Ancient Rights, Usages, and Customs of India.

As Cohn (1996) reminds us, knowledge moved in two directions during the modern colonial period, but I would add that it moved in more than two directions, as the lessons of colonial state formation in Ceylon predated and, in some ways, foreshadowed some of the

Ontological collision

problems associated with alien rule in lands with distinct ontologies of land, governance, and sovereignty. As in the case of the Kandyan Convention, there was an attempt to speak to both ontological traditions, but, as Césaire's point about truly respecting one's adversary informs us, the British (and to a lesser extent, the Kandyans in 1815 and the Nawabs and princes in 1858 India) were not fully able to appreciate the significance of the ontological conflict they found themselves in. Colonial state formation, separate from company state formation, happened first in Ceylon, and as such it offers an especially rich historical case to deepen comparative studies of colonial state formation in India as well, though this is beyond the reach of this current project.

While mainstream historical accounts, including accounts written by Sri Lankan historians, tend to be at relative ease with describing the events of the Kandyan Convention in benign terms, in my reading, I see this spectacle as well as the text as central to understanding the kinds of clashes that produced the territory of Ceylon in the unfolding decades. This chapter offers insights into how British and Kandyan understandings of sovereignty were on very different ontological grounds, leading to an unofficial, unstable harmony of interests between Christian missionaries and the British government, which together were confronting an Orientalized and "backward" native-Other. The confluence of these forces projected a geographical imaginary of the island's disparate regions as contained within "the state," though at this point in history, Ceylon was only at the beginning of "becoming" the modern territorial state, a fact which had implications for Ceylon, for Britain, and for the developing imperial world system.

The state is a symptom of the more insidious violence of colonially administered modernity, complete with the ontological conviction that human society develops linearly and that the darker peoples of the world require European assistance if they are ever to "catch up." If modernity were a palace, coloniality would be the moat that secures the palace; each needs the other to exist. Without the palace, the moat circles nothing, and without the moat, the palace would be burned to ashes. The state, specifically the belief that the state must take the form of "total territorial rule" complete with a seat at the United Nations, exemplifies the continuity

134   *Pluriversal sovereignty and the state*

of structural, ontological, colonial violence in the independent places of the world. Coloniality, writes Nelson Maldonado-Torres (2010: 97), refers to the "long-standing patterns of power that emerged as a result of colonialism, but that define culture, labour, inter-subjective relations, and knowledge production well beyond the strict limits of colonial administrations." As illustrated in this chapter, this can also be seen in the translation of philosophical ways of being that were practised in Ceylon prior to the colonial encounter with "religions" like Buddhism or Hinduism as they are known today.

Notes

1 The beginning of the "ethnic" problems would come with the birth of the plantation economy of the 1830s onwards and, with it, the establishment and rampant proliferation of alcohol-selling taverns, European planters, and migrant South Indian workers. Indeed, in a region well known for its intolerance of alcohol, the fact that 133 arrack taverns opened between 1815 and 1848 and their associated social effects speak to the transformation of the kingdom into an early capitalist "boom" town at a breakneck pace. In the districts of Kandy, Udunuwara, Udapalata, and upper Bulatgama, consumption was as high as 2.2 gallons per head in 1848. See K. M. de Silva, 1965: 16, n. 49.

2 There are different accounts of the leading figure in the Uva Rebellion, as will be discussed in greater detail in Chapter 5. According to newspaper accounts in the early stage of the rebellion, it was believed that one of the main instigators of the rebellion was indeed a Malabar relative of the ousted king named Wilbawe, but in later newspaper accounts and correspondence, this particular person was said to be living in exile in Madras under government arrest. According to these sources, it was a Sinhala Buddhist monk who posed as a Tamil/Malabar relation to drum up support for the rebellion and allied with Ahelepola's nephew Keppitipola, who defected from the British to join the rebels. See *Ceylon Gazette*, May 16, 1818.

3 It is relevant that the two "pure" Sinhalese kings preceding Vijaya both had Nayaka mothers. See Tambiah, 1992: 159.

4 It is worth drawing attention to de Silva's use of "national" in this quote. De Silva's primary research interest is not the rise of nationalism, as he does not view this ostensibly as a characteristic of modern or colonial

Ontological collision   135

society. In his earlier work, however, he does differentiate between a Kandyan sense of nationalism and a modern form of nationalism.

5 It is unclear who this gentleman is, but the historian Geoffrey Powell believes the most likely person is William Tolfrey, the man who replaced John D'Oyly as chief translator of the colonial government after the Kandyan Convention, in which D'Oyly took up the post of government Resident in the newly acquired Kandyan territories. See Powell, 1973: 243.

6 Missionary accounts, as well as the accounts of local converts turned missionary aids, consistently resist what was seen as over-compensation for "false" religion in the text of the Kandyan Convention and the credibility it lent to the "backward" order. One of the most important and influential of these texts was a pamphlet written by the Rev. Spence Hardy, in which he writes: "I rest my argument of the necessity of its [Buddhism's] destruction upon the simple fact that it is opposed to the truth – denies the existence of God – is ignorant of the only way of salvation, by faith in our Lord Jesus Christ ..." See Hardy, 1841. See also Roberts, 1975.

5

The coloniality of the archives

The three decades following the Kandyan Convention speak to an ongoing process of ontological collisions through which modern/colonial state territoriality would take shape. Reading this period as collisions requires us to challenge assumptions that are woven through archival collections, which represent some of the most critical impediments to understanding the gradual envelopment of universal sovereignty and the pieces of pluriversal sovereignty that remain marginalized but present within it. There is already a healthy body of literature in postmodern and post-structural historiography that has sought to draw attention to the impossibility of authoring "objective" histories; this chapter is a subtler critique of the ability to write standpoint histories or national histories while taking for granted the ontological assumptions housed within archival "data" (Munslow, 2010; Jenkins, 1997; Clarke, 2004). In order to do this work, I focus on the various insurrectionary attempts to drive the British out of Kandy and Ceylon that largely defined the middle period of sovereign ontological contestation, outlined in the preceding chapter. Building on the problems identified in the Introduction's discussion of the coloniality of the archives and the representation of colonized people as "pre-political," in this chapter I spend considerable time looking at instances of small and failed rebellions, arguing that they played a role in creating a simmering culture of insurrection that impacted the evolving shape of the colonial state. This was particularly clear by the time of the 1848 Matale Rebellion, in which Governor Torrington's heavy-handed approach at quelling the uprising was informed by his fears of the 1817–1818 Uva Rebellion, but also, as colonial testimonies after

The coloniality of the archives   137

the fact illustrate, by the general culture of insurrection that had been simmering throughout the 1830s and 1840s.

I first discuss the epistemological problem of relying on influential secondary histories of Ceylon, highlighting how even Sri Lankan historians have been complicit with some of the ideological assumptions of colonial modernity as it pertains to representing people as "pre-political" or "pre-modern." In the next section, I develop my own readings of archives in order to draw attention to why the period of relative peace between the Uva and Matale rebellions of 1817–1818 and 1848 respectively needs to be reconsidered in light of what little of the agency of ordinary people may be glimpsed and inferred from available data. In particular, I draw on newspaper accounts, military court martials, and government correspondence "in relief," as outlined in the Introduction, as a way to paint a more complex picture of the transformative period through which we can see the colonial state as the product of both colonizing and anti-colonizing vectors. As Nihal Perera argues (2002: 1706),

> Society and space operate together: they influence and affect each other, but one does not determine the other … If the Lankans were attempting to escape colonialism until the 1850s, from the 1860s they were increasingly focusing on appropriating colonial structures, spaces and symbols and making a livelihood or strengthening their positions within the colonial order.

Perera (2002) maintains that by the 1860s, an element of "reverse-Orientalism" unfolding in Colombo led to the simultaneous Westernization of the nascent national Lankan elite and the indigenization of foreign social and spatial structures. I agree with his reading, as well as with observations by Jayawardena (2010) and Wickramasinghe (2014) which note that modern historians privilege the late nineteenth century and that more focused and nuanced attention to the early nineteenth century is needed. In focusing on insurrectionary activity between 1818 and 1848, I most closely follow along archivally with Jayawardena's important book *Perpetual Ferment* (2010), which also recasts the period between the Kandyan Convention and Matale Rebellion of 1848 as one of constant resistance to foreign British rule. My emphasis in this historical period is slightly different from Jayawardena's (2010) in that I am particularly

138 *Pluriversal sovereignty and the state*

interested in tracing how roughly three decades of simultaneous colonizing and anti-colonizing politics emanating from the sovereign ontological collision worked to produce the colonial satellite state. With reference to the concept of ontological conflict introduced earlier, this is the important period in which we can see the two "galaxies" or ontologies of "sovereignty" colliding and merging into a single framework: that of the modern territorial state. By the end of this period, I argue, the logic of the colonial state had become firmly entrenched, and we can see this in the shift in anti-colonial tactics in the latter half of the nineteenth century.

Elite histories and the coloniality of the archive

The aim of this section is not to re-hash the secondary literature on the broad empirical contours of the history but, rather, to highlight the epistemic violence implicit in the dominant historicizing of the events. I draw on illustrative examples taken from three eminent scholars of Sri Lankan history, G. C. Mendis, Colvin R. de Silva, and K. M. de Silva. Before they are introduced, a brief biographical note is warranted to place these scholars in the political and academic contexts in which they lived and worked.

G. C. Mendis was born in 1894 in Moratuwa, outside Colombo, where his father was the priest of the local Methodist church. Mendis studied and taught in Kandy and was personally engaged in early national political organizing with his older brother, distributing pamphlets and newspapers promoting the Ceylon National Congress. While he was a lecturer at the Ceylon Government Training Centre, he was able to take leave and begin PhD studies at the School of Oriental and African Studies, University of London, under the supervision of Rhys Davids, a Pali scholar who had spent a decade as a colonial civil servant in Ceylon. As a student, Mendis also spent time in Germany, studying with the German Orientalist Wilhelm Ludwig Geiger. Mendis's dissertation was a critical reading of the Sinhalese-Buddhist Pali text *Mahavamsa*, and he went on to write some of the seminal pieces on Ceylonese and Sri Lankan history. Mendis helped to institutionally create the space as well as the texts for the study of history on the island. Among his many

The coloniality of the archives 139

contributions is *The Colebrooke–Cameron Papers: Documents on British Colonial Policy 1796–1933* (1957), which has served as a basis for most historians of the period (E.P., 1969).

Born in 1907, Colvin R. de Silva was a contemporary of Mendis and was also involved in anti-colonial organizing. He was imprisoned for his activism during the independence movement of the 1940s in Ceylon. During that time, he wrote *Ceylon under the British Occupation 1795–1833* (1953), and entrusted the proofs and editing to Mendis (Gunasekara, 1999). A founder of the Lanka Sama Samaja Party – the first communist party on the island – he won a seat in independent Ceylon's first elections in 1947 and was a lawyer and parliamentarian on and off until his death in 1989. Colvin R. de Silva had earned a PhD from University College London, and his dissertation was the material on which his manuscript written in prison was based.

Kingsley Muthumuni de Silva was born in 1931 and thus was in the next generation of Sri Lankan historians. Educated initially at the University of Ceylon at Peradeniya, he completed his doctoral dissertation on missionary organizations in nineteenth-century Ceylon at the University of London. He has written prolifically on Sri Lankan history, ethnic relations, nationalism, conflict, and post-conflict studies.

With this context in mind, I now focus on the ways in which scientific history and the development of society have been under-problematized through the scholarship of these authors. Take, for example, the contestations over the authenticity of the "Cleghorn minute" of 1799 that has served as a historical artefact for both Tamil and Sinhalese nationalists in the late twentieth century. Many of the island's post-independence conflicts have been associated with the contrasting claims of Tamils and Sinhalese to authentic pasts and territories, in which the historical record becomes a contested battleground. Proponents of the claim that the predominantly Tamil-speaking north and east of the island represent a historic and distinct homeland based on an ancient history of Tamil sovereignty point to this minute written by Hugh Cleghorn in 1799. Cleghorn, a visiting academic from England touring the island as part of the British administration that was taking over the Dutch maritime territories of Ceylon at the time, observed that the northern and

140   *Pluriversal sovereignty and the state*

eastern regions of the island were the historic homeland of the Tamil people (K. M. De Silva, 1987). K. M. de Silva lambasted this claim in a conference paper given at an international conference on separatism in 1987, where he argued that Tamil separatist leaders rely on Cleghorn's minute for their claim to statehood: "It was a claim based on a hazy memory of statehood in centuries past, remembered and newly interpreted (and generally misinterpreted) to mean a continuing tradition of independent statehood and an unbroken national consciousness." Cleghorn, de Silva argued, was a foreign academic with no knowledge of or experience on the island, and he probably relied on flawed Dutch archives to come to his conclusion. De Silva further argued that Tamil nationalists rely on only a portion of the minute that supports their claim to a separate homeland in the north and east, while ignoring important errors that draw the historical accuracy into question. Cleghorn wrote:

> Two different nations, from a very ancient period, have divided between them the possession of the island. First the Cingalese [sic] inhabiting the interior of the country, in its southern and western parts, from the river Wallouve (Walawe) to that of Chilow [sic], and secondly the Malabars (Tamils), who possess the northern and eastern districts. These two nations differ entirely in their religion, language and manners.
>
> (quoted in K. M. de Silva, 1987: 7)

According to de Silva, Tamil nationalists tend to ignore the fact that the minute continues: "The former, who are allowed to be the earlier settlers, derive their origin from Siam, professing the ancient religion of that country" (quoted in K. M. de Silva, 1987: 7). De Silva points to this significant empirical misreading of South and South-East Asian history as evidence of the dubious credibility of the minute in its entirety, and rightly so.

De Silva's critique of the Cleghorn minute, however, also betrays his own intellectual investment in a history of the island tinged with a methodological investment that naturalizes – and thus removes from investigation – the norm of total territorial rule. If "unbroken" continuity is a requirement to make a legitimate claim to statehood, then why assume that the British period was not a break in

The coloniality of the archives   141

this chain in the country? To perceive it as a continued chain of governance is to misrepresent even the history of political rule during the Dutch and Portuguese occupations, not to mention the much longer history of fragmented and galactic sovereignty on the island, of which de Silva is well aware. Contemporary Tamil and Sinhala nationalists lay claim to their legitimacy by being grounded in a history of the island that naturalizes a modern norm of territorial exclusivity that is anachronistically rigid and largely indifferent to the colonial encounter.[1]

According to the norms of modern social science research, there is a presumption that objectively analysing history can uncover and prove contemporary claims based on the past. Still, faith in the rigour of the historical method to adequately mitigate the distorting effect of social power is misplaced, in part because of a belief in the historian's ability to be detached from the social past they seek to describe (Seth, 2007: 79–85). As Sanjay Seth (2007: 84) observes, "there is no Archimedean point from which we can survey and know the world without being influenced by our place in it." This highlights the importance of being reflexive about the assumptions, or ontological premises, that the historian brings to the historical narrative.

Consider the representation of nationalism in the following description of the Matale Rebellion, also written by K. M. de Silva (1965: 21):

> Between 8th July and 29th July – the day of the riots at Matale – the mass movement against the taxes was taken over by a small group of men who sought to channel this discontent into an attempt to drive the British out of Kandy. The force that inspired these men was that of Kandyan nationalism, a nationalism poles apart from the nationalism of the 20th century but none the less nationalism for all that. [Governor] Torrington came nearest to understanding this force when he explained that, "By [Kandyan] nationality I mean the feelings, the habits, associations and customs which still obtain among a people who only 34 years ago were for the first time subjected to our authority and whose amalgamation with the Maritime Provinces never appears to have made much progress."

De Silva draws on Torrington's reflection on the events after the fact in the report of the Committee of the Executive Council on

142   *Pluriversal sovereignty and the state*

the Fixed Establishments of Ceylon in 1852. In his observations on nationalism, Torrington importantly reflects on the relatively brief duration (thirty-four years) of British presence in Kandy and their efforts to transform the Kandyan region into a subordinate political administrative region under Colombo's central authority. The important aspect of historical analysis I would like to emphasize is not de Silva's analysis of the colonial government but, rather, the alignment of his analysis with the epistemic perspective of the documents he read. Consider his analysis of why the rebellion emerged in the introduction to his important edited collection of letters between Governor Torrington and the Secretary of State for the Colonies in London, Earl Grey:

> To men in this "pre-political" state of existence, the ruler symbolizes and represents the people and their way of life. The ruler and the system of government which he represents may be evil, corrupt and unjust, but in so far as the society over which he presides is stable and the tradition he represents the norm of life. This norm may not be a very happy one for the common people but because it was the traditional society they would accept its manifold defects as part of man's fate, the more readily when a new form of society had arisen which brought unfamiliar distractions but no compensating advantages evident to themselves. The pretender and his associates provided the people of the Kandyan region with an opportunity to return to the rule of their own "kings," to their norm of life, to the traditional society, and to a world where there were no planters, no migrant Indian labourers and no new revolutionary taxes. The Kandyans could understand monarchy and authoritarian rule but they could make little sense out of the cold and impersonal British administration.
>
> (K. M. de Silva, 1965: 23)

In contextualizing the events of the 1848 failed rebellion, de Silva denies political agency to the individuals participating in the uprising, and he does so in ways that serve to reinforce the normative narrative, of lack and people not being ready for history, that is contained within the colonial archives. Kandyans are seen as both "pre-political" and outside history; unqualified placeholders caught in the maelstrom of the inevitable march to modernity that they are unqualified to perceive. The problem speaks to the issue raised by

The coloniality of the archives 143

Dipesh Chakrabarty in his description of how history structurally superimposes "Europe" upon the rest of the world, and this affliction is not at all unique to K. M. de Silva. Describing the events of the Uva Rebellion a generation earlier in 1817–1818, Colvin R. de Silva (1953: 176) noted:

> With the exception of Nuvarakalāviya, Ūva and Vellassa were perhaps the most backward and least known provinces in the Kandyan Kingdom. They were thinly peopled; and the settled inhabitants were hardly less primitive than the aboriginal Väddas of the Bintänna jungle. The land was sparsely cultivated and the people were poor. Even in the days of Sinhalese independence, the central government had exercised little control over these provinces, the only line between it and the Väddas being the scanty annual tribute of honey and wax. Yet these provinces were thoroughly loyal to the old regime. In 1815, although the British met little or no resistance in this quarter, the people deserted their villages and kept sullenly aloof. These provinces were never properly subdued. For several months after the occupation the people evinced "a certain shyness and coldness" and refused to return to their homes from the jungles in which they had sought refuge.

In this description, the backwardness of the people is doubly described on the basis of distance from two elite orders, first the Kandyan galactic *mandala* order, and second the British administrative order. The history "as it was" perhaps allows for the description of the sparsely cultivated land and poor people, but cannot support the claim of comparative "backwardness" or "primitiveness" of these provinces relative to the Indigenous Väddas, who in this description represent a placeholder for people within the imagined state of nature. There is a presumption in de Silva's description that the distance from civilization – Kandyan or British – and the autonomy enjoyed by the people of Ūva and Vellassa represent a lack of development, but as James C. Scott (2009) has shown, there is considerable precedent for peasants going to great lengths to live away from the reach of a centralizing political authority. The area of upland South-East Asia that Scott writes about is quite distinct from Ceylon, but in light of Scott's body of work on the state and ordinary people at the boundaries of the state, it should not be controversial to say that minimal engagement with the sovereign

144 *Pluriversal sovereignty and the state*

order via tribute at the boundary of Kandyan authority need not be considered to represent a *lack* of political sophistication if one rejects the idea that there is only a linear, universal development of political practice (J. C. Scott, 2009; 1998). In any case, as has been brought to light by more recent work on the period 1815–1850, Väddas actively participated in some very important anti-British organizing– from 1818 to 1848 (J. Wilson, 2017; Jayawardena, 2010). Representation of indigeneity as lacking in development or sophistication is much more a global problem than a regional one alone. Difference, or organizing society in accordance with onto-logical starting assumptions that are distinct from the imagined universality of European thought about reality, is still confused with "primitiveness" and "lack" in these cases. More than just a question of degrees of specificity or choice of wording alone, this example highlights the normative and ontological assumptions about the movement of history and the hierarchies of societies; these are important points of continuity between the values of the colonial archive and the values of post-colonial historians trained in scientific history whose accounts have become seminal to the study of the island.

K. M. de Silva (1965: 23) continues to rationalize the 1848 Rebellion as backward-looking:

> Their aim was a return to the old Kandyan system with its traditional values, which – somewhat naively perhaps – they aspired to cherish by making one of their number king. Theirs was a blind protest against the changes and uncertainties brought by British rule, and they yearned for the old society, the only one they knew and under-stood. They had the support of a substantial section of the population and some at least of the *bhikkhus*, though the aristocracy stood aloof from their movement.

In this interpretation, the people were incapable of imagining a future or enacting meaningful politics, even though the failed actions did provoke the revocation of the governor and legislative changes. G. C. Mendis's account is roughly in line with those of both Colvin R. de Silva and K. M de Silva. Linking the disturbances (as they were called in the government records) to the institutional changes catalysed by the legal and institutional reforms of the 1833

The coloniality of the archives   145

Colebrooke–Cameron review, Mendis (2005: 87) discusses a crowd of some four thousand people petitioning against tax reforms on July 6, 1848:

> Led by two low-country Sinhalese who were professional robbers, mobs sacked public buildings and shops at Kandy, Matale and Kurunagala, as well as some planters' bungalows. These riots can hardly be called a rebellion, but Government which was ignorant of the real conditions of the country misjudged the situation and took severe measures to put them down.

The recurring issue in these histories is perhaps a blend of reliance on the tone of the colonial archives to describe the impossibility of material success, and the latent elitism of the statements. My point here is not to depreciate the foundational work of postcolonial historians, but to highlight how the essential assumptions written into archival accounts texture the reading of the past and reinforce a sense of gradual development that is complacent about normalizing these harmful assumptions about colonized people (Parasram, 2020). For both Colvin R and K. M de Silva, ordinary people are not truly qualified to partake in the elite practice of politics, an idea akin to Rancière's (2001) critique of Western philosophy that argues that the *demos* is unqualified to participate in politics and that there is a proper way to lead or to wage insurrection, or to represent oneself, one that villagers have no experience of. This is precisely the kind of thinking that Rancière challenges by removing politics from the realm of elite debate and positioning it instead in the *partage du sensible*. As Davide Panagia (2010: 98) explains, "the inequality of a *partage du sensible* that establishes a hierarchy between those who know and those who do not know, between those whose speech makes good sounds and those whose utterances are mere noise, holds the potential of its own dissolution." The lay leaders of the Matale Rebellion may have been unqualified to speak in elite circles, yet elite-level conspiracies between Uva and Matale ultimately did not succeed in driving the British from Ceylon either. Moreover, as Jayawardena (2010) and Bandarage (1983) have shown, the Matale Rebellion's initial catalyst was a more general reaction to the rapid economic and social transformations induced by plantation capitalism, and consequently it had broader appeal

146   *Pluriversal sovereignty and the state*

across the island than the previous ones that were more politically grounded in Kandy.

Within their accounts of the Matale Rebellion, Colvin R de Silva and K. M de Silva see a correct way to raise a rebellion and often harken back to the elite-driven attempts during the Uva Rebellion. The inability to convince the *sangha* and the elites in the subsequent rebellions is often highlighted as a major cause of their failure to overthrow the British. Perhaps this is true, but politics, in a radical sense, must be much more than simply the criterion for success; it is the *process* that makes something political, not the outcome. The fact that rebellions throughout the period 1818–1848 failed is not evidence of their failure to enact politics: if it were, then history must indeed be little more than a narrative of victors. Thucydides' oft-cited analysis from the Melian Dialogue, "Right, as the world goes, is only in question between equals in power, while the strong do what they can and the weak suffer what they must" (Thucydides, 2014), is turned on its head by Rancière's understanding of politics as everyday acts of resistance. It is precisely the weak's refusal to "do what they must" that makes something political, by disrupting the normal order of things and forcing a renegotiation. When considering the writings and observations of the colonial archives, one sees clearly that events like these failed rebellions actually had a significant impact on the everyday processes of governance, or what we might more generally describe as the becoming-colonial police order.

The Uva Rebellion

In this section, I look for the enactment of "politics" in places that have not been heard, highlighting the importance of the everyday struggle against colonialism rather than the military victories of those struggles. I range in my illustrations between about 1818 and 1848 to draw attention to the subtler ways in which the actions of the people allegedly "outside" the limit of historical and political consciousness enacted a radical form of politics throughout this important thirty-year period.

The rebellion in Uva of 1817–1818 was fundamentally linked to the fallout from the 1815 Kandyan Convention itself. The details

The coloniality of the archives   147

of the rebellion are well documented in the secondary literature; in summary, however, it is relevant to point to the fact that the British nearly gave up and retreated from the Kandyan territories, as they had done during previous military conflicts in the interior. In order to turn the corner in the military conflict, the British resorted to brutal scorched-earth military strategies, burning villages and destroying agricultural lands and irrigation systems in order to break the will to rebel (Colvin R. de Silva, 1953: 23). The arrival of native reinforcements from India and Molligoda's loyalty to the British kept a line of intelligence and communication open between Kandy and Colombo, so the British remained in the fight (Colvin R. de Silva, 1953; Chandra R. de Silva, 1987: 148). Historical precedent was very much on the Kandyan side in this rebellion, as both the British forces and the Kandyan aristocracy were aware that the ease with which the British had sacked Kandy in 1815 had resulted from a diplomatic arrangement brokered between Ahelepola and D'Oyly – then the chief translator attached to the British government of the maritime provinces. The complicity of the Kandyan aristocracy, as discussed earlier, can be explained by the internal power struggles within the Kandyan galactic system which arguably began with the coronation of Kandy's last king, Vikrama Rajasinha, in 1798. Elite aristocratic attempts to remove the king were not always supported by the masses, and as the king concentrated material power under his control, the principle of galactic sovereignty that balanced power and responsibility between material and cosmological realms was falling out of balance. It was in this context of power concentration that Ahelepola attempted to seize the opportunity to leverage British power to stage a (relatively) bloodless coup, though the aristocracy did not plan for a permanent British presence in Kandy. The preceding military conflicts between Kandy and the British had all ultimately led to the British retreating to the maritime provinces. Following the capture of the "pretender" to the throne in 1818, the British ordered a revision to the Kandyan Convention through the proclamation of November 21, which sought to punish the areas of Kandy that rose in rebellion and reward those that did not.

The proclamation of November 21, 1818 has a triumphant and patronizing tone, chiding those who rebelled for "forgetting" the vast resources of the empire (clause 4) on the one hand, but also

148   *Pluriversal sovereignty and the state*

noting that the rebel king brought forth by Keppitipola was found eventually to not hail from the Nayaka Malabar dynasty, but instead from more humble Sinhala ancestry. This is an important statement because it speaks to the fact that the galactic sovereign order required the king to be of the right lineage in order to occupy the role at the centre of Kandy; otherwise Keppitipola or any of the other rebels would not have needed to hide the identity of the rebel king. In the original 1815 Kandyan Convention (clause 3), all male relations of the Malabar (Tamil) king were deemed "enemies to the government of the Kandyan provinces," and the Malabar claim to the throne of Kandy was deemed to be formally abolished. Clearly this clause did not truly extinguish the social and symbolic importance of the most recent dynasty. Importantly, it altered the wording of the fifth clause of the Convention, which favoured Buddhism, to more broadly offer protection to all religions in the area, opening the door for robust debates among civil servants and missionaries about the relationship between the colonial state and "heathen" religions (Hardy, 1841; Almond, 1988). The major thrust of the November 21 proclamation was to punish the chiefs who rose against the British and reward those who did not by exempting them from paying taxes.

The issue of rugged roads was central to British frustration during the Uva Rebellion. According to the *Ceylon Gazette* of February 28, 1818, it would take British troops nearly nine hours to march as little as eight miles in some parts of the interior, leaving them vulnerable to raids (*Ceylon Gazette*, February 28, 1818). Effort is exerted in this newspaper article to reassure the British public and perhaps the British troops themselves that history would not repeat itself:

> Such is the present state of affairs in the Interior; that it does not bear out any expectation of a speedy end to the insurrection is undeniable, but while the health of the Troops continues to be good and the most powerful efforts of the Rebels occasion no greater loss in casualties than as yet have been sustained, we see no cause for despair of the ultimate success of the British arms against the undisciplined rabble opposed to them; we know that those who predict the most direful results in the present struggle refer to the melancholy Catastrophy [sic] in 1803 as authority for their dismal speculations; but they

The coloniality of the archives 149

surely must omit to advert to the very different state of our Hospital
Returns at that unfortunate Period.

The "catastrophe" in question was the 1803 attempt of the British
to militarily defeat the Kandyans, which ultimately led to the
massacring of an entire regiment and the execution of soldiers
in their hospital beds by the Kandyan forces. The spectre of this
particular defeat haunts accounts within the exchanges between
Colombo and the Colonial Office in London throughout the early
to mid nineteenth century, and is manifested in public discourse in
newspapers as well. It is interesting to observe that in most cases
where "natives" defeated British forces, there appears to have been
a requirement to portray the enemy forces as exotic or especially
barbaric.[2]

As discussed earlier, the British were able to win legal control
over the entire island because of the diplomatic and symbolic
authority wielded by Ahelepola, the condemned *Maha Adikar*
of Sri Vikrama Rajasinha. Ahelepola was a controversial figure
during the Uva Rebellion, often appearing as though he were
playing on both sides. In his own account of what happened
during the beginning of the rebellion, he highlighted that he tried,
on more than one occasion, to alert the British and to dissuade his
countrymen from taking up arms against the government. Symbols
were important in the raising of this rebellion, and part of the
reason why the British were suspicious of Ahelepola was the fact
that his relative Keppitipola was the British-appointed *dessave* of
Uva province after the Kandyan Convention of 1815. After the
Convention, important symbols of sovereignty had "gone missing"
and Governor Brownrigg was looking for them. Keppitipola was
found to be in possession of the royal regalia of the recently ousted
king. When the rebellion began to really heat up, Keppitipola, who
was a signatory to the 1815 Kandyan Convention, was sent by the
government to take concrete steps to crush it. He and five hundred
men went looking for the rebels, and upon finding them, joined
them instead of bringing them to the British. He then returned the
guns he was armed with to the British, reportedly saying that he
did not want to defeat them with their own weapons.[3] According
to Ahelepola, Keppitipola did so using Ahelepola's name so as to

150 *Pluriversal sovereignty and the state*

inspire other Kandyans to rise up as well ("The Case of Eyhelapola Maha Nilime," 1828).

The *Ceylon Gazette* reported on the May 16, 1818 interrogation of Kohnhumbra Ratteralle, a rebel chief captured by Malay troops on behalf of the British. Although the account was clearly translated and probably edited for print, it offers a rare glimpse into the political thinking of a local leader who was engaged in political insurrection at the time. When asked where he was going on the night of his apprehension, Ratteralle answers, "We had received instructions from the Pretender to take the Camps in the neighbourhood and in the event of our success, we were promised great promotion" (*Ceylon Gazette*, May 16, 1818). He confesses that he was the first chief in the area of Welasse to join the rebellion, and when asked why he took up arms against the Government and how long he intended to fight, he answers: "I don't know that any particular period has been contemplated. We intended continuing the struggle to the end of our lives, because we could not expect pardon if we submitted" (*Ceylon Gazette*, May 16, 1818). Ratteralle prefaces some of his comments with "although I am to be put to death" and offers very matter-of-fact answers that betray an allegiance to the older sovereign order. Though it is not clear if Ratteralle would have used the word "pretender" to refer to the leader of the rebellion who was crowned King of Kandy in a dramatic performance of sovereignty that was given legitimacy by symbols including the *dalada* relic, his answers seem to suggest that there was little reason to question the sovereign authority of the newly crowned Kandyan king. At the same time, the deprivations and brutality of the British military tactics that were used to starve the Kandyan population and render it ill by disease would have been acutely felt by May 1818, when Ratteralle would have been questioned.

Symbols of authority were central to the colonial forces as well. While the governor, Robert Brownrigg, was based in the interior during the rebellion, Lady Brownrigg was playing an important diplomatic and symbolic role in Colombo. In the dispatches and newspaper accounts that followed the Uva Rebellion of 1817–1818, a major recurring and underappreciated fact is that the majority of important victories and apprehensions came from the *non*-British troops, either Indian reinforcements, Malay mercenaries, or local

The coloniality of the archives 151

forces from the south. In somewhat rare recognition of this fact, Lady Brownrigg presented official colours to the "Native Militia" in August of 1818. Her speech was simultaneously translated into Sinhalese:

> In presenting this Standard to the Militia of Ceylon, I have great pleasure in expressing how much gratified I have been by the favourage [sic] reports of your attention to the necessary exercise to enable you [to] take the field with effect. Every well disposed man, who wishes for the happiness of his Country and the safety of his family must feel anxious to rally round this Standard, and while their Governor is devoting every moment and thought of his life to put down the Rebellion, and unite this Island under one Government, the Caste of fighting men will all step forward and show the utmost diligence and zeal to support his measures and obtain the grand object of his unceasing endeavours, that of restoring peace and prosperity to Ceylon.
>
> (Brownrigg, 1818)

In Lady Brownrigg's speech we see a performative contestation of sovereignties at play during the Uva Rebellion. Within the interior, still inaccessible and unknowable to the British, who relied heavily on non-European forces to traverse the boundaries, Kandyans were contesting the sovereign claim of the British, using important spiritual symbols that represented Kandyan sovereignty. These included the royal regalia mentioned above, but also the *dalada* relic, which had been stolen back from the British by the rebels. In Colombo, natives who were much further removed from the activities in the Kandyan centre were being encouraged to rally around the British flag to restore "peace and prosperity" while, at the same time, being led to practise scorched-earth military strategy against Kandyan forces who were mostly armed with spears, swords, and bows and arrows. As the rebellion unfolded, with the two sides operating under conflicting ontologies of sovereignty, ordinary people were the ones who suffered the consequences of the ensuing violence. Estimates of the deaths vary, but in general the figures identify about 1,000 deaths on the British side, most of them due to disease rather than direct fighting, and more than 10,000 deaths suffered by the Kandyans, many of them induced by the deprivations associated with the military strategies deployed by the British forces.

152   *Pluriversal sovereignty and the state*

In the aftermath of the Uva Rebellion, Governor Brownrigg sought to ensure control of the Kandyan interior by establishing strategic military fortresses throughout the passages leading to Kandy from different parts of the island. This strategy proved inefficient, as it relied on British troops being stationed within the jungle, where they often fell victim to malaria and fever. Sir Edward Barnes assumed the governorship in 1820 and sought to change the approach to controlling the interior by moving away from periodic fortifications to, instead, altering the transportation infrastructure in such a way that additional access points on more easily traversable roads could guarantee the rapid arrival of military forces from other parts of the island and empire (Colvin R. de Silva, 1953: 25–27).

Although Uva and Matale were the larger uprisings and the subject of the most historical writing within this period, there were important "disturbances" that were quietly noted in the colonial records as well. Table 5.1, created from government records printed in 1849, summarizes these events. Between 1815 and 1848, at least half a dozen organized efforts to drive the British out were recorded.

As described by the former Colonial Secretary James E. Tennent (1850: 162–163),

> We obtained possession of the Kandyan provinces, which completed our tenure of the whole island, in the year 1815. That is 35 years ago, and within that period there have been six treasonable movements of considerable importance against the Government. There has been on the average one such movement in every six years. There was open rebellion in 1817, in 1823, and in 1848. There were three conspiracies detected before their explosion, in 1820, 1834, and 1843, and those are independent of the treasonable plots which were detected and arrests which took place in 1816, 1819, 1820, 1824, 1830, and 1842.

Priests were actively involved in the insurrections throughout this period. As James Wilson (2017) argues, religious ceremonies and symbols connected to Kandyan sovereignty (both Buddhist and Hindu in nature) were critical components in rebellious activities between 1817 and 1848. According to a government report tabled by Tennent at his testimony, the 1817–1818, 1823, 1834, 1842,

Table 5.1 British uprisings 1818–1848 as recorded in government memorandum of February 1849

Year	1818	1823	1824	1834	1843	1848
Duration of rebellion	Beginning of Sept. 1817 to 2nd Nov. 1818[1]	The rising in this year was put down by the local authorities in about a week	The attempt was made in August, and the prisoners were tried in Nov.	The rebellion did not take place, the conspirators being arrested before the completion of their plan	In this case also no rising appears to have taken place	29th July to 10th Oct. was the duration of martial law, but the rebellion was really over in a week or ten days from its commencement – viz., by the end of the first week of August
Number of troops employed	The greatest number of troops in the Kandyan provinces at any time was 6,130	–	The prisoners were taken by a small detachment	–	–	The number of troops in the interior provinces on 14th Aug. was 1,527
Troops killed	According to the Returns and including those who died of their wounds, 94	–	–	–	–	None killed and one wounded according to the official returns, but the newspapers mentioned two killed.[2]
Troops died in Hospital	According to the returns which are not very regular, 428	–	–	–	–	Troops were healthy in general
Punishment of Rebels – Executed	28	2	5	The prisoners were acquitted		18 Court-Martial,

Table 5.1 (continued)

Year	1818	1823	1824	1834	1843	1848
Punishment of Rebels – Banished or transported	25	13	8	The prisoners were acquitted	The man who endeavoured to excite the insurrection was sentenced to imprisonment for fourteen years with hard labour	17 Supreme Court and 28 Court Martial, 45 Total.
Otherwise punished, (imprisonment, lash, etc.)	8	14	–	Prisoners acquitted	–	66 Court Martial
Expense	£177,675 10s.[3]	No expense incurred apparently on these intermediate occasions	No expense incurred apparently on these intermediate occasions	No expense incurred apparently on these intermediate occasions	No expense incurred apparently on these intermediate occasions	Probably under £50,000; this is conjectural however, the whole to be paid by the colony.

1 Martial law was continued in some of the provinces till 3rd Jan. 1821, but the insurrection was virtually ended by the capture of the principal chiefs concerned in it and of the holy relic, on November 2, 1818.

2 Major Forbes states in his "Eleven Years in Ceylon," that the total loss on our side was estimated at 1000 and that of the natives at 10,000.

3 This is the sum at which the Governor, Sir R. Brownrigg, estimated the expense.

Source: "Confidential: Ceylon," 1849. All text (including footnotes) is quoted from this source.

The coloniality of the archives 155

and 1843 resistance attempts were heavily influenced, or even directed, by Buddhist priests. During the Uva Rebellion, the priest Ihagamma was tried by court martial and sentenced to death, but ultimately this sentence was changed to political exile in Mauritius for life. During the 1823 uprising, Kahawatte Unase, a priest from Matale, was tried in criminal court at Kandy and sentenced to death for his role in organizing the uprising. He was hanged on August 5, 1828. In the 1834 conspiracy, three priests, Dembewe Unanse, Tibboteewew Unanse, and Kettacuinburi Unanse, were tried for their role in the conspiracy by the Supreme Court but ultimately acquitted. In the attempts of 1842 and 1843, Chandroyottey Selewananse Saranankere, also a priest, was tried for treason and sentenced to death by the Supreme Court, a sentence ultimately downgraded to prison with hard labour for fourteen years (Tennent, 1850: 162–163).

Though the statistics above describe the disturbance of 1824 as very minor – as indeed it was in terms of the resources expended to quell it – what is worth bringing to light is the particularly dramatic way in which it unfolded. The leader of the attempt, was named as "Mootoo, alias Juan Pulle, alias Kanewada Pulle," claimed to be the rightful heir (in the line of the ousted Sri Vikrama Rajasinha) to the throne of Kandy. According to the available records, Mootoo decried the British government as illegitimate in a rousing speech from a large rock near a village in the Seven Korales. In the discussion that ensued, villagers argued that past rebellions had led only to the loss of land and life. Mootoo attempted to persuade the people that on the basis of his legitimate link to the throne through his South Indian and Kandyan lineage, his relatives were waiting to rise up against the government in different parts of the country following the outbreak of rebellion. Moreover, he argued that the British, too, were in a weakened state at the moment, as they were fighting in Siam. Eleven men followed Mootoo, and they were invited at a later date to receive gifts and endorsements at a nearby village. Fearing treachery, they made their would-be hosts swear upon their swords their loyalty to Mootoo as King of Kandy, and cautiously agreed to go to the village in order to rally more support. Upon arriving, they were invited into a house, which they did not initially enter, but after much persuading and reassurance, Mootoo and three others entered.

156   *Pluriversal sovereignty and the state*

At that point, the door was sealed shut, and a sword and spear fight ensued as they fought their way out of the trap, ultimately surrendering upon the arrival of British troops armed with guns. At the trial, there was a feeble attempt to claim that there was no intention to rebel, but the public spectacle of the whole process undermined the claim. British statistics state that five men were executed and eight were exiled, though they do not name them ("Notes on the Trial of 12 Prisoners," 1824; "Confidential: Ceylon," 1849).

The source of enacting politics in this scenario rested not in Mootoo or the British, but in the villagers who intervened in the prevailing convention of elite-led armed insurrection to put a stop to the rebellion before it began. We catch a glimpse of this in the above-mentioned interrogation of Kohnhumbra Ratteralle, who, although committed to fighting unto death in principle, was willing to engage in a negotiated agreement that would secure the relative safety of his family from war-induced deprivation. By the time of Mootoo's attempt to raise a rebellion in 1823, there had already been nearly constant minor uprisings throughout the territory. Although the government records of 1849 (Table 5.1) note a smaller uprising in 1823 as the only one between 1818 and 1824, the *Ceylon Gazette* of July 29, 1820 (*Ceylon Gazette*, 1820) also reported that there was an ongoing insurrection in Kandy, and that rewards were offered by the governor for information leading to arrests of people disrupting the lines of communication between Kandy and Trincomalee. The emphasis on disrupting lines of communication is important, as the preservation of lines of communication afforded by Molligoda's loyalty to the British throughout the Uva campaign was what made possible the coordination of troops and the eventual arrival of troops from British India. To target lines of communication at the same time as Governor Barnes was co-opting the traditional practice of *rajakariya*, forcing survivors of the rebellion to labour to construct new roads connecting Kandy to Colombo, was a radical political act.

The age of insurrections: 1830s–1840s

There were a number of attempted insurrections in the 1830s as well. According to Colonel Jonathan Forbes, there was an attempt

The coloniality of the archives 157

by an "imposter prince" to "frighten" villagers in 1831; however, the imposter was arrested and was "on his way to the gaols within 24 hours" before anything further could unfold (Forbes, 1850: 17). In 1834 a "very extensive conspiracy" sought to assassinate local government agents and to poison British officers and the governor at a feast ("Appendix No. 5 to Memorandum on Colonial Policy," 1849). Among the conspirators was Molligoda, the brother of the former *adikar* who had remained loyal to the British during the Uva Rebellion (Jayawardena, 2010). On August 6, 1834, the government raided the group ahead of its scheduled plan to disperse across the region and prepare provinces for rebellion. In the process, twenty-seven men were captured. According to government records,

> The motives for this intended rebellion were apparently the same as those which led to all the former ones, viz., a desire on the part of the chiefs and priests to regain the power and influence which they had lost under the British rule; and the manner in which they designed to gain their object, fully proves at the time the justice of Sir R. Brownrigg's remarks respecting the excessive treachery and ingratitude of the higher orders of Kandians, and their extreme ignorance. Their intention was, after the massacre of the English officers, to offer the island either to the French or the King of Siam on condition of their assistance against us, but these new allies were also to be disposed of on the first opportunity.
>
> ("Appendix No. 5 to Memorandum on
> Colonial Policy," 1849)

Interestingly, and no doubt related to the very recent overhaul of the legal system intended to create a single universal judiciary under the Colebrooke–Cameron reforms, when Molligoda and five others were brought to trial on January 12, 1835, the jury was comprised of seven natives from the maritime provinces. According to the government, "though there was no moral doubt of the truth of the facts alleged against them, they were acquitted, and the vote of the seven Kandyans was 'Not guilty'" ("Appendix No. 5 to Memorandum on Colonial Policy," 1849). The government records describe the native jurors as "Kandyans" but from the "Maritime Provinces," probably reflecting the new political geography established in the Colbrooke–Cameron reforms, which were aimed at breaking up

158 *Pluriversal sovereignty and the state*

Kandy administratively. The accused were acquitted by a jury that included natives, which had benefits for the perception of legitimacy during the increasingly liberal turn of the colonial project. As described in the document, "the effect produced upon the natives by the submission of the English Government to the laws which they had themselves made was perhaps better than could have been occasioned by the execution of these men" ("Appendix No. 5 to Memorandum on Colonial Policy," 1849).

News of the crushing British defeat at the hands of the Afghans during what would later be called the First Anglo-Afghan War of 1839–1842 inspired two small-scale and connected attempted rebellions in Ceylon. These were instigated by a priest named Chandrayotty, who was arrested for sedition in 1842, but he was ultimately acquitted because of a lack of evidence (Tennent, 1850). According to James E. Tennent, reports from Badulla asserted that Chandrayotty was "Stirring up the people to sedition" but the central government in Colombo ignored the warnings, a recurring theme since 1815. Major Kelson, the assistant government agent at Badulla, was determined that he was correct in his suspicions, and eventually Governor Campbell sent Major Rogers to investigate the claim. Within a few days, over a hundred people were arrested for high treason. Chandrayotty made a "voluntary" confession leading to his conviction and the acquittal of the other thirteen men put on trial by the British. One of the thirteen men acquitted was known as "Dennis" to the British, but went by the names Alludenia Banada, Gongelegoda Banda, and Kapurobastelagey Dennis Appohamy. It is interesting to note that "Dennis" would go on to play a leading role in the 1848 Matale Rebellion, and it was his younger brother "David," a.k.a. Gongalagode Tikery Banda, a.k.a Kapurubastebanddalagey David Vederalle, who was crowned King of Kandy during the 1848 Matale Rebellion.

According to "wanted" posters that circulated in 1848 in the attempt to capture the two brothers (offering £150 for "David" and £100 for "Dennis"), David was actually employed by the police under the command of a Mr Dalziel during the 1842 attempted rebellion ("The Rebellion," 1848). This meant that his own brother, "Dennis," might well have been one of the men whom

The coloniality of the archives 159

David would have been pursuing in his capacity as a native colonial police officer. Another man named Poorangappoo was among those tried and acquitted in 1842 according to Forbes, and he would later become the sword-bearer for King David during the Matale Rebellion in 1848 (Forbes, 1850: 18). According to Tennent, one of the main charges brought against the conspirators in 1833 was that they had attempted to convince natives employed in the service of the colonial governments to engage in seditious activity and ultimately join in rebellion. The "wanted" posters from 1848 for David and Dennis, issued by the Acting Assistant Colonial Secretary W. Morris, indicate that the men were both between thirty-five and forty years of age, which meant they would have been young children around the time of Kandyan Convention and would have grown up during the military road construction and rise of coffee plantations; an enormously transformative period on the island, though one I do not document in this book.

What can be gleaned from the events during the 1830s and 1840s, small and aborted as they were, is that there was a simmering anti-colonial politics that took strategic form in light of the geographical and technological transformations rapidly unfolding in the interior. The construction of new military-cum-plantation roads in the 1820s was contested by small-scale insurrections, but the completion and maintenance of the roads mitigated the territorial advantage enjoyed by the Kandyans over the British, as well as their Dutch and Portuguese predecessors. Resistance was transformed from attempts at open rebellion into smaller conspiracies during the 1830s- and 1840s. Priests were often at the centre in one way or another, either through crowning kings in sovereign ceremonies or through organizing conspiracies of their own. The transformations within the Kandyan region in the 1830s and 1840s were especially centred on the rapid rise of the coffee plantations. According to Tennent (1850: 167):

> Within the last 10 years [1840–1850] the Kandyan provinces may be said to have been the only portion of the island in which an attempt has been made to convert an Indian [sic] settlement into an English colony, and the scene of those very disasters is now the scene of the planting operations, and the locality of coffee estates throughout the district.

160   *Pluriversal sovereignty and the state*

That a former colonial police officer became the "pretender" of the larger-scale rebellion of 1848 implies either some sort of radical politicizing during the 1840s or a longer-term strategy, both of which speak to radical enactment of anti-colonial politics. During the 1848 Matale Rebellion, villagers focused their attacks on the plantations themselves, even though according to the secondary literature and much of the colonial discourse at the time, the problems were supposed to be related to the Guns, Roads, and Dog Ordinances ("A Few Remarks," 1850).

I am not suggesting that these unfair liberal-colonial legal reforms which imposed flat taxes on villagers and British residents alike were not a source of great irritation, only that the taxes were not the only issues at play. Forty million pounds of coffee were moved along roads built by forced labourers, and because of pressure from the planters, the fledgling state waived the duties and taxes they might have acquired from this commerce, enriching the planters at the expense of villagers. The contentious liberal taxes introduced by the government essentially shifted the burden of paying for public goods from European planters, who had formerly paid a modest tariff, onto the native population in order to make up the deficiencies in the national budget. As Forbes (1850: 12) describes this policy,

> Every male, from age eighteen to fifty-five years of age, is now, by the road ordinance, to work six days or pay three shillings; therefor, if I take the population at a million and a half, and that of the Europeans, not exempted, at half a thousand, we shall at once see that it was removing a moderate indirect taxation from the European capitalist, to inflict large direct taxation on the native.

The unfairness of the taxes became the historical counterpoint to the government's understanding of the circumstances as being exacerbated by "rascally" troublemakers, but both explanations miss the essential politics associated with the simmering trend of anti-colonial resistance that textured the period between 1818 and 1848. Ordinary people were "criminals" and local elites were "backward-looking" in the discourse. According to colonial records, which were also the basis for the secondary histories of the 1848 Matale Rebellion, many of the key players in the rebellion were "criminals" or "thieves," but

The coloniality of the archives　　161

having been a criminal, a thief, or even a murderer hardly disqualifies one from engaging in direct and significant anti-colonial politics. It is true that, among the leadership during the Matale Rebellion, the brothers Dennis and David came from a low-caste background and from the low country and thus had a different, non-Kandyan ancestry, but this is a problem only if one accepts the rationale that Kandyans wanted only to be backward-looking and sought to re-establish the ousted dynasty. Such a starting assumption removes from politics and from history the long tradition of Kandyan sovereign practice and implies that it could not *continue* to exist and evolve alongside British efforts to uniform governance. The final four kings of Kandy were Nayaka Tamils with roots in areas including southern India, as explained earlier, and the very fact that the Sinhalese aristocracy was plotting against the young and allegedly brutal Vikrama Rajasingha implies a sovereign and political regime that was open to change and very much engaged in political practice. The image of a static backward-facing Kandyan political order within the secondary and colonial literature makes no sense when weighed against the pluriversal and cosmopolitan politics that had been unfolding since long before British entry into the region. The violence of universal thinking is enacted through historical remembering; Kandyans are pushed outside of or prior to history and politics. It was certainly the view from the archives, but it persists in the writing of some influential post-colonial histories as well.

By the 1840s, notwithstanding fluctuations in international demand, coffee plantations had become the economic engine of colonial Ceylon, and targeting them was a deliberate political act. Governor Torrington responded to the Matale Rebellion with a very heavy hand, enlisting everyone he could as peace officers, executing prisoners by court martial, and calling for reinforcements from Madras in an effort to prevent an insurrection similar to Uva thirty years before. His methods were hotly controversial in the press at the time, with former colonial officials like J. Forbes decrying publicly the heavy hand dealt to the Kandyans. The planter population and British public resident in Ceylon, however, largely favoured such actions. As one self-described "Colonist" articulated in his condemnation of Forbes's published pamphlet on the subject in a letter to the British Prime Minister,

162   *Pluriversal sovereignty and the state*

> We hear not one word of the bullets or cries of the rebels, which if not fatal or murderous, were only harmless before the courageous daring of our troops. We hear not one word of the Prisoner the rebels succeeded in capturing – an Englishman, and who was cut down by our troops from a stake where the firewood was heaped around him ready for an Auto-da-fe!
>
> ("A Few Remarks," 1850)

A similar sentiment was espoused in the *Morning Star* newspaper by a self-described "Jaffna man living in Kandy," who wrote:[4] "It is said that one or more estates were set on fire by the Rebels, and plundered, that a European planter was unmercifully beaten and wounded and that his wife was carried away by some of these rude fellows" ("Letter to the Editor of the *Morning Star*," 1848). Both of the above statements highlight the political nature of parts of the rebellion, regardless of whether or not there was a strong centralized or elite aspect to the project. The politics of simmering insurgency through this time period affected public perception of the challenges facing the colony, and the self-described "Colonist" quoted above, writing to Prime Minister Peel, goes on to make an important point that speaks to the public feeling and anxieties at the time of the 1848 rebellion:

> That the Pretender was of lowly origin goes for very little; suffice it that he was *crowned King of Kandy* by certain Priests with great Buddhistical ceremony, at their Chief Temple and this was all that the people cared to know. Were not Perkin Warbeck and Lambert Simnel equally dangerous to the English monarch though both of obscure birth? But the intimidation of the innocent alluded to by the Colonel [Forbes], must have been very extensive – extraordinarily so, for a few low country adventurers to exercise, when we are told by respectable Planters that during the nights of the rebellion many gangs of 200 and 300 Kandians marched through their Estates on the way to the scene of the disturbance, all armed in a variety of modes. Did this look like a mere rabble-riot? Was this the intimidation of a few low-country thieves? At any rate in the East where the European power is so much feared, any acts of this kind can bear but one construction.
>
> ("A Few Remarks," 1850)

Planters themselves spoke to the great anxiety about and fear of the natives from the point of view of the European population.

The coloniality of the archives

The "Colonist" highlights the attention to Buddhist ceremony in the coronation and speaks to the lived anxiety of seeing hundreds of armed rebels in the plantation estates. According to one self-identified planter writing on the subject of the debate in London unfolding about the 1848 Matale Rebellion:

> it must be borne in mind that the Coffee Planter of Ceylon was just at that time in a most critical, I may even say a dangerous position. I am not theorizing – I am not *supposing* cases, but I tell you what I *know* to be the real truth, that at the time I am speaking of, the Planting interest of this island was quivering in the balance. We were in truth getting desperate. Protection had made us pay dearly for our land and our labour: our prices had all but broken our hearts. Many an estate was just kept on in the desperate hope that something might turn up in our favour. But had we lost our crops as might have been the case, at that juncture, in our position it would have been absolute ruination. Three fourths of the Plantations in the island must have been abandoned, and how bitter would have been our disappointment to have seen the home markets for our produce rise, as it has recently done and we unable to profit by the golden opportunity.
>
> (A Ceylon Planter, 1850)

The author writes that the coffee fruit was just at maturation, and the timing of the uprising would have also scared away many of the migrant Indian labourers who would have been just arriving for work after their deadly journey through the jungle. In the court martial account from September 14, 1848 discussed above, we see mention by the accused of their willingness to send away the plantation workers with food, suggesting that these "criminals" were nonetheless calculating political actors with a sophisticated understanding of the rhythm of the planting season and the economic sensitivities of the global coffee markets. The difficulties the planters faced by virtue of the diminished global demand for coffee in 1848 were no secret and were well discussed in newspapers and government gazettes. Planters were members of the British public in the interior, and to think that ordinary workers, thieves, or villagers were simply unaware of these developments relies on the ontological assumption of their primitiveness and lack of political sophistication, charges that ought to be dispensed with if one is to understand the rhythms of decolonial activism that textured the

164 *Pluriversal sovereignty and the state*

development of the colonial state. An observation of this nature from a planter is very illuminating, as it brings the intersection of territory, capitalism, and politics to the foreground. If we break with the prevailing scholarly consensus that the ordinary masses would have had no understanding of modern politics and economy, it is possible to conceive that those who rose up were well aware of the sensitive timing of their uprisings. As noted in government records of the failed attempt of 1842, it was knowledge of British exploits and their brutal defeat by the Afghans that inspired the events,[5] which suggests that knowledge of the empire's exploits was not a secret.

Neither should it lead one to deduce that everyone in the Kandyan region was of a single mind with respect to rebellion. During the Matale Rebellion, ordinary people were caught between rebel forces and a government that was especially paranoid and trigger-happy in light of fears that the rebellion could blossom into something as large as, or perhaps larger than, what had transpired in 1817–1818. Part of that fear on the side of the government manifested itself in the trial and execution of "natives" by court martial, a controversial practice during the uprising that drew harsh condemnation of the miscarriage of justice and the brutality with which people were tried and often executed. According to Forbes (1850: 21–22), a former lieutenant-colonel, the use of court martial was excessive, unnecessary, and unlawful:

> I aver in common sense and common justice, that those who are made liable to the penalties of martial law, are also entitled to its privileges: if so, the inhabitants of Ceylon were entitled to be tried by a general court-martial, legally constituted, for crimes clearly and distinctly specified, and according to the common and statue law of England, and cognisable by such a tribunal. The oath which the members of all courts-martial take, leaves, I think no doubt of what the prisoners had a right to expect, and without which, in my opinion, trials for "high treason" were at best but solemn mockery.

The most important point of the Matale Rebellion is not whether the government was or was not justified in the heavy-handed tactics it used to quell the rebellion; rather, it is what, amid the genuine sense of the British population, planters, and bureaucrats, it *felt*

The coloniality of the archives   165

was necessary in light of the rebels' political actions. The enactment of politics, whether planned by elites or more grassroots-based, affected the kinds of policy choices pursued by the government and shaped the development of the state in the process.

While many people did take up arms and raid the plantations, as discussed above, it is important to note that others, according to their testimonies at the court martials, were caught between contending violent situations. In the case of the court martials of Nikolla Punchyrall, Melpitia Appoohame, Alutgamma Banda, and Allawelle Goda Leortin of September 6, 1848, all were found guilty of high treason and were shot to death the following morning. In the translations of their testimonies at their trials, the narrative that emerges is one of villagers seeking to escape both the rebels and the government by leaving their home villages. Upon leaving, they were conscripted into serving the rebel forces in the jungle. Faced with execution for treason by the authority of the rebel king on the one hand, and with execution for "high treason" by the authority of the British government if they were captured, these ordinary people caught in the midst of the conflict utterly lacked any element of choice ("Confidential Despatch: Court Martial," 1849).[6] I would argue that leaving the contestations between the British and the Kandyan expressions of sovereignty in this moment was both a political and a logical course of action, though in the unfortunate case of these young men, execution awaited them at any turn.

Conclusion

In this chapter, I have strived to show first that the logic of coloniality permeates seemingly objective recordings of "facts" in the form of archives. Building on my argument concerning archiving in relief from the Introduction, I have argued that the epistemic violence of representation that positions ordinary Kandyans between 1815 and 1848 scripts them as non-political and mute, but approaching the same historical documents with decolonial investments allows us to reinterpret the political significance of uprising and rebellion beyond the question of whether or not they were successful. Relatedly, influential secondary historical accounts are complicit

166 *Pluriversal sovereignty and the state*

with the representation of a past that takes for granted core modern/colonial assumptions such as native inferiority or the "fatal impact thesis" that sees British victory as inevitable, rather than precarious and contingent on the unpredictable insurrectionary politics within a contentious political space.

Drawing on the method of archiving in relief, I have sought to engage differently with colonial archival records in order to draw attention to elements in the discarded background of the history that demonstrate the political agency of both elite and ordinary people who resisted colonial attempts to contaminate and transform Kandy into Ceylon between 1815 and 1848. In so doing, I seek to challenge the conventional narrative that presents the time between the Uva and Matale rebellions as "quiet." If we take a more radical understanding of politics, we can better apprehend the simmering insurrectionary politics of the early period of British presence in which the logics of Kandyan galactic sovereignty and British imperial sovereignty were in the process of colliding with and transforming one another.

Notes

1 I describe it as indifferent because of course the colonial encounter is present in all histories, but the idea of total territorial rule, the main subject of this book, is generally treated as an assumed constant.
2 In the sources consulted in the preparation of this book, accounts of British military failures in North America, Ceylon, India, and Afghanistan all sought to explain and rationalize the losses by citing the savagery of the native Other and the moral virtue of the British forces.
3 Why Keppitipola returned the guns to the British upon defecting to the rebels is a mystery, though perhaps it was to instil a sense of national, Kandyan pride in the traditional warfare tactics that had protected Kandy through hundreds of years of colonial advances until this point.
4 It is not clear whether the author was British or not. That he identified as a "Jaffna" man might suggest that he was perhaps a Tamil man from Jaffna writing in English, but it is not clear enough to determine from the letter.
5 In the First Anglo-Afghan War, Dr William Brydon was the only survivor of the 16,000-strong British Indian army retreating from Kabul in 1842. The infamous Rudyard Kipling penned a popular poem in the

The coloniality of the archives 167

aftermath: "When you're wounded and left on Afghanistan's plains / An' the women come out to cut up what remains, / Just roll to your rifle, and blow out your brains, / And go to your Gawd like a soldier" (quoted in Freemont-Barnes, 2009: 1).

6 Though I have not engaged with the political-economy aspect of state transformation and the subject of migrant Tamil plantation workers in this book, it is relevant to note that, on occasion, reference is made in the testimonies to Tamil workers and kanganies (higher-caste overseers and recruiters of migrant labourers) who encountered the rebels as well. In the proceedings of a court martial of September 14, 1848, those charged reported that they had heard word that the pretender king had control of the northern region of Ceylon as well as Kandy. They permitted migrant Tamil labourers and kanganies to leave the plantations they were attacking with food. This is an important point, because the general colonial narrative was that the Tamil workers were held in utter contempt by the Kandyan locals and seen as "simpler" people than the devious or lazy Kandyan locals. This narrative is doubly strengthened by the fact that the new taxes that were supposed to have been the motivation for the uprisings in 1848 were in part related to the road tax, in which migrant labourers were excluded from having to pay to upkeep the roads on the basis that they were migrants. See "Confidential Despatch: Court Martial," 1849; "Ordinance No. 8," 1848; Duncan, 2007.

Conclusion: pluriversal sovereignty and research

In 1948, the reins of state power passed formally from the British to the newly independent government of Ceylon. Shortly thereafter, a critical mass of the national elite saw fit to disenfranchise the so-called "Indian-Tamils" or "Estate Tamils" who worked in the coffee and later tea plantations in the interior.[1] In effect, as the people of Ceylon achieved political-institutional freedom at the scale of the state, one of the first applications of state power targeted a long-marginalized population and rendered hundreds of thousands of them stateless. From the late nineteenth century to the early twentieth century, a rising national class of elites became influential in colonial politics. Many who would go on to form parties of government and opposition participated in young national roundtables and associations debating impending constitutional reforms ahead of formal independence. Men like Sir John Kotelewala (the third Prime Minister), S. W. R. D. Bandaranaike (the fourth Prime Minister), G. G. Ponnambalam (leader of the All Ceylon Tamil Congress), and J. R. Jayewardene (President 1978–1989) were at times jovial comrades in the late colonial period, as evidenced by transcripts of roundtable conferences in the 1940s ("The Roundtable Conference," 1944). While it seemed the national elite would keep a tight grip on political power, by 1956 Sinhala-Buddhist nationalism, which had arisen from the grassroots and rural areas, was the force to be reckoned with. The Freedom Party that won that election was led by S. W. R. D. Bandaranaike, but the real power came from its grassroots popular front. Notwithstanding the late colonial solidarities brokered between ethnic groups and across ideologies, postcolonial

Conclusion: pluriversal sovereignty and research 169

anti-Tamil propaganda among politicians vying for political influence over the post-colonial state manifested themselves in a series of pogroms targeting Tamil civilians in 1958, 1965, 1971, and 1978, and most significantly in "Black July" of 1983. On July 23, 1983, a small group of rebels ambushed thirteen Sri Lankan soldiers in Jaffna, and within two days of national media coverage Sinhalese civilians were waging a street-level campaign of terror against Tamil businesses, property, and bodies. In the words of the Minister of Development (cited in Yiftachel and As'ad, 2004: 658) in 1983:

> Sri Lanka is inherently and rightfully a Sinhalese state ... this must be accepted as a fact and not a matter of opinion to be debated. By attempting to challenge this premise, Tamils have brought the wrath of the Sinhalese on their own heads; they have themselves to blame.

Seen as the critical juncture that marked the official beginning of Sri Lanka's civil war, the collective punishment of bodies deemed enemies of or external to an ethno-nationalist state was resisted using a modern, dialectical strategy: the creation of an opposing modern ethno-nationalist state, Tamil Eelam.

The logic of total territorial rule and postcolonial sovereignty had, by the time of independence, become normalized. By the late twentieth century, it had become fetishized, essentialized as the only legitimate marker through which a formerly colonized people could live in peace and freedom. This is not a moral judgement, but rather a description of a global political requirement of modern total territorial rule as a necessity for self-determination. There are non-state expressions of sovereignty that exist today, including sub-national self-determination movements of Indigenous peoples around the world, Palestine, and the Tibetan government in exile, but the gold-standard measure of independence remains the territorial nation state (McConnell, 2009, 2010; Murphy, 1996; Shani, 2008). In the Sri Lankan context, we have not seen the extinguishing of the important pre-colonial norms of *rajamandala* and Buddhification, but rather their contamination and transformation into a modern, colonial, statist exoskeleton tasked with the objective of protecting a nation on modern, universal grounds. The process of Buddhification, as described

170   *Pluriversal sovereignty and the state*

in Obeyesekere's and Tambiah's work, was historically one of integration and inclusion rather than ethnically determined exclusion. Its application in the post-colonial period appears to serve precisely the opposite purpose, and this is historically related to the normalization and de-politicization of the state. To speak of the colonial contamination of the state is to describe the tension between universal sovereignty and pluriversal sovereignty. The colonial encounters did not destroy millennia of sovereign practice; rather, from 1815 to 1848, the ontological dimensions of the struggle for sovereignty were transformed alongside the material realm within which anti-colonial and colonial violence was unfolding.

I have focused on sovereignty in this book, but of course sovereignty is just one piece of a much more complex picture that was manifested through transformations in political economy, the judicial and governmental systems, religious education, and migration patterns in the late nineteenth century. For the generations of children practising "civil" Christianity in the mid to late nineteenth century, who were educated in missionary schools and challenged missionaries and government officials in public debates, writing, and institutions, the opportunities afforded by the structure of the still-forming liberal-colonial state offered more promising results for ending British rule than did the armed insurrectionary movements of their elders. As Nihal Perera (2002) argues, by the turn of the twentieth century, the centre of Buddhism on the island had shifted from Kandy to the outskirts of Colombo so as to allow for more effective lobbying of the colonial government towards independence.

The footpaths of Ceylon, which had been turned successively into military roads, commercial plantation roads, and railways during the nineteenth century, had increased the speed of transportation and the "modernization" of the island. In the context of the monumental changes of the nineteenth century and the limited success of armed uprisings, the rise of an anti-colonial national consciousness that strove to inhabit the existing apparatus of the colonial state and economy while putting "internal" problems arising from colonialism later was understandable, and not at all unique to Ceylon. In the garb of this historical version of anti-colonialism,

Conclusion: pluriversal sovereignty and research   171

the rising movements described by Obeyesekere as "protestant Buddhism" (Gombrich and Obeyesekere, 1988) and its Hindutva cousin in India have adopted a fetishized modern form that has become complicit with singular narratives: *uni*versal aspirations, rather than the pluriversal histories that have fragmented and diversified practices named as "Hindu" or "Buddhist" only through the modern, colonial encounter.

Throughout this book, I have strived to show how before the universe of total territorial rule, there was a pluriverse of uncolonized options that operated with diverse ontological starting points and trajectories. The treatment of the "nation state" as a universal container in which to exist is perhaps one of the most normalized expressions of the violence of universal colonial politics. However, the politics of the pluriverse teaches that the temporal hegemony of universality does not imply the extinction of pluriversal realities. Pluriversal thinking engages with pasts to challenge the histories and the normative assumptions and exclusions within them, and ultimately to resuscitate important diversity that can help build decolonial futures. Articulating this in a different vocabulary, Robbie Shilliam (2015) has called it rejecting the "colonial science" of categorical separation in favour of a "decolonial science" of rebinding and rehabilitation.

As a contribution to global social theory, pluriversal sovereignty offers a theoretical approach that starts with the premise that the ontologies and epistemologies of colonized people matter not just for their communities, but in the making of the modern/colonial world order. This forces a reconsideration of imperial encounters because in understanding the colonized as co-constitutors of the modern/colonial condition (albeit on unequal terms), we must reconsider how we measure and border empire both physically and temporally. If colonial violence is encoded into the practice of *being* a modern state, then there is little hope of imagining a truly post-colonial state without fundamentally rethinking and diversifying the ontologies underscoring how human beings live with one another and the rest of the natural world. For example, in light of the ontological contestations unfolding in early nineteenth century Ceylon, and what the British learned from these encounters, we ought to reconsider

172 *Pluriversal sovereignty and the state*

the birth of the Raj in South Asia and position it first in Ceylon rather than as a statist project relevant only to India after the First War of Independence or Sepoy Rebellion and the subsequent Royal Proclamation that established direct British rule in India only in 1858. Rather, a generation earlier it was trial and error, with the emphasis on error, that largely defined direct British rule in its early days in Ceylon. Unlike in India, where generations of East India Company officials had developed relationships and an understanding of Mughal state behaviour, in Ceylon, the Buddhist *rajamandala* system to which they were exposed was poorly understood. Orientalist scholars were still trying to understand the differences between *buddhagama* and their own particularly Brahminical understanding of the varied practices they would later call "Hinduism."

This book has taken up the question of how the process of "becoming" the modern territorial state worked to legitimize a universal understanding of how to exist free from colonial rule. I have taken as the object of analysis the territorial state itself, offering a critical re-reading of the early British encounter with Ceylon to show how, through ontological, religious, and political struggles, the logic of "total territorial rule" gradually became de-politicized such that it was a passive terrain upon which anti-colonial struggles would eventually unfold in the nationalistic ways we are all familiar with. By using a decolonial theoretical approach to intervene conceptually within bodies of social science theory concerned with questions of state, territory, and sovereignty, I have argued that a decolonial reading brings to light the material and conceptual violence of universal thought in the form of colonial state formation. This manifestation of violence has sought to push the multiple and diverse ways of organizing social, political, and spiritual life outside the "limit" of a reality that, in turn, treats Eurocentric ontological starting points as "given" or "common sense."

It is my sincere belief that the significance of postcolonial crises of sovereignty cannot be understood using universal reason, which has underscored some of the most colonial forms of scholarship in literatures which discuss "failed" states or justify notions like "democratic peace theory" and even make cases for the recolonization of

Conclusion: pluriversal sovereignty and research   173

parts of the planet. So much work in social science in general, and international relations in particular, has been concerned with the territorial state and its universal ontology that pluriversal sovereignty and political agency have been glossed over in discourses of pre-political people or what we more generally critique as modernity and development. Nonetheless, it is clear that through a lens of universality, the norm of "total territorial rule" in the nation state remains the only acceptable one within the colonial international system of the twentieth and twenty-first centuries. While controlling the state was of monumental importance in the twentieth century and nothing written here is meant to suggest otherwise, a core part of the problem today is that inheriting and controlling the reins of the state became an end in itself rather than a means to a greater end of building free societies.

Controlling the state has been mistaken for decolonization, and while I have sought to show this through a close look at early nineteenth-century sovereign ontological contestations in Ceylon, this approach to decolonial international relations can be applied elsewhere. The coloniality of the state thus calls into question the degree to which a government, simply by exercising Weberian sovereignty over a territorially bounded imaginary national community, can truly lay claim to being "post-colonial." If one untethers colonialism from a temporal period and examines its material processes in economic, political, and social terms, independence can be only the beginning of a much longer process of decolonization that requires a fundamental rethinking of how human communities are constituted.[2] We modern political subjects are, as James C. Scott argues, "hypnotized by the state"; we think about the past as mediated through a statist lens without due regard for the ways in which the modern territorial nation state and the system of states came to be (J. C. Scott, 2009; Agnew, 1994; Elden, 2010a). Understanding the colonial context through which material practices emerged – such as large-scale agricultural production for export, centralization of political sovereignty, private ownership, or elite-level representative government (instead of participatory democracy) – can enliven debates today about what decolonization ought to look like in terms of practice, as well as within scholarly discussions.

174 *Pluriversal sovereignty and the state*

The legal relationship between the British "sovereign" and the sovereign obligations of rule in Kandy presented a long-standing problem where the British attempted to rationalize the Kandyans' more-than-modern ontology of sovereign practice by using what they believed to be an unproblematic and universally applicable understanding of sovereignty as it had developed in their own traditions. Thus, the British partially fulfilled the requirements of Kandyan sovereignty but understood them merely as necessary to placate the uncivilized superstitions of locals rather than as serious obligations. Drawing on Tambiah's galactic sovereignty model, I have strived to show that the political ontological clash of the Kandyan Convention represented a kind of galactic collision, the consequences of which were not immediately apparent, though the contemporary problems of ethno-nationalism can be seen to be part of its logical outcome. I have proposed using a metaphor of galactic collision to theorize the many collisions between Kandyan and British ontologies of sovereignty between about 1815 and 1848 in order to understand how these imperial encounters together normalized the territorial colonial state. Galaxies are porous: when they collide they do not bounce against one another, but pass through each other several times before merging. Their gravity keeps the stars operating around a galactic core, but the forces of gravity within any one galaxy inevitably interact with the other galaxy during the encounter. If the 1815 Convention represents the first collision and "passing through" of sovereign ontologies, then by the 1850s, Ceylon had reached the ensuing period of galactic unification.

The history of spatial organization, as explained in the Introduction, can be thought of in three general periods. The first marks the galactic *mandala* system and its genealogy in South and South-East Asia. The second is the moment of ontological tension and colonial contamination at which a Kandyan-Buddhist galaxy meets and passes through a British-Christian galaxy – roughly 1815–1848. By the time of the third phase in the late nineteenth and early twentieth centuries, the colonial structure of universal territorial rule has become a naturalized structure within which to struggle. This is analogous to the frame shown in Figure C.1, where

Conclusion: pluriversal sovereignty and research 175

Figure C.1 Convergence of Milky Way and Andromeda galaxies. NASA artistic prediction, May 31, 2012. Taken from https://www.nasa.gov/mission_pages/hubble/science/milky-way-collide.html (accessed May 23, 2023).

the Milky Way and Andromeda galaxies have collided more than once, and have formed something new.

We have yet to leave this period, but there is no reason to believe that it is a finale. Elements of both the Milky Way and the Andromeda galaxy exist within this new galaxy, and like its predecessor galaxies, the new one is not solid, stable, or unchanging. Elements of pluriversal sovereignty similarly remain within the contemporary state system; however, its modern contamination is in need of decolonial treatment, as the practice of Buddhification has taken on violently ethno-nationalist connotations as recently calcified ethnicities continue to vie for total territorial rule. Such decolonial treatments may, and perhaps must, begin within the context of a state; the limits of the modern state cannot be the limit of the potential application of multiple approaches to understanding and practising sovereignty.

Notes

1 Colvin R. de Silva was an important exception. During the parliamentary debate on the Citizenship Act that would disenfranchise the Tamil workers in the interior, de Silva denounced the "racialism" of the act. See "Colvin the Fighter," 2020.
2 In some parts of the world, including Turtle Island, where I live and work, it is wholly insufficient to think about decolonization in reference to only human communities.

References

Abeysekara, Ananda. 2002. *Colors of the Robe: Religion, Identity, and Difference*. Columbia: University of South Carolina Press.

"After the Slaughter: Tamil Tigers Contemplate Life without Prabhakaran." 2009. *The Economist*, May 28. Accessed November 23, 2010. www.economist.com/node/13754093.

Agnew, John. 1994. "The Territorial Trap: The Geographical Assumptions of International Relations Theory." *Review of International Political Economy* 1/1: 53–80.

——. 1995. "The Hidden Geographies of Social Science and the Myth of the 'Geographical Turn." *Environment and Planning D: Society & Space* 13: 379–380.

——. 2010. "Still Trapped in Territory." *Geopolitics* 15/4: 779–784.

Ahluwalia, Pal. 2005. "Out of Africa: Post-Structuralism's Colonial Roots." *Postcolonial Studies* 8/2: 137–154.

Alfred, Taiaiake. 1999. *Peace, Power, Righteousness: An Indigenous Manifesto*. Toronto: Oxford University Press.

Almond, Philip C. 1988. *The British Discovery of Buddhism*. Cambridge: Cambridge University Press.

Anderson, Benedict. 1983. *Imagined Communities*. London: Verso.

Anghie, Antony. 1996. "Francisco de Vitoria and the Colonial Origins of International Law." *Social and Legal Studies* 5/3: 321–336.

"Appendix No. 5 to Memorandum on Colonial Policy: Memorandum of Former Insurrectionary Attempts at Ceylon, 1849." 1849. The National Archives, shelfmark: CO/882/1/4.

Armitage, David. 2013. *Foundations of Modern International Thought*. Cambridge: Cambridge University Press.

Ault, Rev. William. 1814. "Rev. William Ault to Mother, 1814." (Wesleyan) Methodist Missionary Society Archive, School of Oriental and African Studies, University of London, box 628 (1), Ceylon Various Papers Various Dates, no. 1005.

178   *References*

Bailey, Rev. J., Secretary to the Mission. 1833. *Statement of the Ceylon Mission of the Church Missionary Society for the Year M.DCCC.XXXII W.* Ceylon: Cotta Church Mission Press.

Bandarage, Asoka. 1983. *Colonialism in Sri Lanka: The Political Economy of the Kandyan Highlands, 1833–1886.* Berlin: Moutan.

Barkawi, Tarak. 2016. "Decolonising War." *European Journal of International Security* 1/2 (July): 199–214. DOI: 10.1017/eis.2016.7.

Bartelson, Jens. 1995. *A Genealogy of Sovereignty.* Cambridge: Cambridge University Press.

Bennet, J. W. 1843. *Ceylon and its Capabilities: An Account of its Natural Resources, Indigenous Productions, and Commercial Facilities.* London: W. H. Allen & Co.

Bernard, Dorene. 2017. "Reconciliation and Environmental Racism in Mi'kma'ki." *Kalfou* 5/2: 297–302.

Bhambra, Gurminder K. 2014. *Connected Sociologies.* London: Bloomsbury.

——. 2016. "Comparative Historical Sociology and the State: Problems of Method." *Cultural Sociology* 10/3: 335–351.

——. 2022. "Relations of Extraction, Relations of Redistribution: Empire, Nation, and the Construction of the British Welfare State." *The British Journal of Sociology* 7/1: 4–15.

Blaney, David. 1996. "Reconceptualizing Autonomy: The Difference Dependency Theory Makes." *Review of International Political Economy* 3/3: 459–497.

Blaser, Mario. 2013. "Ontological Conflicts and the Stories of Peoples in Spite of Europe: Toward a Conversation in Political Ontology." *Current Anthropology* 54/4: 547–568.

Bodhi, Bikkhu (trans.). 2000. *The Connected Discourses of the Buddha: A New Translation of the Samyutta Nikaya*, vol. 2. Boston: Wisdom Publications.

Boldt, Andreas. 2014. "Ranke: Objectivity and History." *Rethinking History* 18/4: 457–474.

Branch, Jordan. 2011. "Mapping the Sovereign State: Technology, Authority, and Systemic Change." *International Organization* 65/1: 1–36.

Bridgalle, William. 1828. Bridgalle to Wesleyan Methodist Church, March 25 1828. (Wesleyan) Methodist Missionary Society Archive, School of Oriental and African Studies, University of London, Special Series, Correspondence (H-2715), box 1814–1867, Ceylon: 446 – 1828, no. 108.

Brighenti, A. 2010. "On Territorology: Towards a General Science of Territory." *Theory, Culture, and Society* 27/1: 52–72.

Brownrigg, Elizabeth. 1818. "Lady Brownrigg Speech to Native Militia." *Ceylon Gazette* August 8, 1818.

References 179

Byng, George Stanley (seventh Viscount Torrington). "Copy of a Letter from Viscount Torrington to the Right Honourable H. Laboucherie, M.P., Jan. 17, 1857." 1857. The National Archives, shelfmark: PRO/30/29/23/10.

Camilleri, Joseph A. 1990. "Rethinking Sovereignty in a Shrinking, Fragmented World." In R. B. J. Walker and Saul H. Mendlovitz (eds) *Contending Sovereignties: Redefining Political Community*, 13–44. Boulder: Lynne Rienner Publishers.

Carnoy, Martin. 1984. *The State & Political Theory*. Princeton: Princeton University Press.

"The Case of Eyhelapola Maha Nilime, a Kandyan Chief Detained at Mauritius as State Prisoner." 1828. Letter submitted to His Majesty's Commissioner of Inquiry, January 17. The National Archives, shelfmark: CO/416/20.

Casinader, Niranjan, Roshan de Silva Wijeyeratne, and Lee C. Godden. 2018. "From Sovereignty to Modernity: Revisiting the Colbrooke Cameron Reforms – Transforming the Buddhist and Colonial Imaginary in 19th Century Ceylon." *Comparative Legal History* 6/1: 1–31.

Césaire, Aimé. 2000 [1955]. *Discourse on Colonialism*. Translated by Joan Pinkham. New York: Monthly Review Press.

Ceylon Gazette. 1820. Reprinted and reproduced online at *A People's History 1793–1844 from the Newspapers* by Roger Houghton. Accessed September 21, 2016. http://www.houghton.hk/.

Ceylon Gazette. February 28, 1818. Reprinted in the *Madras Courier*.

Ceylon Gazette. May 16, 1818.

A Ceylon Planter. 1850. "Is Ceylon to be Sacrificed at the Shrine of a Party? A Letter Addressed to Sir R. Peel, Bart M.P." Colombo, 1850. British Library, shelfmark: 8023.cc.7.(7.).

Chakrabarty, Dipesh. 2000. *Provincializing Europe*. Princeton: Princeton University Press.

——. 2007. *Provincializing Europe*. Reissue. Princeton: Princeton University Press.

——. 2009. "The Climate of History: Four Theses." *Critical Inquiry* 35/2: 197–222.

——. 2010. "The Legacies of Bandung: Decolonization and the Politics of Culture." In Christopher Lee (ed.) *Making a World after Empire: The Bandung Moment and its Political Afterlives*, 45–68. Athens: Ohio University Press.

Chatterjee, Partha. 1986. *Nationalist Thought and the Colonial World: A Derivative Discourse*. Minneapolis: University of Minnesota Press.

——. 1993. *The Nation and its Fragments: Colonial and Postcolonial Histories*. Princeton: Princeton University Press.

——. 1997. *Our Modernity*. Dakar: Sephis & Codesria.

180 *References*

Chatterjee, Partha and Pradeep Jeganathan (eds). 2001. *Community, Gender and Violence*. Subaltern Studies 11. New York: Columbia University Press.

Chitty, Simon Casie. 1972. *The Ceylon Gazetteer Containing an Accurate Account of the Districts, Provinces, Cities, Towns, Principal Villages, Harbours, Rivers, Lakes of the Island of Ceylon*. Colombo: M. D. Gunasena.

Clarke, Elizabeth. 2004. *History, Theory, Text: Historians and the Linguistic Turn*. Cambridge, MA: Harvard University Press.

Cohn, Bernard S. 1996. *Colonialism and its Forms of Knowledge: The British in India*. Princeton: Princeton University Press.

"Colvin the Fighter." 2020. *Daily News*, February 18. Accessed November 27, 2022. www.dailynews.lk/2020/02/18/features/211718/colvin-fighter.

"Confidential: Ceylon. Appendix No. 6 to Memorandum on Colonial Policy: Comparative Statistics of the Different Insurrections and Insurrectionary Attempts which have Taken Place in Ceylon." Printed at the Foreign Office, February 1849. The National Archives, shelfmark: CO/882/1/5.

"Confidential Despatch: Court Martial." November 14, 1849. The National Archives, shelfmark: CO/54/263.

Coulthard, Glen. 2014. *Red Skins White Masks: Rejecting the Colonial Politics of Recognition*. Minneapolis: University of Minnesota Press.

Coulthard, Glen and Leanne Betasamosake Simpson. 2016. "Grounded Normativity/Place-Based Solidarity." *American Quarterly* 68/2: 249–255.

Crawquill, Julian. 1839. "Colonies and Colonization." *The Colombo Magazine* 1/1 (January): 16–18. British Library, shelfmark: 8023cc7.

De Alwis, Malathi. 1995. "Gender, Politics and the 'Respectable Lady.'" In Pradeep Jeganathan and Qadri Ismail (eds) *Unmaking the Nation: The Politics of Identity & History in Modern Sri Lanka*, 138–156. Colombo: Social Scientists' Association.

———. 2002. "The Changing Role of Women in Sri Lankan Society." *Social Research* 69/3: 675–691.

———. 2010. "The 'China Factor' in Post-War Sri Lanka." *Inter-Asia Cultural Studies* 11/3: 434–446.

De la Cadena, Marisol. 2010. "Indigenous Cosmopolitics in the Andes: Conceptual Reflections beyond 'Politics.'" *Cultural Anthropology* 52/2: 334–370.

———. 2015. *Earth Beings: Ecologies of Practice across Andean Worlds*. Durham, NC: Duke University Press.

Deloria, Vine, Jr. 1973. *God is Red: A Native View of Religion*. New York: Putnam Publishing Group.

De Silva, Chandra Richard. 1987. *Sri Lanka: A History*. New Delhi: Vikas Publishing House.

De Silva, Colvin R. 1953. *Ceylon under the British Occupation 1795–1833*, vol. 1: *Its Political and Administrative Development*. Colombo: The Colombo Apothecaries' Co., Ltd.

References 181

De Silva, K. M. (ed.). 1965. *Letters on Ceylon 1846–1850: The Administration of Viscount Torrington and the "Rebellion" of 1848; The Private Correspondence of the Third Earl Grey (Secretary of State for the Colonies 1846–52) and Viscount Torrington*. Kandy: K. V. G. de Silva.

——. 1981. *A History of Sri Lanka*. London: C. Hurst & Company.

——. 1984. "University Admissions and Ethnic Tensions in Sri Lanka: 1977–1982." In R. Goldman and A. J. Wilson (eds) *From Independence to Statehood: Managing Ethnic Conflict in Five African and Asian States*, 97–100. London: Frances Pinter.

——. 1987. "Separatist Ideology in Sri Lanka: A Historical Appraisal of the Claim for the 'Traditional Homelands' of the Tamils of Sri Lanka." Paper presented at the International Workshop on Separatist Movements sponsored by the International Centre for Ethnic Studies, Kandy, July 1–3.

DeVotta, N. 2004. *Blowback: Linguistic Nationalism, Institutional Decay, and Ethnic Conflict in Sri Lanka*. Stanford: Stanford University Press.

——. 2009. "The Liberation Tigers of Tamil Eelam and the Lost Quest for Separatism in Sri Lanka." *Asian Survey* 49/6 (November–December): 1047–1048.

Duncan, James. 1990. *The City as Text: The Politics of Landscape Interpretation in the Kandyan Kingdom*. New York: Cambridge University Press.

——. 2007. *In the Shadow of the Tropics: Climate, Race, and Biopower in Nineteenth Century Ceylon*. Aldershot: Ashgate Publishing House.

Dussel, Enrique. 1995. *The Invention of the Americas: Eclipse of "the Other" and the Myth of Modernity*. Translated by Michael D. Barber. New York: Continuum.

Eisenstadt, S. N. 1974. "Studies of Modernization and Sociological Theory." *History and Theory* 13/3: 225–252.

——. 2000. "Multiple Modernities." *Daedalus* 129/1: 1–29.

Elden, Stuart. 2009. *Terror and Territory: The Spatial Extent of Sovereignty*. Minneapolis: University of Minnesota Press.

——. 2010a. "Land, Terrain, Territory." *Progress in Human Geography* 34/6: 799–817.

——. 2010b. "Thinking Territory Historically." *Geopolitics* 15/4 (2010): 757–761.

——. 2013. *The Birth of Territory*. Chicago: University of Chicago Press.

E. P. 1969. "Review of G. C. Mendis, *Problems of Ceylon History and Ceylon Today and Yesterday*." *The Journal of the Ceylon Branch of the Royal Asiatic Society of Great Britain & Ireland*, New Series, 13: 94–97.

Escobar, Arturo. 2015. "Thinking-Feeling with the Earth: Territorial Struggles and the Ontological Dimensions of the Epistemologies of the South." *Revisita de Antropologia Iberoamericana* 11/1: 11–32.

182   *References*

Ethirajan, Anbarasan. 2019. "Sri Lanka's Muslims 'Demonised' after Easter Bombings." *BBC News*, August 13. Accessed October 15, 2022. www.bbc.com/news/world-asia-49249146.

Etipola, R. B. 1952. *Queen Elizabeth of Ceylon and the Kandyan Convention, 1815*. Kandy: Kandy Printers. British Library, shelfmark: 8157.c.56.

Fanon, Frantz. 2004 [1961]. *The Wretched of the Earth*. Translated by Richard Philcox. New York: Groves Press.

Federici, Silvia. 2004. *Caliban and the Witch: Women, the Body, and Primitive Accumulation*. Brooklyn: Autonomedia.

"A Few Remarks upon Colonel Forbes' Pamphlet on Recent Disturbances in Ceylon in a Letter to Sir R. Peel, Bart, M.P. & C by Colonist, April 12th 1850." 1850. British Library, shelfmark: 8023.cc.7.(1.).

Forbes, J., Late Lieutenant-Colonel 78th Highlanders. 1850. *Recent Disturbances and Military Executions in Ceylon*. Edinburgh and London. British Library, shelfmark: 8022.d.26.

Foucault, Michel. 2009. *Security, Territory, Population: Lectures at the Collège de France 1977–1978*. Translated by Graham Burchill. New York: Palgrave Macmillan.

Frank, Andre Gunder. 1966. "The Development of Underdevelopment." *Monthly Review* 18/4: 17–34.

Freemont-Barnes, Gregory. 2009. *The Anglo-Afghan Wars 1839–1919*. Oxford: Osprey Publishing.

Gehl, Lynn. 2014. *The Truth That Wampum Tells*. Halifax: Fernwood Publishing, 2014.

Giddens, Anthony. 1987. *The Nation-State and Violence*. Berkeley: University of California Press.

Go, Julian. 2013. "For a Postcolonial Sociology." *Theory and Society* 42/1: 25–55.

Gogerly, D. J. 1863. "Buddhism in Ceylon." (Wesleyan) Methodist Missionary Society Archive, School of Oriental and African Studies, University of London, Special Series, Biographical (H-2723), box 664 (3), Various Papers/Ceylon 1857/59/66, no. 1996.

Gokhale, Balkrishna Govind. 1973. "Anagarika Dharmapala: Toward Modernity through Tradition in Ceylon." *Contributions to Asian Studies* 4: 30–39.

Gombrich, Richard and Gananath Obeyesekere. 1988. *Buddhism Transformed: Religious Change in Sri Lanka*. Princeton: Princeton University Press.

Goswami, Manu. 2004. *Producing India: From Colonial Economy to National Space*. Chicago: University of Chicago Press.

Grinde, Donald A., Jr., and Bruce E. Johansen. 1991. *Exemplar of Liberty: Native America and the Evolution of Democracy*. Los Angeles: American Indian Studies Centre Publications.

References 183

Grosfoguel, Ramón. 2007. "The Epistemic Decolonial Turn: Beyond Political Economy Paradigms." *Cultural Studies* 2/3: 211–223.

——. 2013. "The Structure of Knowledge in Westernized Universities: Epistemic Racism/Sexism and the Four Genocides/Epistemicides of the Long 16th Century." *Human Architecture: Journal of the Sociology of Self-Knowledge* 11/1: 73–90.

Grovogui, Siba. 1996. *Sovereigns, Quasi-Sovereigns, and Africans: Race and Self Determination in International Law*. Minneapolis: Minnesota University Press.

——. 2002. "Regimes of Morality: International Morality and the African Condition." *European Journal of International Relations* 8/3: 315–338.

Guha, Ranajit. 1997. *Dominance without Hegemony: History and Power in Colonial India*. Cambridge, MA: Harvard University Press.

——. 2002. *History at the Limits of World History*. New York: Colombia University Press.

Gunasekara, Kalasuri Wilfred. 1999. "G. C. Mendis – One of Sri Lanka's Pioneer Scientific Historians." *Daily News*, October 28. Accessed December 8, 2016. https://goo.gl/Pp3187.

Gunawardana, R. A. L. H. 2004 [1990]. "The People of the Lion: Sinhala Identity and Ideology in History and Historiography." In Jonathan Spencer (ed.) *Sri Lanka: History and the Roots of Conflict*, 45–86. London: Routledge.

Gupta, Akhil. 1992. "The Song of the Nonaligned World: Transnational Identities and the Reinscription of Space in Late Capitalism." *Cultural Anthropology* 7/1: 63–79.

Haraway, Donna. 1988. "Situated Knowledges: The Science Question in Feminism and the Privileging of Partial Perspective." *Feminist Studies* 14/3: 575–599.

Hardt, Michael. 2002. "Sovereignty." *Theory & Event* 5/4. Accessed October 23, 2016. http://muse.jhu.edu/journals/theory_and_event/v005/5.4hardt.html.

Hardy, R. Spence. 1841. *The British Government and the Idolatry of Ceylon*. London: Crofts and Blenkarn.

Harris, Elizabeth. 2006. *Theravada Buddhism and the British Encounter: Religious, Missionary and Colonial Experience in Nineteenth Century Sri Lanka*. London: Routledge.

——. 2012. "Memory, Experience, and the Clash of Cosmologies: The Encounter between British Protestant Missionaries and Buddhism in Nineteenth Century Sri Lanka." *Social Science and Missions* 25: 265–303.

Harvard, William. 1833. *Memoirs of Elizabeth Harvard, Late of the Wesleyan Mission to Ceylon with Extracts from her Diary and Correspondence by her Husband*. London: John Mason. British Library, shelfmark: T.1587.(7.).

184 *References*

"Heroes in the Struggle for Independence." 2012. *Sunday Times*, February 5. Accessed February 7, 2012. www.sundaytimes.lk/120205/FunDay/fut_01.html.

Hill, Gord. 2009. *500 Years of Indigenous Resistance*. Oakland: PM Press.

Hill, Susan. 2008. "'Travelling Down the River of Life Together in Peace and Friendship, Forever': Haudenosaunne Land Ethics and Treaty Agreements as the Basis for Restructuring the Relationship with the British Crown." In Leanne Simpson (ed.) *Lighting the Eight Fire: The Liberation, Resurgence, and Protection of Indigenous Nations*, 23–44. Winnipeg: Arbeiter Ring Publishing.

Hobsbaum, Eric. 1997. *On History*. New York: The New Press.

Hunt, Sarah. 2013. "Ontologies of Indigeneity: The Politics of Embodying a Concept." *Cultural Geographies* 21/1: 27–32.

Hyndman, Jennifer and de Alwis, Malathi. 2004. "Bodies, Shrines, and Roads: Violence, (Im)mobility and Displacement in Sri Lanka." *Gender, Place & Culture* 11/4: 535–557.

Ismail, Qadri. 1995. "Unmooring Identity: The Antinomies of Elite Muslim Self-Representation in Modern Sri Lanka." In Pradeep Jeganathan and Qadri Ismail (eds) *Unmaking the Nation: The Politics of Identity & History in Modern Sri Lanka*, 55–105. Colombo: Social Scientists' Association.

James, C. L. R. 1938. *The Black Jacobins: Toussaint L'Ouverture and the San Domingo Revolution*. London: Secker & Warburg.

Jayawardena, Kumari. 1995. *The White Woman's Other Burden: Western Women and South Asia during British Rule*. New York: Routledge.

——. 2010. *Perpetual Ferment: Popular Revolts in Sri Lanka in the 18th and 19th Centuries*. Colombo: Social Scientist's Association of Sri Lanka.

Jayawardena, Kumari and Malathi de Alwis (eds). 1996. *Embodied Violence: Communalising Women's Sexuality in South Asia*. New Delhi: Kali.

Jeffries, Sir Charles. 1962. *Ceylon: The Path to Independence*. London: Pall Mall Press.

Jeganathan, Pradeep. 1995. "Authorizing History, Ordering Land: The Conquest of Anuradhapura." In Pradeep Jeganathan and Qadri Ismail (eds) *Unmaking the Nation: The Politics of Identity & History in Modern Sri Lanka*, 108–137. Colombo: Social Scientists' Association.

Jeganathan, Pradeep and Qadir Ismail (eds). 1995. *Unmaking the Nation: The Politics of Identity & History in Modern Sri Lanka*. Colombo: Social Scientists' Assocation.

Jegathesan, Mythri. 2019. *Tea and Solidarity: Tamil Women and Work in Postwar Sri Lanka*. Seattle: University of Washington Press.

Jenkins, Keith (ed.). 1997. *The Postmodern History Reader*. London: Routledge.

References

"The Kandyan Convention Proclamation of 2 March 1815." 1815. In G. C. Mendis (ed.) *The Colebrooke–Cameron Papers: Documents on British Colonial Policy in Ceylon 1796–1833*, vol. 2, 227–230. Oxford: Oxford University Press.

Kayaoglu, Turan. 2010. "Westphalian Eurocentrism in International Relations Theory." *International Studies Review* 12: 193–217.

Klem, Bart and Thiriumi Kelegama. 2020. "Marginal Placeholders: Peasants, Paddy and Ethnic Space in Sri Lanka's Post-War Frontier." *The Journal of Peasant Studies* 47/2: 346–365.

Korf, Benedikt. 2009. "Cartographic Violence: Engaging a Sinhala Kind of Geography." In C. Brun and T. Jazeel (eds) *Spatializing Politics: Culture, Politics, and Geography in Postcolonial Sri Lanka*, 100–121. New Delhi: Sage.

Kranz, Frederick (ed.). 1988. *History from Below*. Oxford: Basil Blackwell.

Krasner, Stephen. 1988. "Sovereignty: An Institutional Perspective." *Comparative Political Studies* 21/1: 66–94.

——. 1999. *Sovereignty: Organized Hypocrisy*. Princeton: Princeton University Press.

Krishna, Sankaran. 1999. *Postcolonial Insecurities: India, Sri Lanka, and the Question of Nationhood*. New Delhi: Oxford University Press.

Lai, Larissa. 2014. *Slanting I, Imagining We: Asian Canadian Literary Production in the 1980s and 1990s*. Waterloo: Wilfred Laurier University Press.

Lake, David A. 2003. "The New Sovereignty in International Relations." *International Studies Review* 5/3: 303–323.

Lal, Vinay. 2001. "Walking with the Subalterns, Riding with the Academy: The Curious Ascendency of Indian History." *Studies in History* 17/1: 101–134.

Lawrence, Bonita and Kim Anderson. 2005. "Introduction to 'Indigenous Women: State of Our Nations.'" *Atlantis: Critical Studies in Gender, Culture, and Social Justice* 29/2 1–8.

Lawrence, Bonita and Enakshi Dua. 2005. "Decolonizing Anti-Racism." *Social Justice* 32/4: 120–143.

Lee, Christopher. 2010. "Between a Moment and an Era: The Origins and Afterlives of Bandung." In Christopher Lee (ed.) *Making a World after Empire: The Bandung Moment and its Political Afterlives*, 1–39. Athens: Ohio University Press.

"Letter to the Editor of the *Morning Star* by a Jaffna Man Residing in Kandy, Aug. 10, 1848." 1848. British Library, shelfmark: 14172.k.4.

Lynch, James. 1808–1958. Letters, Papers, Pamphlets, Memoirs of Rev. James Lynch, 1808–1858. (Wesleyan) Methodist Missionary Society Archive, School of Oriental and African Studies, University of London, Special Series (H-2723), box 628 (1), Ceylon J. Lynch 1808–1814, no. 991.

186 *References*

Mackey, Eva. 2016. *Unsettled Expectations: Uncertainty, Land and Settler Decolonization*. Halifax: Fernwood Publishing.

Maldonado-Torres, Nelson. 2006. "On the Coloniality of Being: Contributions to the Development of a Concept." *Cultural Studies* 21/2: 240–270.

——. 2010. "On the Coloniality of Being: Contributions to the Development of a Concept." In Walter Mignolo and Arturo Escobar (eds) *Globalization and the Decolonial Option*, 94–124. New York: Routledge.

Maritain, Jacques. 1969. "The Philosophical Attack." In W. J. Stankiewicz (ed.) *In Defense of Sovereignty*, 41–64. London: Oxford University Press.

Marx, Karl. 1853. "The British Rule in India." *New York Daily Tribune*, June 25. Reprinted in *On Colonialism: Articles from the New York Tribune and Other Writings by Karl Marx and Frederick Engels*, 40. New York: International Publishers.

Matsunaga, Jennifer. 2016. "The Two Faces of Transitional Justice: Theorizing the Incommensurability of Transnational Justice and Decolonization in Canada." *Decolonization: Indigeneity, Education & Society* 5/1: 24–44.

McConnell, F. 2009. "De Facto, Displaced, Tacit: The Sovereign Articulations of the Tibetan Government-in-Exile." *Political Geography* 28/6: 343–352.

——. 2010. "The Fallacy and Promise of the Territorial Trap: Sovereign Articulations of Geopolitical Anomalies." *Geopolitics* 15/4: 762–768.

Mendis, G. C. (ed.). 1957. *The Colebrooke–Cameron Papers: Documents on British Colonial Policy in Ceylon 1796–1833*, 2 vols. London: Oxford University Press.

——. 2005 [1952]. *Ceylon under the British*. 2 vols. New Delhi: Gautam Jetley.

Metcalf, Thomas. 1998. *Ideologies of the Raj*. New Delhi: Cambridge University Press.

Mignolo, Walter. 2002. "The Geopolitics of Knowledge and the Colonial Difference." *The South Atlantic Quarterly* 101/1: 57–96.

——. 2007. "Delinking: The Rhetoric of Modernity, the Logic of Coloniality and the Grammar of De-Coloniality." *Cultural Studies* 21/2: 449–514.

——. 2011. *The Darker Side of Western Modernity: Global Futures, Decolonial Options*. Durham, NC: Duke University Press.

Mohanty, Chandra. 2003. "'Under Western Eyes' Revisited: Feminist Solidarity through Anti-Capitalist Struggles." *Signs* 28/2: 499–537.

Moloney, Pat. 2011. "Hobbes, Savagery, and International Anarchy." *American Political Science Review* 105/1: 189–204.

References 187

Morgenthau, Hans. 1948. *Politics among the Nations*. New York: Alfred A. Knopf.

M'sit No'kmaq et al. 2021. "'Awakening The Sleeping Giant': Re-Indigenization Principles for Transforming Biodiversity Conservation in Canada and Beyond." *Facets* 6/1: 839–869.

Munro, Martin and Robbie Shilliam. 2011. "Alternative Sources of Cosmopolitanism: Nationalism, Universalism and Créolité in Francophone Caribbean Thought." In Robbie Shilliam (ed.) *International Relations and Non-Western Thought: Imperialism, Colonialism and Investigations of Global Modernity*, 159–177. New York: Routledge.

Munslow, Alun. 2010. *The Future of History*. London: Palgrave.

Murphy, A. B. 1996. "The sovereign State System as Political-Territorial Ideal: Historical and Contemporary Considerations." In T. Bierstreker and C. Weber (eds) *State sovereignty as Social Construct*, 81–120. Cambridge: Cambridge University Press.

Nandy, Ashis. 1995. "History's Forgotten Doubles." *History and Theory* 34/2: 44–66.

A Narrative of Events which Have Recently Occurred in the Island of Ceylon, Written by a Gentleman on the Spot. 1815. London: T. Egerton Military Library, Whitehall.

"NASA's Hubble Shows Milky Way is Destined for Head-On Collision." 2012. NASA, May 31, 2012. Accessed May 23, 2023. https://www.nasa.gov/mission_pages/hubble/science/milky-way-collide.html.

"No Mention of Prabhakaran in Rajapaksa's Victory Speech." 2009. *Times of India*, May 19. Accessed October 18, 2016. http://timesofindia.indiatimes.com/world/south-asia/No-mention-of-Prabhakaran-in-Rajapaksas-victory-speech/articleshow/4550436.cms.

"Notes on the Trial of 12 Prisoners Regarding the Attempted Rebellion of 1824. Tried in Kandy." 1824. The National Archives, shelfmark: CO/416/20.

Obeyesekere, Gananath. 2006. "Buddhism, Ethnicity, and Identity: A Problem in Buddhist History." In Mahinda Deegale (ed.) *Buddhism, Conflict and Violence in Sri Lanka*, 134–162. New York: Routledge.

——. 2017. *The Doomed King: A Requiem for Sri Vikrama Rajasinha*. Colombo: Sailfish.

——. 2020. *The Many Faces of the Kandyan Kingdom 1591–1765*. Colombo: Sailfish.

Onuf, Nicholas. 1991. "Sovereignty: Outline of a Conceptual History." *Alternatives* 16: 425–446.

"Ordinance No. 8, 1848 (Road Ordinance)." 1848. The National Archives, shelfmark: CO/56/5.

Osiander, Andreas. 2001. "Sovereignty, International Relations, and the Westphalian Myth." *International Organization* 55/2: 251–287.

References

Pagden, Anthony. 1993. *European Encounters with the New World*. New Haven: Yale University Press.

——. 2005. "Fellow Citizens and Imperial Subjects: Conquest and Sovereignty in Europe's Overseas Empires." *History and Theory* 44: 28–46.

Panagia, Davide. 2010. "'*Partage du sensible*': The Distribution of the Sensible." in Jean-Philippe Deranty (ed.) *Jacques Rancière: Key Concepts*, 95–104. Durham: Acumen.

Parasram, Ajay. 2012. "Erasing Tamil Eelam: De/Re Territorialization in the Global War on Terror." *Geopolitics* 17/4: 903–925.

——. 2014. "Postcolonial Territory and the Coloniality of the State." *Caribbean Journal of International Relations & Diplomacy* 2/4: 51–79.

——. 2018. "Hunting the State of Nature: Race and Ethics in Postcolonial International Relations." In Brent J. Steele and Eric Heinze (eds) *Routledge Handbook of Ethics and International Relations*, 102–115. London: Routledge.

——. 2020. "Engaging *Capitalism and Slavery* as Decolonial Text." In Kirrily Freeman and John Munro (eds) *Reading the Postwar Future: Textual Turning Points from 1944*, 113–128. London: Bloomsbury.

Parasram, Ajay and Nissim Mannathukkaren. 2021. "Imperial Afterlives: Citizenship and Racial/Caste Fragility in Canada and India." *Citizenship Studies*. DOI: 10.1080/13621025.2021.1984494.

Parasram, Ajay and Lisa Tilley. 2018. "Global Environmental Harm, Internal Frontiers, and Indigenous Protective Ontologies." In Robbie Shilliam and Olivia Rutazibwa (eds) *Routledge Handbook of Postcolonial Studies*, 302–317. New York: Routledge.

Perera, Nihal. 1998. *Society and Space: Colonialism, Nationalism, and Postcolonial Identity in Sri Lanka*. Boulder: Westview Press.

——. 2002. "Indigenising the Colonial City: Late 19th-Century Colombo and its Landscape." *Urban Studies* 39/9: 1703–1721.

Perera, S. G. 1944. *The Jesuits in Ceylon*. Madura: De Nobili Press.

"Philoyenues," 1817. Letter to Unnamed "Sir" on the Baptism of two High Priests from Ceylon. (Wesleyan) Methodist Missionary Society Archive, School of Oriental and African Studies, University of London, Special Series, Biographical (H-2723), box 628(1), Ceylon Papers of A. Clark Var. Dates, no. 1002.

"Plan to Resettle Tamil IDPs in the Midst of Army and Sinhala Settlements." 2009. *Sri Lanka Guardian*, August 24. Accessed September 3, 2010. www.srilankaguardian.org/2009/08/plan-to-resettle-tamil-idps-in-midst-of.html.

Powell, Geoffrey. 1973. *The Kandyan Wars: The British Army in Ceylon 1803–1818*. London: Lee Cooper.

Pratt, Mary Louise. 2008. *Imperial Eyes: Travel Writing and Transculturation*. New York: Routledge.

"Proclamation by the Queen in Council to the Princes, Chiefs and People of India (published by the Governor-General at Allahabad, November 1st 1858)." British Library, shelfmark: IOR/L/PS/18/D154.

"Proclamation of 2nd March, 1815." In *Revised Edition of the Ordinances of the Government of Ceylon*, vol. 1: *1799–1882*, 16–18. Colombo: G. J. A. Skeen, Government Printer.

"Proclamation of 21st November, 1818." In *Revised Edition of the Ordinances of the Government of Ceylon*, vol. 1: *1799–1882*, 18–21. Colombo: G. J. A. Skeen, Government Printer, 1894.

Quijano, Aníbal. 2007. "Coloniality and Modernity/Rationality." *Cultural Studies* 21/2–3: 168–178.

Ramnath, Maia. 2011. *Decolonizing Anarchism: An Antiauthoritarian History of India's Liberation Struggle*. Oakland: AK Press.

Rancière, Jacques. 2001. "Ten Theses on Politics." *Theory & Event* 5/3: 1–18.

——. 2010. *Dissensus: Politics and Aesthetics*. Ed. and trans. Steven Corcoran. New York: Continuum.

"The Rebellion." 1848. *Morning Star*, September 14.

Ricardo, David. 1817. *On the Principles of Political Economy and Taxation*. London: John Murray.

Roberts, Michael. 1975. *Facets of Modern Ceylon History through the Letters of Jeronis Pieris*. Colombo: Hans Publishers Limited. British Library, shelfmark: X.800/27313.

Rogers, John D. 2004. "Early British Rule and Social Classification in Lanka." *Modern Asian Studies* 38/3: 626–631.

Rojas, Cristina. 1995. "Identity Formation, Violence, and the Nation-State in Nineteenth-Century Colombia." *Alternatives* 20: 195–224.

——. 2002. *Civilization and Violence: Regimes of Representation in Nineteenth Century Colombia*. Minneapolis: University of Minnesota Press.

——. 2016. "Contesting the Colonial Logics of the International: Towards a Relational Politics for the Pluriverse." *International Political Sociology* 10/4: 369–382.

"The Roundtable Conference: A Conference of Leaders of Various Communities Held to Discuss the Parliamentary Commission on the Constitutional Reforms of Ceylon." 1944. Young Ceylon, August. The National Archives, shelfmark: FCO/141/2339.

Ruggie, John. 1986. "Continuity and Transformation in the World Polity: Towards a Neorealist Synthesis." In Robert Keohane (ed.) *Neorealism and its Critics*, 131–158. New York: Columbia University Press.

References

———. 1993. "Territoriality and Beyond: Problematizing Modernity in International Relations." *International Organization* 47/1: 139–174.

Said, Edward. 1978. *Orientalism*. New York: Random House.

Sassen, Saskia. 2015. "Making Territory Work Analytically beyond its Connection to the State." In Stephen Legg, "The Birth of Territory: A Review Forum." *Journal of Historical Geography* 50: 109–188.

Scott, David. 1999. *Refashioning Futures: Criticism after Postcoloniality*. Princeton: Princeton University Press.

Scott, James C. 1987. *Weapons of the Weak: Everyday Forms of Peasant Resistance*. New Haven: Yale University Press.

———. 1998. *Seeing Like a State: How Certain Schemes to Improve the Human Conditions Have Failed*. New Haven: Yale University Press.

———. 2009. *The Art of Not Being Governed: An Anarchist History of Upland Southeast Asia*. New Haven: Yale University Press.

Seneviratne, H. L. 1977. "Politics and Pageantry: Universalisation of Ritual in Sri Lanka." *Royal Anthropological Institute of Great Britain and Ireland* 12/1 (April): 65–75.

———. 1987. "Kingship and Polity in Buddhism and Hinduism." *Contributions to Indian Sociology* 21/1: 147–155.

———. 2001. "Buddhist Monks and Ethnic Politics: A War Zone in an Island Paradise." *Anthropology Today* 17/2: 15–21.

Seth, Sanjay. 2007. *Subject Lessons: The Western Education of Colonial India*. Durham, NC: Duke University Press.

Shaffer, Linda. 1994. "Southernization." *Journal of World History* 5/1: 1–21.

Shani, Giorgio. 2008. "Towards a Post-Western IR: The *Umma, Khalsa Panth,* and Critical International Relations Theory." *International Studies Review* 10/4: 722–734.

Sharp, Joanne. 2009. *Geographies of Postcolonialism*. London: Sage.

Shaw, Karena. 2008. *Indigeneity and Political Theory: Sovereignty and the Limits of the Political*. New York: Routledge.

Shekhawat, V. S. 2010. *Sri Lanka: The Politics of Tamil Eelam*. Jaipur: Ram Kishore Sharma.

Shilliam, Robbie. 2011. "Non-Western Thought and International Relations." In Robbie Shilliam (ed.) *International Relations and Non-Western Thought: Imperialism, Colonialism and Investigations of Global Modernity*, 1–11. New York: Routledge.

———. 2015. *The Black Pacific: Anti-Colonial Struggles and Oceanic Connections*. London: Bloomsbury.

Simpson, Audra. 2014. *Mohawk Interruptus: Political Life across Borders of Settler States*. Durham, NC: Duke University Press.

Simpson, Leanne (ed.). 2008. *Lighting the Eighth Fire: The Liberation, Resurgence, and Protection of Indigenous Nations*. Winnipeg: Arbeiter Ring Publishing.

References

——. 2013. *Islands of Decolonial Love*. Winnipeg: ARP Books.

——. 2017. *As We Have Always Done*. Minneapolis: University of Minnesota Press.

——. 2020. "The Brilliance of Beaver: Learning from an Anishnaabe World." *Ideas*, April 16. Accessed April 27, 2020. https://www.cbc.ca/radio/ideas/the-brilliance-of-the-beaver-learning-from-an-anishnaabe-world-1.5534706.

Singh, Bhagat. 2007. *The Jail Notebook and Other Writings*. New Delhi: LeftWord Books.

Sivasundaram, Sujit. 2007. "Tales of the Land: British Geography and Kandyan Resistance in Sri Lanka, c. 1803–1850." *Modern Asian Studies* 41/5: 925–965.

Steuart, James. 1850. "Appendix: On the British Protection of Buddhism in 1844." In *Observations on Colonel Forbes' Pamphlet on the Recent Rebellion in Ceylon*. Colombo: Examiner Press. British Library, shelf-mark: 8244.b.3.(2.).

Tagore, Rabindranath. 1917. "Nationalism in Japan." In *The Complete Works of Rabindranath Tagore*. Accessed August 20, 2013. https://goo.gl/32uj72.

Tambiah, Stanley Jeyaraja. 1976. *World Conqueror and World Renouncer: A Study of Buddhism and Polity in Thailand against a Historical Background*. Cambridge: Cambridge University Press.

——. 1977. "The Galactic Polity: The Structure of Political Kingdoms in Southeast Asia." *Annals of the New York Academy of Sciences* 293/1: 69–97.

——. 1992. *Buddhism Betrayed? Religion, Politics, and Violence in Sri Lanka*. Chicago: University of Chicago Press.

——. 2013. "The Galactic Polity in Southeast Asia." *HAU: Journal of Ethnographic Theory* 3/3: 503–534.

Taylor, Peter. 1994. "The State as Container: Territoriality in the Modern World System." *Progress in Human Geography* 18/2: 151–162.

Tennent, James Emerson. 1850. "Tennent to Committee." In *Minutes of Evidence Taken before the March 25 1850. Third Report from Select Committee on Ceylon (Session 1850)*. Accessed July 12, 2011. https://goo.gl/MeYCyM.

Teschke, Benno. 2002. "Theorizing the Westphalian System of States: International Relations from Absolutism to Capitalism." *European Journal of International Relations* 8/1: 5–48.

Thompson, E. P. 1966 [1963]. *The Making of the English Working Class*. New York: Random House.

Thucydides. 2004. *History of the Peloponnesian War*. Trans. Richard Crawley. Project Gutenberg, 2004. Accessed May 19, 2023. https://www.gutenberg.org/ebooks/7142.

References

Tilly, Charles. 1985. "War Making and State Making as Organized Crime." In Peter B. Evans, Dietrich Rueschemeyer, and Theda Skocpol (eds) *Bringing the State Back In*, 169–191. Cambridge: Cambridge University Press.

——. 1990. *Coercion, Capital, and European State*s: *AD 990–1990*. Cambridge: Basil Blackwell Publishers.

Venugopal, Rajesh. 2018. *Nationalism, Development and Ethnic Conflict in Sri Lanka*. Cambridge: Cambridge University Press.

Vimalananda, Tennakoon. 1984. *Sri Wickrema, Brownrigg, and Ehelepola: being Letters Addressed to the Home Government from 1811–1815 by Major General John Wilson and Lieut.-General Robert Brownrigg, Governor of Ceylon*. Colombo: Gunasena. British Library, shelfmark: V 26078.

Walker, R. B. J. and Saul Mendlovitz. 1990. "Interrogating State Sovereignty" in R. B. J. Walker and Saul Mendlovitz (eds.) *Contending Sovereignties: Redefining Political Community*, 1–13. London: Lynne Rienner Publishers.

Wallerstein, Immanuel. 1974. *The Modern World System: Capitalist Agriculture and the Origins of the European World-Economy in the Sixteenth Century*. New York: Academic Press.

Watson, Paul. 2004. "Leaving Luna Alone." Sea Shepherd Conservation Society, June 18. Accessed September 2, 2014. www.seashepherd.fr/news-and-media/editorial-040618–1.html.

Weber, Max. 1919. "Politics as a Vocation." In *Anthropological Research on the Contemporary*, 1–27. Accessed August 20, 2013. http://anthro pos-lab.net/wp/wp-content/uploads/2011/12/Weber-Politics-as-a-Vocation.pdf.

Weckowicz, Helen Liebel. 1988. "Ranke's Theory of History and the German Modernist School." *Canadian Journal of History/Annales Canadiennes d'Histoire* 23 (April): 73–93.

Wesleyan Methodist Missionary Society. 1950. (Wesleyan) Methodist Missionary Society Archive, School of Oriental and African Studies, University of London, Special Series–Notes and Transcripts, box 570, fiches 90–93.

"Why Can't We Go Home? Military Occupation of Land in Sri Lanka." 2018. Human Rights Watch,_October 9. Accessed May 2021. https://www.hrw.org/report/2018/10/09/why-cant-we-go-home/military-occupation-land-sri-lanka.

Wickramasinghe, Nira. 1995. *Ethnic Politics in Colonial Sri Lanka: 1927–1947*. Delhi: Vikas Publishing House.

——. 2006. *Sri Lanka in the Modern Age: A History of Contested Identities*. Honolulu: University of Hawai'i Press.

——. 2009. "After the War: A New Patriotism for Sri Lanka?" *The Journal of Asian Studies* 68/4 (November): 1045–1054.

References   193

———. 2014. "Sujit Suvassundaram, Islanded: Britain, Sri Lanka and the Bounds of an Indian Ocean Colony." *South Asia: Journal of South Asian Studies* 37/3: 542–543.

———. 2015. *Sri Lanka in the Modern Age: A History*. New York: Oxford University Press.

Wickremeratne, Swarna. 2006. *Buddha in Sri Lanka*. New York: State University of New York Press.

Wijeyeratne, Roshan de Silva. 2011. "Appendix B: Violence, Evil and the State in Sri Lanka: Revisiting an Ontological Approach to Sinhalese Nationalism." In Bruce Kapferer, *Legends of People, Myths of State: Violence, Intolerance, and Political Culture in Sri Lanka and Australia*, 291–318. New York: Berghahn Books.

———. 2014. "The *Mandala* State in Pre-British Sri Lanka: The Cosmographical Terrain of Contested Sovereignty in the Theravada Buddhist Tradition." In A. Wagner and Richard K. Sherwin (eds) *Law, Culture, and Visual Studies*, 573–598. United States: Springer Publishing. E-Book.

Wijimanne, A. 1996. *War and Peace in Post-Colonial Ceylon 1948–1991*. New Delhi: Orient Longman Limited.

Williams, Eric. 1964 [1944]. *Capitalism and Slavery*. London: Andre Deutsch Limited.

Wilson, A. J. 2000. *Sri Lankan Tamil Nationalism: Its Origins and Development in the Nineteenth and Twentieth Centuries*. Vancouver: UBC Press.

Wilson, James. 2017. "Reappropriation, Resistance, and British Autocracy in Sri Lanka, 1820 – 1850." *The Historical Journal* 60/1: 47 – 69.

Yiftachel, O. and G. As'ad. 2004. "Understanding 'Ethno-Cratic' Regimes: The Politics of Seizing Contested Territory." *Political Geography* 23/6: 647–676.

Index

Page numbers in bold indicate table. Page numbers followed by n denote notes.

Abeysekara, Ananda 32, 76
absolute authority 30n2, 123
adikars 89, 105, 108, 113
African sovereigns 52
agama 98
Agganna Sutta ("The Discourse on What is Primary") 106
Agnew, John 8–9, 50, 70
Ahelepola, Wijayasundara Wickramasinghe Chandraskara Amarkoon Wasala Ranamuka Mudiyanse 86–7, 88, 121–2, 147
  Rajasinha, Vikrama, Sri and 10–11, 110, 149
  Uva rebellion and 149–50
Ahluwalia, Pal 46n3
alcohol-selling taverns 134n1
Ali (Mohammed's nephew) 96
Ambedkhar, B. R. 32
anarchism 74n2
Anderson, Benedict 31n6, 50–1
Anghie, Antony 49, 60–1
Anglican missionaries 92–3, 95
anti-Tamil propaganda 169
Anuradhapura kingdoms 106

Appohamy, Kapurobastelagey Dennis 158–9
Appoohame, Melpitia 165
archives, colonial 136–67
  age of insurrections: 1830s–1840s 156–65
  biases of 15–19, 23
  elite histories and 138–46
  introduction 136–8
  representation of ordinary people in 26–7
  Uva rebellion 146–52, 155–6
Arthashastra 106
Aryan racial blending 119
Äsala Perahera 112–14
Asgirya monasteries 114
Ashokan-inspired practice of sovereignty 9
Asiatic Researches (journal) 115
Asiatic Society of Bengal 115
autonomy 124
  absolute 53
  Colebrooke–Cameron reforms and 17
  galactic model of power and 124–5
  Kandyan 17

Index

monastic tradition and 108–10
of principalities 55
through self-government to
   Tamil-dominated regions 6
value placed on 36
Aztec-Maya-Caribbean genocide
   37

Bailey, John, Rev. 93, 94–5
Banada, Alludenia 158–9
Banda, Alutgamma 165
Banda, Gongalegode 130, 158–9
Bandarage, Asoka 145–6
Bandaranaike, S. W. R. D. 6, 168
Bandung conference 34
Barnes, Edward, Sir 20–1, 152,
   156
Bartelson, Jens 54, 58
Basu, Ramram 25–6
Batavian Republic 80
1757 Battle of Plassey 12
Bay of Bengal 80
B-C Pact 6–7
Belgium 52
Bellarime, Robert 60
Bennet, J. W. 21
Bhabha, Homi 41
Bhambra, Gurminder
   concept of "nation" 66–7
   on European modernity 38
   on multiple modernities 120
   on state formation 50–1
bhikkhus 99, 144
biases
   of the colonial archives 15,
      23
   institutional 6
Bible 96
"Black July" (of 1983) 169
Blaney, David 35–6, 37
Blaser, Mario 103, 116–17, 118,
   120, 122
bodhisattva 76, 110, 113, 122

bodhisattva king 76, 110, 113, 122
Bodin, Jean 53
body politic 55
book of Genesis 96
Brahma (god of creation) 99
Branch, Jordan 63
Bridgalle, William 90
British East India Company
   12–13, 61, 96, 115–16
*The British Government and the
   Idolatry of Ceylon* 100
British India *see* India
British Indian army 166n5
British invasion of Kandyan
   territories 9, 83–4
British missionaries 89–90, 91–3,
   97
British Raj 96
British uprisings (1818–1848)
   153–4
Brownrigg, Lady 150–1
Brownrigg, Robert, Sir 76, 86, 87,
   88, 108
   Ahelepola and 11
   on 1834 insurrection 157
   Kandyan Convention and 10,
      125–6, 128, 129
   sovereign handover and 121–3
   UVA rebellion 149–52
Brydon, William, Dr 166n5
buddhagama 13, 121, 172
Buddhification 11–12, 169–70
   Buddhist revival 14
   Buddhist system of sovereignty
      107–10
   pre-European Ceylon and
      110–15, 123, 124
   see also sovereignty
Buddhism
   British administrators and
      missionaries' understanding of
      98–101
   European scholarship on 80

196 *Index*

Buddhism (*cont.*)
 fifth clause of the Kandyan
  Convention and 148
 interaction with state 76–7
 Protestant 29, 171
 Sinhala-Buddhist nationalism 3,
  4, 5, 106, 107, 139–41, 168
Buddhist conception of sovereignty
 see Buddhification
Buddhist genealogy of sovereignty
 10, 91, 95, 99, 115, 124
Buddhist guardian deities 114–15
Buddhist monks 76
 in charge of *Äsala Perahera* 114
 Christian missionaries and
  99–101
 influence on uprisings 155
 Kandyan Convention and 125
 protests against B-C Pact 6
 Tamil/Malabar relation and
  134n2
Burgher 17
Burke, Edmund 61
Byng, George, Governor 130

Cakkavatti Sinhanada Sutta
 ("The Lion's Roar of the
 Wheel-Turning Emperor")
 106
Cameron 30n1
Campbell, Governor 158
capitalism 51–2
caste relations in Kandyan galactic
 order 105, 106–7
Catholic Church 75–6
Catholicism 90, 95
 conversion to 81–2, 90–1, 110
ceremonial legitimacy 131
Césaire, Aimé 98–9, 133
Ceylon Gazette (newspaper)
 148–50, 156
Ceylon National Congress 138
Ceylon territory, described 13

*Ceylon under the British
 Occupation 1795–1833*
 (de Silva) 139
Chakrabarty, Dipesh 22–3, 25, 143
Chandrayotty (priest) 158
Chatterjee, Partha 18, 73n1
Chelvanayagam, S. J. V. 6
Chitty, Simon Casie 83
Christian-British understanding of
 sovereignty 10, 12–13
 Christian genealogy of
  sovereignty 10, 70, 91, 96,
  124
 see also Kandyan Convention
Christian education 94–7
 see also missionary, education
Christian-monotheistic ontology
 95–6
church 96, 138
 authority of 55
 Catholic 75–6
 state and 55, 75–6, 78, 79, 97
Church Missionary Society 93
Cicero 60
Citizenship Act 176n1
civic Christianity 90, 95
civil disobedience 6, 35, 41
"civilizing" natives 91–2
civil war 1, 3–4, 6, 169
Cleghorn, Hugh 139–40
coercion 51–2
coffee plantations
 capitalist economy and 71,
  134n1, 145–6
 European planters 162–4
 raiding 165
 rise in 20–1, 44, 159–61
 Tamil plantation workers
  167n6
Cohn, Bernard 78, 132–3
Colbrooke–Cameron Commission
 (of 1829–1833) 7–8
Colebrooke 30n1

Index

The Colebrooke–Cameron Papers: Documents on British Colonial Policy 1796–1933 (Mendis) 138–9
Colebrooke-Cameron reforms 17, 30n1, 145, 157–8
Colombia 40
Colombo Magazine 23
colonial contamination 169–70
  post-colonialism 32–5, 46n3
  violence of universality and 35–44
colonial governmentality 30n1
coloniality
  concept of 133–4
  manifestations of violence 118–19
  modernity and 73, 80–9
  state formation and ontological conflict 115–19
  violence of universality and 35–7
commerce
  capitalism and 52
  coffee plantations and 160
  empire and 62–3
  rapid construction of roads and 21
commonwealth 55
Congo 52
Constant, Benjamin 52, 62
Crawquill, Julian 23
critical theory 43
cultural relativism 120
Cusicanqui, Silvia Rivera 42

Dalada Temple 114
dalada (tooth) relic 113, 150
  ontological dissonance and 128–30
  theft by rebels 150–1
Danbulla Temple 130
Davids, Rhys 138
Davies, Major 85

de Alwis, Malathi 92
de-centralization 112–13
decolonization 34, 36, 44, 71–3, 173
degovernmentalization of the cosmos 38
de la Cadena, Marisol 22, 24
de-linking 41
demilitarization of the state 52
denial
  of colonial violence of universality 68
  of political authority 36, 40
de Silva, Chandra R. 106
de Silva, Colvin R. 102n6, 139, 145, 146
de Silva, Kingsley Muthumuni 85–6, 89, 139
  describing Uva rebellion 143–5
  on Kandyan sense of nationalism 134n4
  on Matale rebellion 141–3, 146
  on representative government 17
  on Tamil nationalists 140–1
dessaves (ministers) 122
devales 125
Devanampiyatissa, King 81
de Vitoria, Francisco 49
dhamma 100
disavas (officials) 113
Diyavadana Nilame (Water-Bearing Official) 114
Dona Catherina (mother of Rajasinha II) 118
Donoughmore Commission 4
Donoughmore Report (of 1928) 30n3
D'Oyly, John 10, 87, 88, 135n5, 147
Dravidian foreigners 111
Dravidian South Asia 81
Duncan, James 108
Dussel, Enrique 37, 38, 42

198 *Index*

Dutch
  archival sources 106–7, 140
  arrival in Kandy 11–12
  Maritime Provinces of Ceylon 80
  Protestants 76
Dutch East India Companies 12

Easter terrorist attacks, 2019 4
economic compulsion 51–2
education
  Christian 94–7
  missionaries 13, 91–7, 101n4,
    170
  religious 91–2, 94–7
  Westernized 102n8
Eisenstadt, Shmuel 120
Elden, Stuart 50, 57, 59–60, 63–4
elite histories and coloniality of
    archives 138–46
  de Silva, Colvin R. 139, 146
  de Silva, Kingsley Muthumuni
    139–46
  Mendis, G. C. 138–9, 144–5
elite-led nationalism 34–5
Elliott, Christopher 24
empire 5, 60–3
  ethno-nationalism and 14
  parameters of 78
  relational state formation and
    63–7
  territorial assumptions and 8,
    14, 34, 36, 59, 60–3
English language, learning 90,
    91–2
Enlightenment 69, 94, 97
epistemic disobedience 41, 43
ethnic nationalism 3–7, 9, 15, 34,
    67, 105, 169, 174, 175
ethno-religious nationalism 9, 14
Eurocentric Orientalist scholars
    13
European geopolitics and British
    invasion 82

European planters, uprisings
    against 160–5
external sovereignty 34, 54–5

Fanon, Frantz 34
Ferdinand, Archduke 62
First Anglo-Afghan War 158,
    166n5
First War of Independence 132
Forbes, Jonathan, Colonel 156–7,
    159, 160, 161, 164
France 25, 71, 82
Freedom Party 168–9

"galactic polity" system 9
galactic sovereignty 86, 98–9
  collision and political ontology
    126–31
  galactic *mandala* system 68, 103,
    104–10, 123, 174
  historical and political context
    104–10
Gandhi, M. K. 32
Gautama, Siddharta 99
Geiger, Wilhelm Ludwig 138
genealogical traditions 46–7
  see also specific entries
general will 55
geopolitics of knowledge 37–8, 42
George, King of England 76, 124
German imperialism 66
Giddens, Anthony 50, 51–2
Gifford, Hardinge, Sir 129
global South 42–3, 70
Gogerly (Christian missionary) 100
Goswami, Manu 7, 21
Government Christians 95
Goyigama caste 113
Greece, ancient 115
Grosfoguel, Ramón 36
Grovogui, Siba 52
guerilla warfare 83, 85
Guha, Ranajit 24, 26–7

Index

Haraway, Donna 38
Hardy, Spence, Rev. 100, 135n6
Harris, Elizabeth 13–14, 100
Harvard, Elizabeth 75, 91–3, 99
Hastings, Warren 78, 115
Haudenosaunee Great Law of
  Peace 68
heathen females 91–2
heathenism 99
Hebrew Bible 95
Hindu genealogies 91, 95, 99
Hindu India 106
Hinduism/Hindus 172
  Christian Truth and 93
  European scholarship on 80
Hobbes, Thomas 33, 35, 53, 55–6,
  59–60, 63–4, 65, 66
homogenous nationalism 73n1

idolatrous worship 129–31
idolatry 75, 91, 92, 99
Ihagamma, priest 155
imposter sovereign 22
India 156
  ancient Greece and 115
  British officials' understandings
    of state functions 78, 172
  Indian immigrants 115
  Indian migrant labourers 163
  legal diversity in colonial
    61–2
  native reinforcements from 147,
    161
  Orientalist scholars in 115
  Royal Proclamation and 132
Indigenous ontologies
  of "sovereignty" 50
  of territory 67–8
industrial capitalism 51–2
institutional biases 6
insurrections (1830s–1840s)
  156–65
intellectual emancipation 38

international relations
  diplomacy and 55
  internal conditions of peace
    within Europe and 52
  Kandyan agency and 84
  territorial assumptions of 8–9,
    50, 53–5
  understanding of state
    sovereignty 35–6, 63–70
ISIS 4
Islam 95–6
Islamic genealogies 91, 96
Ismail, Qadri 57

Jaffna kingdom 107
Japanese nationalism 51
Jayawardena, Kumari 19, 91,
  102n6, 137, 145–6
Jayewardene, J. R. 168
Jeganathan, Pradeep 57
Jinnah, Mohamed Ali 32
jiv-atma and *param-atma*
  (transcendental soul and
  divine essence) 80
Jones, William, Sir 62
Judaeo-Christian-Islamic
  genealogies 91
Judaism 95–6

Kandy
  autonomy of 17
  British invasion of 9, 83–4
  laws of 88, 126
  South Indian Hindu influence
    on 12
  surrender of 84
Kandyan aristocracy
  diplomatic manoeuvres of 77,
    85–9, 117
  internal power struggles and 147
  Kandyan Convention and 121,
    129
  Sri Vikrama's falling-out with 108

200 *Index*

Kandyan Convention (of 1815) 10,
  30n1, 76–7, 78–9, 83, 84, 87,
  89, 92, 115
  Buddhification 110–15
  galactic sovereign collision and
    political ontology 127–31
  galactic sovereignty 104–10
  introduction 103–4
  multiple ontologies vs multiple
    modernities 119–21
  as political ontology 121–7
  political ontology and the
    pluriverse 115–19
  revision to 147–8
Kayaoglu, Turan 64
Kelegama, Thiriumi 3
Kelson, Major 158
Keppitipola and UVA rebellion
  102n6, 134n2, 148–50
king-as-*bodhisattva* 76, 110, 113,
  122
Kipling, Rudyard 167n5
Kotelewala, John, Sir 32, 168
Kotte kingdom 107
Krasner, Stephen 54
Kristiyāni Prajnapti ("The
  Evidence of Christianity") 100
Kumarihari (Ahelepola's wife) 88
Kusumasana Devi, Queen 118

Lanka Sama Samaja Party 139
Law of Kamma 100
Leortin, Allawelle Goda 165
Leviathan (Hobbes) 33, 55, 56, 60
Liberation Tigers of Tamil Eelam
  (LTTE) 1–3
Locke, John 37, 65
Lynch, James, Rev. 90

MacDowall, General 85–6
Madras Presidency 80, 82
Maha Adikar (Prime Minister) 10,
  86, 111–12, 121–2, 149

Mahavamsa 138
Maitland, Thomas, Sir 82, 84
Malabars 26, 31n5, 84, 111, 126,
  134n2, 148
Malay mercenaries 85, 86, 150–1
Maldonado-Torres, Nelson 134
Malwatta monasteries 114
Maquinna, Ambrose 116
Maritain, Jacques 55, 56–7, 58,
  64–5
Marx, Karl 36, 50, 51–2, 69
Matale rebellion (1848) 19, 130,
  136
  conditions leading to 145–6,
    158
  representation of nationalism
    in 141
  Torrington on 24, 26
  unlawful quelling of 164–5
Mauryan Empire 104
Melian Dialogue 146
Mendis, G. C. 30n2, 89, 138–9
Metcalf, Thomas 94, 101n5, 115,
  119, 132
Mignolo, Walter 19, 36, 45, 69
migrant labourers 163, 167n5
military-cum-plantation roads and
  rebellions 159–60
Mill, James 65, 94
missionaries
  on Buddhist tradition 23
  conversion to Christianity and
    81
  distinction between India and
    Ceylon 80
  education 13, 91–7, 101n4,
    170
  pluriversal lived realities of the
    people and 75–9
  publications 16
  religious politics of 89–94
  women 91–2
  see also religious education

Index

modernity 69
  coloniality and 73, 80–9
  multiple ontologies *vs* multiple
    119–21
Modernity/Colonialty/
  Decoloniality (MCD) research
  group 41–3
modern nationalism and empire
  51
Mohammed 96
Molligoda 88, 102n7, 121–2, 147,
  156, 157
monotheism 13–14, 91, 95–6
Mootoo, rebellion raised by
  155–6
moral order 110
Morgenthau, Hans 54
Morning Star (newspaper) 162
Morris, W. 159
Mowachat/Muchalaht First Nation
  116–17, 118
Mughuls 96, 101n3
Muhandiram (headman from lower
  country) 86
multiple ontologies *vs* multiple
  modernities 119–21
Muslim traders 103, 105
Muttusami 111–12

Napoleon 61
Narendrasinha 111
nation
  conceptualization of 66–7
  imperial expansion and
    wellbeing of 66–7
  states 51–2, 171
nationalism 55
  elite-led 34–5
  empire and 14, 51
  ethnic 3–7, 9, 15, 34, 67, 105,
    169, 174, 175
  ethno-religious 9, 14
  homogenous 73n1

Japanese 51
Kandyan sense of 134n4
postcolonial 8
representation of 141–2
Sinhala-Buddhist 3, 4, 5, 6, 106,
  107, 139–41
Tamil 2–3, 139–40
Native Militia 151
native Other 133, 166n2
Nawab of Bengal 12
Nayaka(s) 101n1, 110, 124
  embracing Buddhism 112
  kings 11, 12, 107, 111
  Malabar dynasty 148
  Tamil dynasty 83, 161
Nehru, Jawaharlal 32
non-aligned movement 34
North, Fredrick 82, 85

Obeyesekere, Gananath 11, 77,
  87–8, 103, 114–15, 122, 125,
  171
ontological collision 126–31
  Buddhification 110–15
  galactic sovereign collision and
    political ontology 126–31
  galactic sovereignty 103–10
  genealogy and 115, 117
  introduction 103–4
  on becoming Kandyan
    111–12,
  Kandyan Convention as political
    ontology 121–6
  multiple ontologies *vs* multiple
    modernities 119–21
  political ontology and the
    pluriverse 115–19
Onuf, Nicholas 34–5, 54–5, 58
Orientalism (Said) 46n3
Orientalist scholars 13, 115, 172
Osiander, Andreas 64
Osnabrück Treaty 63–4
Otherness 115

Index

paganism 91–2, 98
Pagden, Anthony 37, 49, 52, 65
  views on empire 60–3, 65
Pal, Bipin Chandra 31n6
Pali (language) 100
Panagia, Davide 145
Peace Treaties of Westphalia 49, 53, 64
Peel, Robert, Sir 162
Perahera 113–14, 130
Perera, Nihal 76–7, 80, 137, 170
Perpetual Ferment (Jayawardena) 19, 137
Philoyvenues 99
Pilimatalava (Rajasinha's advisor) 10, 85–6, 102n6, 110, 111–12
plantation economy 134n1
pluriversal realities and universal gaze 75–101, 171–2
  Christian missionaries 89–94
  introduction 75–9
  modern/colonial religious education 94–7
  modernity and coloniality 80–9
pluriverse 67, 73, 120
  political ontology and 115–19
political agency 18, 25, 142, 166, 173
political citizenship 25
political economy of knowledge 42
political ontology
  galactic sovereign collision and 126–31
  Kandyan Convention as 121–6
  pluriverse and 115–19
Polonnaruwa kingdoms 106
Ponnambalam, G. G. 32, 168
Poorangappoo 159
Portuguese
  arrival in Ceylon 81
  Catholic influence on Kandy 11–12
  colonization 75–6

post-colonialism 32–5, 46n3
post-modernism 46n3
post-positivist research 46n3
post-structuralism 46n3
Powell, Geoffrey 135n5
Prabhakaran, Velupillai 2
Pratt, Mary Louise 38
press, influence on rebellion 24–5
pretender to the throne 22, 131, 142, 147, 150, 160, 162, 167n6
Proclamation, Queen's 132
Protestantism 29, 76, 89, 95, 171
provincialization 69–70
Pulle, Juan 155–6
Pulle, Kanewada 155–6
Punchyrall, Nikolla 165
punishment of rebels **153–4**

Quijano, Aníbal 37

rajakariya 20, 85, 105, 108, 156
rajamandala system 9, 78, 104, 109, 169–70, 172
  see also galactic sovereignty
Rajapaksa, Gotabaya 4
Rajapaksa, Mahinda 1, 3–5
Raja Pratapadiya-Charit (Basu) 25–6
Rajasinha, Kirti Sri 111, 112
Rajasinha, Rajadhi, Sri 85, 111, 112
Rajasinha, Vijaya, Sri 111
Rajasinha, Vikrama, Sri 161
  Ahelepola and 10–11, 110, 149
  capture and exile of 111
  executions ordered by 10–11, 28, 102n6, 126
  Kandyan aristocracy and 108, 147, 161
  Pilimatalava and 102n6
  rule of 83, 84–7, 112
Rajasinha II, King 111, 118

Index

Rajput systems of sovereignty 119
Ramnath, Maia 74n2
Rancière, Jacques 18–20, 145, 146
Randala nobility (a subgroup of the Goyigama caste) 107
Ratteralle, Kohnhumbra 111, 150, 156
regime of representation 40
relational state formation 63–70
religious ceremonies 152
religious education
  to girls 91–2
  modern/colonial 94–7
  see also missionary, education
religious symbols 152
re-politicization
  of state 28
  of territory 72–3
reverse-Orientalism 137
rituals 112–13
  dramas 114
  of sovereign handover 122
  of state 108–9, 112–13
roads
  commerce and rapid construction of 21
  rebellions and 159–60
Rogers, Major 158
Rojas, Cristina 37, 38–9, 40, 41, 49, 60–1
roundtable conferences 168
Rousseau 53, 55
Royal Proclamation 132
Ruggie, John 53, 54, 58

Said, Edward 46n3
Sangha 125
Sanskrit 115
Saranankere, Chandroyottey Selewananse (priest) 155
Sassen, Saskia 57, 59
scientific positivism 94
scientific rationalism 96, 97

scientific thinking 94
Scott, David 30n1
Scott, James C. 33, 74n2, 143–4, 173
secularism 13, 96, 97
self-rule 44
Senanayake, D. S. 32, 44
Seneviratne, H. L. 6, 113–14
Sepoy Rebellion 132
Seth, Sanjay 102n9, 141
Shani, Giorgio 69–70
Shaw, Karena 33, 35, 37, 56
Shilliam, Robbie 46n4, 69, 89, 171
Siddipathi, Wikrema, Sri 130
Simnel, Lambert 162
Sinhala 81, 100
  aristocracy 84, 86, 108, 111, 112, 117, 161
  folklore 88
  kingdoms 81, 110
  non-Kandyan 105
  Sinhala-Buddhist nationalism 3, 4, 5, 106, 107, 139–41, 168
  Sinhalese identity, cultural 107
Sinhalese-language skills 125
Sirisena, Maithripala Yapa 4
Sitavaca, King of 81–2
Smith, Adam 61
social order 113
sovereignty
  Buddhist obligations and 11
  concept of 55–7, 58–9
  defined 54
  Eurocentric 48–9, 56–7, 68–70
  European genealogy of 41, 45, 50
  Hobbes on 35
  indivisibility and 61
  internal 34, 54–5
  Rajput systems of 119
  rise of, and postcolonial nationalism 8
  territory and 53–60
  see also Buddhification; state sovereignty

204 *Index*

Soviet Union 69
spiritual legitimacy 130
spiritual primitiveness 91
spiritual realm 113
Spivak, G. C. 15
Sri Lanka Freedom Party 6
Sri Menanti 123
state, defined 53
state sovereignty
  Eurocentric statism 27
  international relations'
    understanding of 63–70
  rapid proliferation of 36
  relational state formation
    63–70
  state-nations 51–2
Steuart, James 129–30
Sumangala, Wariyapola, Sri 122,
  123, 129
surrender of Kandy 84
symbolism 108–10

Tambiah, S. J. 9, 103, 104–6, 111,
  130
Tamil-language skills 125
Tamil(s) 31n5, 105, 107
  anti-Tamil propaganda 169
  in Kandyan galactic order
    103
  kingdom 81, 83, 107, 161
  migrant labourers 44, 167n5
  nationalism 2–4, 139–41
  separatism 140
  Sri Lanka–Tamil Eelam civil
    war 6
  Tamil Eelam 1, 3–4, 6, 169
  workers and kanganies 167n6
Tawantinsuyana (Inca), Latin
  America, genocide of 37
taxes 19, 26, 64, 86, 141, 142,
  148, 160, 167n6
Tennent, James Emerson, Sir 24,
  25, 152, 158, 159

territory
  evolution within Europe 59–60
  formulations 81
  meaning of 57
  sovereignty and 53–60
  territorial jurisdiction 64
  "territorial sovereignty" in
    translation 64
  territorial trap 50
  tracing development of 46, 50,
    53–8, 69
Thirty Years War in 1648 54, 56
Thucydides 146
Tilly, Charles 50
Tolfrey, William 135n5
Torrington, Governor 24, 26,
  130–1, 136, 141–2, 161
transcendent authority of
  sovereignty 65
Treaty of Amiens 80, 82
Treaty of Münster 63–4
Turtle Island 68, 72–3, 176n2

universal gaze of the monotheist
  British missionary 90–1
universalization of history 73
universal ontology of race 119
universal sovereignty
  empire 60–3
  introduction 48–52
  relational state formation
    63–70
  sovereignty and territory 53–60
universal temporality 116
uprisings 1818–1848 **153–4**
  see also Matale rebellion (1848);
    Uva rebellion (1817–1818)
Uva rebellion (1817–1818) 19,
  79, 111, 129, 134n2, 136–7,
  146–56
  British adoption of concept of
    rajakariya 20
  Brownrigg, role of 150, 152

Index

diplomatic arrangement by
  Ahelepola during 147, 149
end of 132
Lady Brownrigg, role of 150–1
newspaper accounts of 134n2
quelling of 147–9
theft of *dalada* relic by revels
  151

Vedda (Indigenous) peoples 107,
  143–4
Vederalle, Kapurubastebanddalagey
  David 158–9
Venugopal, Rajesh 1
Victoria, Queen 131, 132
viharas 125
Vimaladharmasuriya I 11, 110–11
violence of universality 37–44,
  46n4
  coloniality and 35–7
virtual power relations 109
Vitoria 49–50, 61

Warbeck, Perkin 162
Weber, Max 50, 53, 66
Wesleyan missionaries 91–2, 125
Western-Christian universalist
  93–4
Western intellectualism 37–8
Westernized education 102n8
Westphalia 63
  "myth" 64
  Peace Treaties of 49, 53, 64
  sovereignty 54
Wickramasinghe, Nira 4, 31n3,
  75–6, 107, 137
Wickremeratne, Swarna 78
Wijeyeratne, Roshan de Silva 103,
  108–9, 112
Wilbawe, king 111, 134n2
Wilson, James 152
women missionaries 91–2
World Systems Theory 36

Milton Keynes UK
Ingram Content Group UK Ltd.
UKHW021417061223
433893UK00009B/134